WHY SACRAMENTS?

WHY SACRAMENTS?

ANDREW DAVISON

First published in Great Britain in 2013

Society for Promoting Christian Knowledge
36 Causton Street
London SW1P 4ST
www.spckpublishing.co.uk

British Library Cataloguing-in-Publication Data
A catalogue record for this book is available from the British Library

ISBN 978–0–281–06392–5
eBook ISBN 978–0–281–07134–0

Typeset by Graphicraft Limited, Hong Kong
First printed in Great Britain by Ashford Colour Press

eBook by Graphicraft Limited, Hong Kong

For
Matthew, Russell, John, Robert, Anna and John,
with thanks

cella tua docebit te universa

O Word immortal of eternal God,
only-begotten of the only Source,
for our salvation stooping to the course
of human life and born of Mary's blood;
Sprung from the ever-virgin womanhood
of her who bare thee, God immutable,
incarnate, made as man with man to dwell,
and condescending to the bitter rood;
Save us, O Christ our God, for thou hast died
to save thy people to the uttermost,
and dying tramplest death in victory;
one of the ever-blessed Trinity,
in equal honour with the Holy Ghost,
and with the eternal Father glorified.

(Attributed to the emperor Justinian (483–565),
translated by Thomas Alexander Lacey (1853–1931))

Contents

Foreword by Stephen Foster   ix

Acknowledgements   xi

1 Why sacraments?   1

2 Baptism   13

3 Sacramental character   23

4 The Eucharist   30

5 The anatomy of the sacraments I: signs, matter and form   55

6 How many sacraments?   66

7 Confirmation   75

8 Ordination   82

9 The anatomy of the sacraments II: setting, intention,
   minister and recipient   96

10 Marriage   102

11 Anointing   120

12 Confession   129

13 The sacraments and the Holy Spirit   142

Conclusion: sacraments and the Incarnation   148

Notes   152

Bibliography   173

Index of biblical references   175

Index of names and subjects   177

Foreword

In the Michaelmas term of 2012, Andrew Davison kindly approached me and asked if there might be a small group of students at Ridley Hall who would be willing to read, in draft, the chapters of this book and discuss them with him. I was delighted that four of us were able to meet with him on a weekly basis. It was a rewarding process, and hopefully one which in some small way has added to the finished product.

It is sometimes forgotten (not least by evangelicals) that the reformers saw both word and sacrament as the key marks of the true Church. The sacraments are founded on Christ's commands, which we must obey, and they are his gifts to us which we must guard and treasure. The contemporary amnesia of a theology of the sacraments within some parts of the Church must then be a matter of concern. A book which serves as a theological introduction to the sacraments is therefore to be warmly welcomed, and merits a broader readership than might be first thought.

In that regard, it is important to stress that this is no dry, step-by-step exposition of sacramental ritual. Instead one is engagingly immersed within theology and practice, with the interrelation of the sacraments and realities of life demonstrated in an intuitive, compelling way. Along the way one absorbs a large amount of Christian doctrine, deftly woven into the issues which are discussed.

For those familiar with Reformed theology, it will be apparent that there are elements of this book with which we did not agree. The discussion on the number of the sacraments, unsurprisingly, was particularly vigorous, and a good example of unity in difference! However, each of the chapters is helpful, stimulating and positively challenging; and we were surprised at just how much common ground there was. The wealth of material is marshalled expertly, and fresh insights are introduced incisively and persuasively.

One of the tragedies of the history of the Church is the way in which those sacraments Christ instituted to bring people into his Church, and to build up his Church in health and unity, have been the focus of persistent disunity. Our prayer as we discussed this book together was, and is, that it would serve the goal of greater unity in Christ's Church. I hope you find it as unifying and as edifying to read as we have.

Stephen Foster
Ridley Hall, Cambridge

Acknowledgements

This is a book about the sacraments, so I begin by thanking my parents, who had me baptized and encouraged me as I went on to be confirmed, receive Communion for the first time and, eventually, to be ordained. I am also grateful to the priest who heard my first confession, and to those who have anointed me on the couple of times when I have been very sick. I am thankful for the opportunities I have had to baptize and anoint, and to preside at marriages. Celebrating the Eucharist in the communities to which I have belonged since my ordination has been a constant joy. I express my particular gratitude and admiration to all at Westcott House.

When I was an exchange student at the Anglicum in Rome, I attended lectures on sacramental theology by Professor Robert Christian OP. They were comprehensive, thought provoking and fun, in the best tradition of the Dominicans. He would not agree with everything I say from my Anglican perspective, but he might notice from what I have written that I valued his lectures.

Some of these chapters began life as lectures at St Stephen's House, Oxford. Students and colleagues there, and at Westcott House, Cambridge, have been the best of interlocutors. Any errors or infelicities remain my own. I owe a particular debt to a group of ordinands at Ridley Hall, Cambridge, who read chapters in draft from week to week, and offered reactions and encouragement. They were a reminder of the cheerful, thoughtful seriousness of evangelicalism.

I am grateful to others who have read and commented on the manuscript, and especially to Anna Matthews for her insights.

1

Why sacraments?

The sacraments are actions, often humble, through which God works and acts upon us. They are everything that we are, and purposefully so: physical, material, speaking, cultural. For some Christians, they form the bedrock of the spiritual life; for others they are further from the centre. This book asks a question: 'Why sacraments?' It asks why we suppose that God acts this way.

The answer comes by means of an observation: the reasons for the sacraments are the reasons for the Incarnation. At root, they both come down to one reason: *salvation*. Christ was incarnate to save us, and the sacraments are means by which God works our salvation.[1]

The sacraments are occasions when we encounter Christ. Or, since the emphasis should rest on him, not on us, the sacraments are occasions when Christ reaches out to us. This book explores the idea that the sacraments are all about Christ and his Incarnation, his Passion and resurrection. They are all about Christ, who came to be all things for us: 'who became for us wisdom from God, and righteousness and sanctification and redemption' (1 Cor. 1.30). A fourteenth-century Orthodox theologian wrote that,

> As he acts in each of his sacraments, Christ becomes all things to us: our Creator as he washes us in baptism, in the oil of confirmation as the one who anoints us for the contest, and as our ally when he feeds us in the Eucharist.[2]

This book grows out of a simple observation on reading one of Thomas Aquinas's surveys of Christian theology. He discusses the 'reasons' for the Incarnation and hot on its heels he discusses the 'reasons' for the sacraments. It does not take a particularly trained eye to notice that these two sets of reasons line up closely. Oddly, Aquinas himself does not make much of this similarity, although he certainly notices it: the 'first and universal cause' of salvation, he writes, is the Incarnation of the Word and this salvation reaches us

1

in ways that are 'harmonious' with the Incarnation.[3] In what follows in this book we will take some detours from time to time, but the goal is simply this: to explore the link between the sacraments and the Incarnation.

Sacramentality in the life of Christ

In one of his miracles, Christ explores the dynamic of making profound but hidden things visible. Presented with a paralytic, Christ forgives his sins (Matt. 9.2–5). This provokes an accusation of blasphemy from the teachers of the law. Christ replies with a question: 'Which is easier, to say . . . "Your sins are forgiven", or to say, "Stand up and take your mat and walk"?' Christ has already said one of these things; he goes on to say the other: 'stand up, take your mat and go to your home', which the paralytic does. Jesus explains the logic of what he is up to in his actions: the healing reveals that he does have 'authority on earth to forgive sins' (Mark 2.9–11).

The forgiveness of sins is an inward and invisible grace. It is profoundly important, and we may well be able to see some of its effects. As an event, however, forgiveness goes unseen. In his exchange with the teachers of the law, Christ underlines the fact that human beings need 'outward and visible signs' to accompany 'inward and invisible grace': if we are to be captivated, if we are to have our doubts and fears allayed, if we are really going to get the point. A sacrament is classically defined as just such 'an outward and visible sign of an inward and invisible grace'.

Before we move on from this passage, we might notice another feature. Christ refers to himself as 'the Son of Man'. While biblical scholars are not entirely in agreement as to what is most significant about this title, it certainly has a sense of true and representative humanity. Christ shows us what it means to be fully human. The episode ends with the crowds giving praise to God and marvelling that God should have 'given such authority to human beings' (Matt. 9.8).

We might reflect on our response to the conclusion of this passage. God has given such power to humanity. Do we think, 'Ah, yes, such power to humans – but this is no game-changer, not really, because Jesus, the human being in question, is God, so God isn't giving anything new to anyone'? If so, we had better watch our Christology (a theological account of who Christ is). Jesus was indeed God, but

2

that did not make him any less human. He was the 'Son of Man': the most fully and most representative human being of all. When Jesus forgave sins, a human being really did forgive them.

This means we can get sacraments wrong in two ways in relation to the Incarnation. If we suppose that human agents extend the work of salvation in the sacraments without reference to Christ, we blunder. If, however, we reject the idea that human beings and human agency are drawn into the work of salvation at all – so, for instance, as to reject a sacramental approach – then we are in just as much danger of missing what the Incarnation was about, only in the opposite direction. Once the Word has become flesh, the domain of divine action is found among human beings and is given to human beings: in a remarkable way, it is placed into our hands.

The sacraments consist of words and gestures, and in this Christ's life offers us a sacramental pattern. In the Gospels he is forever making gestures, using physical things, and aligning them with words. He took a child, placed him or her in the middle of his disciples, and made a talking point about life in his kingdom. He touched lepers to make them whole and touched a funeral bier to overcome the contamination of death and raise the widow's son to life; he lifted another dead child, this time a little girl, to her feet, saying, 'Little girl, get up!' (Mark 5.41). To heal the sick he spat, made mud and smeared it; he put his fingers in ears and he told a paralysed man to carry his mat. He made pilgrimages and offered sacrifices. He turned water into wine. He rode symbolically upon a donkey. He made a whip from cords and drove the moneychangers from the Temple. He ate and drank, sang and slept. When the disciples of John the Baptist asked if he was really the Messiah, he told them simply to observe his actions: 'the blind receive their sight, the lame walk, the lepers are cleansed, the deaf hear, the dead are raised, and the poor have good news brought to them' (Matt. 11.5). To refute a bunch of self-righteous men intent on stoning a woman to death, he bent down and drew on the ground (John 8.1–11). His teaching is full of practical imagery and local colour: the camel and the gate called the Eye of the Needle, the rubbish dump in Jerusalem called Gehenna, and rural farming images in the parables. As his interpretation of the Passion, as Tom Wright has written, Christ did not leave words but a meal;[4] he also washed his disciples' feet. He rose from the dead, and we should not forget that at root the word for the resurrection means just that: he stood up. After the resurrection he cooked for his disciples and breathed on them.

The words connected with some of his healings were considered so important that some are recorded in the original Aramaic: *Talitha cum* ('Little girl, get up!') and *Ephphatha* ('Be opened'). When he stilled the storm he spoke to the wind and sea, saying, 'Be still!' He addressed demons, saying, 'Be silent' and 'come out'. To the paralysed man he said, 'Stand up and take your mat and walk' and to his friend, dead in the tomb, 'Lazarus, come out!' (Mark 5.41; 7.34; 4.39; Luke 4.35; Mark 2.9; John 11.43)

Jesus understood perfectly well the gesture of the men who knocked a hole in a roof, and of Zacchaeus when he climbed the tree. He was not embarrassed by the woman who kissed him, anointed him and wiped him with her hair. It upset others but not Jesus; his annoyance on that occasion was with Simon the Pharisee, for offering him no kiss, washing or anointing.

Christ redeemed the world not by word of command or act of will, but by action, by wood, iron, flesh and blood, by the death of the body and its resurrection. C. S. Lewis underlines this point, obliquely but profoundly, in his novel *Perelandra*. At a certain point the hero, who is a Christ figure, Elwin Ransom, has a showdown with the figure who represents the devil. The reader – or at least the author of this book, perhaps an overly pious reader at the time – expects some *spiritual* triumph: perhaps prayer, at which an angel appears, or fire from heaven, or the banishment of evil to the pit of hell, or at least to some nearby pigs. Instead, Ransom and his adversary fight. They do not even fight particularly elegantly: this is no fencing match. They grapple one another and, in the process of wrestling, Ransom is bitten. It is more or less a catfight, and the story hinges on it. Who knows what Lewis had in mind here. I took it as a forceful reminder that spiritual evil shows itself in physical ways – in hungry bodies and overcrowded houses – and that evil is similarly overcome in physical ways: by good people rolling up their sleeves, by sacrifices (such that if I give money away, I *cannot* eat in quite such a good restaurant when I am on holiday) and, most foundationally of all, by a man on a cross.

Relating the sacraments to the Incarnation

Before moving on, we can add a few more items to our list of relations between Christ and the sacraments. One is to propose Christ as the instigator of the sacraments. This idea has a chequered history. It is not particularly convincing, if we take it to mean that Jesus instituted each sacrament just as it might be celebrated in your parish church next week. Approached with a little more sense of historical development, however, this link is a good one. We will return to it in Chapter 6, when we consider the number of the sacraments, along with a more controversial proposal: the idea, offered as an imaginative exercise, that Jesus was also himself a recipient or participant in something like each of the sacraments.

The word 'sacrament' itself means a certain sort of bond. In Christian usage the bond is to Christ. In his own words, the purpose of his life, death and resurrection was a 'new covenant [or testament] in [his] blood' (Luke 22.20). A covenant or testament is a form of bond, and so are the sacraments. Christ came because God wished to unite himself to the human lot, redeem it and transform it. The sacraments continue to forge and strengthen that bond down the centuries. As witness to this link, the word 'covenant', or bond, was on Christ's lips as he instituted Holy Communion, and baptism is so significant a bond that it warrants description in terms of adoption.

For an illustration of sacraments as a bond, consider a scene from the Bayeux Tapestry. In one scene, Harold makes a solemn promise to William (or so the Norman embroiderers *say*: William's claim to the throne of England depends on this). The Latin accompanying scene uses the word *sacramentum* (*Ubi Harold sacramentum fecit Willelmo Duci*: 'Here Harold makes his oath to William the Duke'). This is no oddity or play on words; it is the original sense of the word *sacramentum*. A sacrament, at least at its linguistic root, is an oath, or covenant or testament. The Romans used the word *sacramentum* of the oath that a Roman soldier made to the emperor. A verbal and outward sign (the soldier's oath) both betokened and forged something real but invisible: a bond to the emperor that was as strong as death. Sometimes this oath was signified by a tattoo. Augustine made a play on this, likening the sign of the cross in baptism to the soldier's tattoo.

Others have found a link between Christ and the sacraments in the very definition of a sacrament. Whatever form of words we might use to characterize a sacrament, perhaps 'an outward and visible sign of an inward and spiritual grace', that form of words is likely also to describe Christ very well. Consider, for instance, how well this particular example of a definition lines up with how Christ is described in the eucharistic preface for Christmastide: 'In this mystery of the Word made flesh ... we see our God made visible and so are caught up in the love of the God we cannot see.'[5] Nowhere is grace more visible and outward than it is in the flesh and blood, the actions and words, of Jesus. For this reason he has been called the 'primordial sacrament'.[6]

Alongside this 'Christmas' emphasis, on God among us, there is also an Easter emphasis, which links the sacraments to Christ through his death and Passion.[7] As a lecturer I heard once put it, not all of the human race could be present at the cross for those three hours on the first Good Friday, but everyone – everywhere and at all times – can approach the cross through the sacraments: through baptism and the Eucharist primarily, but also in each of the other rites that we also call sacraments. With anointing, for example, the sick person, within the family of the Church, seeks both the healing that comes from the cross ('by his bruises we are healed', Isa. 53.5; cf. 1 Pet. 2.24) and the transformation of the meaning of suffering that comes with wanting to share with Christ (Phil. 3.7–14). In marriage the couple participate in the love of Christ for his Church, which was shown on the cross to be stronger than death (cf. Song of Sol. 8.6). The couple offer their lives to God by offering their lives to one another, following the example of the perfect offering of Christ.

In her book *The Cross: Word and Sacrament*, Adrienne von Speyr linked the seven sacraments to Christ upon the cross through his 'seven last words'.[8] Among artists, the great 'Flemish primitive' Rogier van der Weyden illustrated that link, between the cross and the sacraments, in his *Seven Sacraments* altarpiece of around 1445, which is now in the Royal Museum of Fine Arts in Antwerp.[9]

The painting depicts the interior of a church. In the centre of the painting, Christ hangs on a cross, surrounded by John and the three Marys. Behind, in the chancel, a priest celebrates the Eucharist, and in six side chapels, three to the right and three to the left, each of the other six sacraments are being celebrated. The messages are stacked one upon another. The sacraments bring us into the presence of the crucified Lord. We are not likely literally to die in a bed in a side chapel of a church, as seems to be the case with one man. Nonetheless, if we are incorporated into the Church through baptism then, wherever we may be, we die in the bosom of Christ's body. Above the side chapels fly angels. In every celebration of a sacrament, heaven and earth are brought close, mirroring that moment when Christ was suspended upon the cross between heaven and earth. This is among the most theological of paintings, although even having praised it vigorously we might wonder whether this interpretation makes enough of the resurrection.

Overlap

Our topic is the overlap between sacraments and the Incarnation. Overlap is itself a good theological topic, and the Incarnation is a good area in which to explore this. The Incarnation itself is all about overlap. It is the *greatest* of overlaps: a person who is completely God is also completely human. From this many other overlaps follow, such that they keep multiplying: Jesus is the redeemer who is also the first fruits of redemption; he puts us right with God and is himself the first human being right with God; he is creator and created – both his mother's child and, in another sense, his mother's parent; he is all holy and yet 'made . . . sin' (2 Cor. 5.21); he is both the priest and the victim – and, as Augustine once noted with obvious delight, he is also the one to whom sacrifice is offered (as God), and one with us for whom sacrifice is offered (as a human being).[10] Christ is 'the mediator between God and humankind' (1 Tim. 2.5), but by means of overlap rather than by standing halfway between the two. He is mediator as *fully human* and *fully divine*: fully both, truly them together.

We see some of the same multiplication of overlaps in the sacraments. They are both a sign and what is signified, a promise and what is promised; by them God redeems us, but through them he also raises the means of our salvation to a new dignity: bread, water, wine, oil. In anointing, our suffering is mapped onto Christ's; in marriage an earthly union mirrors a heavenly one; in the Eucharist Christ is both priest and offering.

A problem with materiality

The place of the sacraments in the life of the Church, and of the individual Christian, does not necessarily seem very obvious for some. It will be worthwhile, then, to face some of the objections that might be raised to a thoroughly sacramental view of the Christian life.

The sacraments are 'outward and visible signs' and for some this 'outwardness' is the problem. Sacraments are material and 'religious', whereas Christianity seems to be inward and 'spiritual'. Christianity seems, on this account, to have swept away rite and the ministry of intermediaries such as priests or, for that matter, intermediaries such as bread and wine.

In reply we can start with the Old Testament, where faith in God is very much rooted in physical things and physical actions, in times and places. We see this in the ritual of the Temple and the regulations concerning sacrifices; we see it in circumcision and in instructions to bind the law to one's forehead and on the posts of one's door, not to mention in daubing blood there.

The message of the New Testament is of 'God among us'. We should hardly expect that the new covenant – of Christ's body, of his blood – would make the practice of faith less physical. Indeed, the message of 'the Word made flesh' makes faith more physical for Christians, not less, and more tangible, not more abstract. A perennial danger lurks at the door, to *replace* the flesh with the spirit: a sort of reverse Incarnation where we convert the Word made flesh back into word alone.[11]

For Christians, that is a mistake, rooted in neither the Old nor New Testament but rather in the Gnostic heresy. Human beings are more than souls, and God came to us as a human being, as human beings are. From the start, the pagan threat to Christianity was not in outwardness but in excessive inwardness. Protestantism is no stranger to or enemy of the sacraments, but a certain strain of Protestantism is, with its tendency to exalt the abstract over the concrete: for instance in a disembodied 'message' of the gospel in isolation from the practices of the Church[12] or in the sacramental theology of Zwingli, who sought to reduce sacraments to the means by which God communicates ideas to us. We are not, however, disembodied minds. In the words of Schleiermacher, the greatest Protestant theologian of the nineteenth century, we must at all costs avoid the 'over-intellectual bareness of the Zwinglian view'.[13]

We are not angels, as Thomas Aquinas pointed out, and God chose to deal with us as we are: as human beings, not angels. Christ redeemed us on the cross, for which he was willing, as Aquinas reminds us, to be 'made a little lower than the angels' (Heb. 2.9): quite a lot lower, in the degradation of the crucifixion. The materiality of the cross points away from any purely spiritual, mental or ethereal view of God's dealings with us. It follows, for Aquinas, that it 'belongs to human beings, but not to angels, to dispense the sacraments and to take part in their administration.'[14] His point is that we were not redeemed immaterially, so neither does that redemption come to us immaterially.

Part of the problem here is in the very idea of a sharp distinction between matter and spirit. The Christian tradition will not let the 'spiritual' be simply spiritual or the 'material' be simply material. It shows this by constantly taking material things and dragging them into church (babies, love and marriage, bread and wine, the dead), and by constantly taking spiritual things and enacting them materially. This does not *create* an entanglement between the spiritual and the material; it recognizes one that already exists. Friedrich Schelling (1775–1854) saw that the spiritual, when only 'spiritual', is banal, even evil: 'Evil is in a certain respect completely spiritual, for it carries on the most emphatic war against all being, indeed it would like to negate the ground of creation.'[15] Slavoj Žižek joins the dots here and concludes that 'Evil is much more spiritual than Good'.[16] Evil dreams a dream and lets suffering happen as an 'unavoidable consequence' over there; good rolls up its sleeves and tends the sick, one actual person at a time.

If the purely spiritual is best avoided, then the purely material is just as much a fiction (despite what the New Atheists might claim). Matter, at every turn, presents itself as spiritually charged: in peril, gift and redemption, in life and death, sickness and love. Matter is *extraordinarily spiritual*. As Conor Cunningham has recently discussed, the problem with the anti-spiritual materialism of the Christianity-hating scientist is that hardly anything is more metaphysical and more spiritual – frankly, more *weird* – than matter.

The shortcomings of pan-sacramentality

Another objection to the sacraments lies at the opposite pole from the dislike of materiality. It claims that sacraments are unnecessary since everything is already holy and therefore already 'sacramental'. This position was not unknown even in the Middle Ages. The pantheist Amaury de Bène argued around 1200 that since 'God is immense', he must be in every place, and in every thing, and is therefore as present in all ordinary bread as he is in the bread of the Eucharist. He took this to its logical conclusion, and supposed that if God, who is holy, is present in all things and in all people, then really there is no sin. Other theologians were not slow in pointing out where the flaws might lie in his position.

The 'pan-sacramental' objection is problematic because it is historically naive. It lives on borrowed capital: on the capital, indeed, of what it seeks to deny. It saws off the branch on which it is sitting. Historically speaking, cultures in general, at all times and in all places, simply have not supposed that the world is good, wonderful and holy. We have that conviction from the Christian, and Jewish, roots of our culture. What is more, Christianity taught and insisted upon this goodness to a considerable degree *through the sacraments*. These particular rites ground our sense that God made, and works through, all things. Remove the foundation of the distinct sacraments and we can wonder how long before we revert to the pre-Christian, and non-Christian, and otherwise very common, assumption that the world is something to flee from and that materiality is about as far from God as one can get.

More than this, there is a toughness to the seven sacraments that is bound to be missing in some general appeal to the pan-sacramentality of the world. At its *most* theological, pan-sacramentality rests on a vague invocation of the Incarnation as some sort of universal affirmation. It sticks with the cradle and does not follow Christ to the cross. Because of that, it does not have the resurrection either, and must, ultimately, give the world over to futility and dissolution, for all it celebrates it now. Here Henri de Lubac set the right tone, insisting that the Christian faith starts with the Incarnation but it does not end there: 'Incarnation, death, and resurrection: that is, taking root, detachment, and transfiguration. No Christian spirituality is without this rhythm in triple time.'[17] We want all people to recognize God in all things, but the sacraments go further, linking this to judgement, redemption and transfiguration. They make the idea of God-in-all more credible because they have a realistic sense of sin and the tragic *distance* of some situations from God. We can have a profound sense of God in nature, for instance, as long as that is placed within a larger theological whole, just as we can rightly say that 'God speaks in everything' as long as we hold that he even more perfectly speaks to us in the Scriptures.[18]

Salvation is shaped at our end

God acts, in the last analysis, out of love and generosity, and the only rule of his action is the law of his own nature. This manifests itself in actions towards his creatures that are marked by *fittingness*, as Aquinas put it. That fittingness is measured not only by who God is, but also by what God has made us to be. That is central to what God is up to in the sacraments. He is working with us in ways that have us in mind. The shape of the 'means of grace' comes from our end as well as coming from God's.

Why should we bother with the sacraments? Well, why would God bother with them? The answer is that God thought it fitting to reach human beings in a human way. Calvin approached this with his idea of 'accommodation': in his action towards us, God accommodates himself to what we are. In revealing himself, for instance, he uses human modes and means: he reveals himself in human history, human language and human culture.

Evelyn Underhill approached this in her book *The Mystery of Sacrifice*. In the Eucharist (as in other sacraments)

> God the Supernatural seeks man [and woman, of course] by natural vehicles and lowly ways, and man, the creature of the borderland, makes his small response by the same means . . . and thus man learns to recognise the constant mysterious intermingling, yet utter distinctness, of his natural and supernatural life.[19]

The Church sees the same divine commitment to the human condition in the sacraments as it finds in the revelation of the Scriptures. Only the wildest of short-lived sects supposes that when it comes to the communication of saving truth God *principally* deals with people directly, in the sense of speaking to them without mediation. While, by and large, Christians have not wanted to deny direct individual communication, nonetheless they recognize that the sufficient and foundational way in which God has vouchsafed his truth to us is through the Scriptures. The Bible deals with what is 'necessary for salvation',[20] not private revelations.

In working with the spoken and written word, God commits himself to the messiness, and glory, of much that is definitively human: language, writing, communality, culture, transmission, safeguarding, interpreting, and so on. Involving culture, God begins to redeem

11

culture.[21] Already this is physical; the work of salvation takes in scribes and printing presses, not just ideas. The pattern set down with the Scriptures is also to be found in the sacraments. Like the Bible, they involve words and physicality. The work of salvation takes in water, bread and wine, and human hands and voices. And behind both of these facets to God's work – word and sacrament – lies the Incarnation of Christ, the Word made flesh.

2

Baptism

The sacraments are about nothing less than salvation. That is their point and purpose. We see this most clearly with baptism, which is the first and foundational sacrament. The Christian faith goes further: not only is baptism about salvation, but salvation is about baptism: 'no one can enter the kingdom of God,' Christ said, 'without being born of water and Spirit' (John 3.5). In Acts, Peter preaches 'Repent, and be baptized . . . so that your sins may be forgiven' (Acts 2.38). Turning to the Epistles, we read in 1 Peter that 'baptism . . . now saves you' (1 Pet. 3.21). One of Paul's great themes is that through baptism we are saved by incorporation into Christ's death and resurrection (for instance in Rom. 6.4, with Col. 2.12 and Gal. 3.27 as parallels). The so-called 'longer ending to Mark', whether by Mark or not, is very early. In it Jesus is recorded as saying, 'The one who believes and is baptized will be saved' (Mark 16.16). When, then, we confess with the Nicene Creed belief in 'one baptism for the forgiveness of sins', we are simply summarizing this biblical tradition.[1] On this, the magisterial reformers were unwavering. In Luther's words, 'it is solemnly and strictly commanded that we must be baptized or we shall not be saved'.[2]

Luther's entire message was centred on the gospel message that we are saved by grace, to which we respond through faith, and not by our works. That he also insisted on baptism is a good reminder, therefore, that baptism brings salvation not as a human work, but as a divine work.[3] Luther addresses all who are seeking God: be baptized, he says. That does not mean that only those who have been baptized can or will be redeemed from their wrongdoings, although this may seem to be the logic. The sacraments are God's guarantees, not his straitjacket. God has established a good order in his Church, and has appointed the Church to be the herald and the body of his Son upon earth. All the same, God can also work outside those channels, although if we were to rely upon such exceptions we would be looking a gift horse in the mouth.[4]

The belief that, in the normal run of things, God works principally through baptism, but can and does work beyond it, was established in the early Church in relation to martyrdom. Preparation for baptism was taken very seriously, and sometimes people on such a programme were martyred for that identification with Christ before they had been baptized. The consensus placed a 'baptism of blood' alongside the baptism of water. After all, Christ had said that beyond his baptism in water there was 'another baptism' with which he was to be baptized, referring to his Passion and death (Luke 12.50). Most Christians enter into Christ by imitating his baptism in the Jordan. Others, however, enter into Christ's death and resurrection by an even more direct imitation: by martyrdom.[5]

'No' and 'yes'

The New Testament describes salvation using a variety of images. They are notably both 'positive' and 'negative'. Salvation is a matter both of embracing something wonderful and of leaving other things behind; it is a journey *to* somewhere glorious, but also a journey *from* somewhere perilous. The words 'save' and 'salvation' have both of these dimensions. Salvation is clearly a marvellous thing, but it also implies something to be saved from. The Greek word *sotzo* ('to save') is used throughout the New Testament. It means to rescue or preserve from danger or destruction. It can also mean to heal. It is the word you would use for plucking someone out of the sea or a burning building. If we take salvation seriously then we cannot neglect the sense that we have got ourselves into a very bad predicament.

The genius of the Christian doctrine of salvation is to gather all of these aspects under a fundamentally positive banner. We are saved *from* something, making salvation a matter of rescue, but, at heart, God is not reactive. We are saved *from* something, but salvation leaves us better off at the end than we ever were at the beginning. Nothing about what God extends to us in Christ consists of making the best of a bad job, as some sort of salvage operation.

If we want to explore the interweaving of remedy and gain in salvation, we should turn to Christ and the Incarnation. Sure enough, we find there both 'flee from the wrath to come' (Luke 3.7) and 'I came that they may have life, and have it abundantly' (John 10.10).

14

There was an aspect of 'no' and an aspect of 'yes' to the presence of the Son of God among us. Christ came both to judge and to bring life. The Incarnation is a 'no' and then a 'yes', but the 'no' was for the sake of the 'yes'. Paul made this clear in a wonderful passage at the beginning of 2 Corinthians: 'the Son of God, Jesus Christ, whom we proclaimed among you ... was not "Yes and No"; but in him it is always "Yes". For in him every one of God's promises is a "Yes"' (2 Cor. 1.19–20). There is plenty of 'no' in relation to Christ – he came to judge as well as to bring life – but following Paul's injunction we must understand the 'no' in relation to the 'yes'.

The German theologian Karl Barth would have claim to be the greatest theologian of the twentieth century precisely because he saw all of this. After the First World War, he reacted to the flimsiness of contemporary Protestant theology – Protestant theologians largely supported the war – with a *Theologie der Krisis*: 'crisis theology'. He was using a good New Testament word here: *krisis* means judging, sundering, separating. A Church too comfortable with the world had to be called back to all of that. But, for all that judgement, Barth knew that the beginning and end of the gospel is the grace of God. In a beautiful passage he compares God's saving treatment of the human race to the music of Mozart: there is a 'no' and a 'yes', the 'no' is always embraced by the 'yes', and the 'yes' means all the more because of the 'no'.[6]

As we think about baptism, the pre-eminent sacrament of salvation, we should both take the 'no' seriously but also hold it in relation to the overarching 'yes'. Baptism appears to be the cosiest of sacraments, often involving pink-cheeked babies and a welcome into the family of the Church. Alongside this, the 'no' reminds us that baptism is also magnificent and terrible. We should put it no less forcefully than this: if baptism is about life then it is also about death. Baptism is the most extreme of remedies, since it kills us. In baptism we share in the death of Christ and in his resurrection. If this seems hyperbolic, consider how central it is for Paul that we die with Christ, and when he says so, baptism is often close at hand. Salvation is rescue from a shipwreck, but the paradox is that baptism saves us by drowning. Baptism by full immersion points most closely to this, and our more common rite of pouring water points to this. Submersion is like plunging into the death of Christ, and early baptismal pools have something of the shape of a tomb.[7]

15

Extreme measures suggest an extreme problem. Ephesians puts it clearly: the human predicament is of 'having no hope and [being] without God in the world' (2.12). The 'no' of baptism is a constant indication to avoid the threat of Pelagianism: the idea that we can sort ourselves out; that grace is a more or less useful supplement; that salvation is tinkering. Theologically speaking, baptism is a serious matter, but the early Church knew that, since conversion was also a serious matter. In those early days, baptism could mean persecution and martyrdom. That is where identification with Christ and his people could lead. In many parts of the world, it can lead there still. Salvation is a gift and yet it is costly at the same time. Dietrich Bonhoeffer wrote about this, and his opposition to Hitler was later to cost him his life. In one of his definitive books, *The Cost of Discipleship*, he explains that God's grace is not cheap:

> Costly grace is the treasure hidden in the field; for the sake of it a man will gladly go and sell all that he has. It is the pearl of great price to buy which the merchant will sell all his goods.

He goes on to describe both the 'no' and the 'yes':

> Such grace is costly because it calls us to follow, and it is grace because it calls us to follow Jesus Christ. It is costly because it costs a man his life, and it is grace because it gives a man the only true life. It is costly because it condemns sin, and grace because it justifies the sinner. Above all, it is costly because it cost God the life of his Son: 'ye were bought at a price,' and what has cost God much cannot be cheap for us. Above all, it is grace because God did not reckon his Son too dear a price to pay for our life, but delivered him up for us. Costly grace is the Incarnation of God.[8]

Continuity and discontinuity

Crossing our distinction between positive and negative in baptism is the distinction between continuity and discontinuity. Approached this way – and we must approach it this way – baptism is no gentle sacrament. It is the sacrament in which we die. This is not as gloomy as it sounds: hope of the second coming withstanding, it is the destiny of everyone to die (Heb. 9.27); in baptism we get this dying over and done with. We can then approach physical death, whenever it comes, with a lighter heart. At our most confident, we might brush it off as secondary to the death we have already been through in baptism. In less confident mood, we might at least be able to approach death with some of the comfort of thinking, 'Been there, done that.'

The end of the Christian's life is redeemed by insertion into a series of repetitions. Our physical death loses something of its sting by becoming a derivative repetition of a death that has already taken place, first of all on the cross and then at the font. To show this, churches in the catholic tradition place the Paschal candle, which is lit in the middle of Easter night to represent the resurrection, by the font at baptisms. The same large candle is then brought to stand by the coffin at a funeral. Similarly, Easter night is the principal feast at which to bless water, which is then used in baptism and can be sprinkled on the coffin at a funeral.[9]

A pivotal Old Testament story to read at Easter is the crossing of the Red Sea during the exodus, since it connects death, water and new life. In baptism, we die to the powers of evil, represented in this reading of the story by the Egyptians.[10] If in later life the Christian is troubled by the threat of bodiless, spiritual evil, it is wise to turn back to baptism and remember that the devil and his angels are for the Christian overwhelmed by the waters of Christ's death, and therefore by the water of our baptism.

Baptism is a sharing in the death of Christ, and it is also about sharing in his resurrection. In the interpretation of the Red Sea story, this is represented by the land of milk and honey. (In earlier rites, newly baptized babies were given milk and honey to drink after baptism.) Resurrection is the 'yes' that grows out of baptism's 'no', and overshadows that 'no'. We typically dress babies in white for their baptism. This is appropriate, as it is an Easter sacrament whenever it is celebrated. The early Church had even more powerful symbolism for an adult baptism. Candidates dressed in 'ordinary' clothes before baptism but changed into white garments after. If changing is impractical today, it may be possible to wrap a white or brightly coloured robe around the new Christian after baptism. The Church of England includes this option in the *Common Worship* rite, accompanied by the words 'You have been clothed with Christ. As many as are baptized into Christ have put on Christ.'

Alongside death and resurrection, we also understand baptism in terms of washing, adoption and in-grafting. Like other images, washing contains elements of continuity and discontinuity: the body remains; the dirt is removed. Overall, continuity has the upper hand, except that it is one of the tragedies of sin that, to extend this metaphor, we can become more attached to the dirt than to our humanity lying underneath. Seen sensibly, however, washing tells us something important about the relation of continuity and discontinuity in salvation: the clean body is in a sense even more what it is than the dirty body. Life in Christ is about growing into our humanity.

Christians in the early Church so rejoiced that baptism washes away sin and its consequences that some would leave baptism until the end of their lives. The sacrament functioned almost like their one token for a really decent dry cleaner: better not use it glibly. The bishops and other teachers opposed this, not least because those who leave baptism for the eleventh hour may die at half past ten. More than that, baptism is the gateway into the abundant grace of God: a beginning, not an end. People do go astray after baptism, however. We need to admit that, and will return to it when we come to the sacrament of confession and absolution.

Rebirth and adoption are another way in which continuity and discontinuity are combined in baptism. In John 3, the uncomprehending Nicodemus asks Jesus, 'How can anyone be born after having grown old? Can one enter a second time into the mother's womb and be born?' (John 3.4). He is right to be perplexed. Far more than he could imagine at the time, the impossible actuality of human *re*birth rests on an even more impossible entering into the womb. 'Can one enter a second time into the mother's womb and be born?' Indeed, but how could the Son of God enter into a mother's womb *a first time* and be born? The possibility of newness in baptism rests on God's most profound 'new thing': the Incarnation. The mediaeval hymn for before the Gospel at Christmas Midnight Mass puts this beautifully, opening *Præter rerum seriem, parit deum hominem, virgo mater*: 'Beyond the order of things, someone is born of a virgin, who is both divine and human'.[11] The Incarnation marks the arrival of something new, something unguessed at. So does baptism. This newness at the heart of baptism makes it the supreme sacrament of forgiveness, for forgiveness is the most novel and creative of all gestures, which is why it is supremely divine. (We will return to these themes when we consider the sacrament of confession.)

18

We can gather all of these themes together in the idea of offering. In baptism we offer our lives, our whole selves, to God. Or, if we are the parents of a child, we offer that child to God, just as parents did throughout the Old Testament, and just as Mary and Joseph did when they presented Christ in the Temple on the fortieth day. This offering is total, since baptism is a death.

In baptism, God offers us his all, and a new life. Central to the ways the Church has described this dynamic is to say that God makes us his sons and daughters. That is one reason why infant baptism is so appropriate: we offer God our sons and daughters, and he returns them to us, as both our own children and now his also.

Baptism unites us to Christ in his life, death and resurrection, and it does this by making us part of his body. Baptism unites us to Christ through the Church and is the door to the other sacraments. 'Baptism opens the gate of heaven,' wrote the Venerable Bede.[12] We will consider this theme of incorporation more fully in the chapter on the Eucharist.

Infant baptism

Christians – Protestants as well as Catholics, Orthodox and Anglicans – baptize infants. The teachers of the Reformation – Luther, Calvin, Cranmer and Zwingli, for instance – were in a habit of bringing the practices of the Church under careful scrutiny and yet they each accepted the rightfulness of baptizing infants. Those who rejected infant baptism, the *anabaptists* (or 'rebaptizers'), were a small minority among the Protestant reformers. Only with the growth of Pentecostalism has an insistence on 'believer's baptism' become a numerically significant Protestant position.

Already, in writings of the early Fathers and councils of the early Church, the baptism of children was seen as important. In a passage worth quoting for the beauty of its account of Christ's identification with all of humanity, Irenaeus of Lyons spoke in the second century of 'infants' being 'born again to God' through Christ:

> he became like us in every way so that whoever we are, we could be restored to God: He was made an infant for infants, to make infants holy; a child among children, sanctifying childhood; a young man among young people, becoming an example to them, and sanctifying them to the Lord. So he was a grown-up among older people,

that he might be a perfect teacher for all . . . sanctifying older people, and becoming an example to them also. And thus he came even to death, that he might be 'the first-born from the dead, having pre-eminence among all', the Author of Life, who goes before all and shows the way.[13]

Augustine upheld infant baptism in his *Literal Commentary on Genesis*[14] and in a treatise on the baptism of infants.[15] This tradition, going back in explicit form to the second century, is consistent with the New Testament witness. Infant baptism may well have been practised from the very earliest days, since we hear of *whole households* being baptized, a phrase that would include infants and children in the ancient world (Acts 16.15, 33; 18.8; 1 Cor. 1.16). We also know from the funeral epitaphs of Christian children that they were initiated into the Church as infants from early in the history of the Church.[16] The canons of the Church of England forbid any minister from obstructing the baptism of an infant.[17] A priest can insist on a reason-able programme of preparation for the family before baptizing a child, which might be all the more important if the family are not regular churchgoers. However, this cannot be used as an obstacle to baptism.

Programmes of preparation, called catechesis, have been import-ant since the earliest days of the Church. A child that is baptized a Christian should be raised a Christian, and that means bringing them to church. We have to trust parents over this, and honour their sense that, with baptism, they are doing the right thing by their child. This will often succeed in building a bridge between a family and the Church.

No one can be rebaptized

Baptism is the means by which we enter into Christ's Church and receive the grace of being born again. For this reason baptism cannot be repeated under any circumstances. If a Christian were to leave the Church to become a Muslim or Mormon, and then return, he or she would not need to be baptized again. The first and only baptism would hold good. Adults who have been baptized as infants, who later wish to take hold of their faith in a new and intentional way, need not and indeed cannot be rebaptized. Instead, first and foremost, they should be confirmed. They can also reaffirm their baptismal

vows,[18] as traditionally the whole Church does each Easter. Here, we
are reconnecting with the real foundation of our salvation, which is
God's faithfulness, rather than trying to shore anything up by virtue
of our own faith.

This absolute ban on rebaptism was worked out by the early Church
in the days of persecution. If a Christian renounced Christ out of
fear of torture, but then repented, he or she did not need to be
rebaptized. Nor did those who had originally been baptized by heretics, using water and the name of the Trinity, need to be rebaptized.
In the words of Augustine of Hippo,

> both the perfection of the sacrament is honoured and the delusion
> of their mind is corrected . . . nor, because his error [that of the her-
> etic] is to be condemned, is the baptism of Christ to be therefore
> extinguished . . . the truth of the sacrament is to be distinguished
> from the error of the person who believes amiss . . . therefore, when
> any one grounded in any error, even outside the Church, has been
> baptized with the true sacrament, when he or she is restored to the
> unity of the Church, a true baptism cannot take the place of a true
> baptism.[19]

Occasionally, someone is unsure if he or she has been baptized as
an infant. We can also imagine the situation where a baptism is
carried out in an emergency and there is later some doubt about
whether the candidate really got wet at all, or whether the minister
completely fluffed the words. The Book of Common Prayer of 1552
put this picturesquely:

> If they which bring the infants to the Church do make an uncertain
> answer to the Priests questions, and say that they cannot tell what they
> thought, did, or said, in that great fear and trouble of mind (as often-
> times it chanceth) . . .

In such cases, the Church administers *conditional baptism*. This is
precisely not rebaptism; in fact it is its opposite. So careful is the
Church to avoid any hint of rebaptism that the words are changed.
To continue with our quotation from 1552, the form of words there
is: 'If thou be not baptized already, *N.* I baptize thee in the name of
the Father, and of the Son, and of the Holy Ghost. Amen.'

Baptism deserves to feature prominently in each Christian's awareness and sense of identity. We might foster a 'baptismal piety': towards
the font and towards holy water offered at the church door, if that

is our tradition, in concern for baptismal candidates and those in preparation for baptism, in marking the anniversary of our baptism as a day of celebrating, in approaching Easter as the baptismal season and reaffirming our baptismal vows, and in celebrating every Sunday as the day of resurrection.[20]

3

Sacramental character

The purpose of the sacraments is to unite us to God, who has united himself to us in the Incarnation. The word 'Christian' itself means this: we have taken on Christ and become his, who has taken us on, and become ours. In this chapter we will see how central this idea is to the theology of the sacraments, through which God works so that we may come 'to the full stature of Christ' (Eph. 4.12).

Each of the sacraments can be understood in terms of union with Christ, but four, in particular, are marked out as 'forming Christ in us', to use the language of Paul (cf. Rom. 8.29; Gal. 4.19). In the technical language of sacramental theology, they are said to impart the 'character' of Christ. These are baptism, confirmation, marriage and ordination.

Our English word 'character' comes from a Greek word, *karaktes*. We find it only once in the whole of the New Testament, in the arresting opening of the Letter to the Hebrews, one of the Bible's most poetic accounts of the Incarnation:

> Long ago God spoke to our ancestors in many and various ways by the prophets, but in these last days he has spoken to us by a Son, whom he appointed heir of all things, through whom he also created the worlds. He is the reflection of God's glory and the exact imprint of God's very being, and he sustains all things by his powerful word.
>
> (Heb. 1.1–3)

The word *karaktes* signifies so much that it is difficult to render it into English. We can say that Christ is the 'exact imprint of God's very being' (NRSV), the 'very stamp of his nature' (RSV) or the 'impress of God's own being' (NJV). In the Greek of the first century, the word *karaktes* meant a stamp or engraving tool, and the mark that it leaves, perhaps embossed in wax on a letter or treaty.[1] The Geneva Bible therefore translated this passage as the 'engraved form of his person'. From this we can take two separate ideas, one objective and mainly from the Greek and the other subjective and mainly from the English, although the two ideas are closely related.

The Greek *karaktes* highlights a change. The sacraments that impart character leave a 'stamp' upon the soul. They 'conform' us to Christ, which is to say that they change our form or shape at the deepest level, in a thoroughly objective way. The English 'character', on the other hand, reminds us that this should not be an abstract fact without consequences. Our 'character' is who we are and how we naturally behave, especially how we behave in a difficult situation, when the chips are down. The sacraments have both of these dimensions. The objective change suggested by the Greek should show itself in observable changes, as suggested by the English.

All of the sacraments are about transformation: the 'sacraments of character' change who we are; the other sacraments nurture or repair that character. When we co-operate with God through the sacraments, they bring the character of Christ to fruition; they engrain it in our attitudes and reflexes (what the theological books call our 'habitual disposition'). They do not free us all at once from the urge to do wrong, but over time that is their goal.

Just as the sacraments bring transformation, they also invite action. In a sense they even require it. This is clearest with the four 'sacraments of character': having received them, an individual has a duty to live as a Christian (baptism and confirmation), a husband or wife (marriage), or a deacon, priest or bishop (ordination). The other three sacraments send us away with a charge for that particular moment. With confession, for instance, the challenge comes from the words of Christ: 'your sins are forgiven' (Mark 2.5); 'go, and *sin no more*' (John 8.11 AV, emphasis added). The Eucharist propels us out into the world, just as we have brought the world and its needs to the Eucharist to offer them to God. The beautiful fifth-century Liturgy of Malabar asks:

> Strengthen for service, Lord, the hands
> That holy things have taken;
> Let ears that now have heard thy songs
> To clamor never waken.
> Lord, may the tongues which 'Holy' sang
> Keep free from all deceiving;
> The eyes which saw Thy love be bright
> Thy blessèd hope perceiving.

The feet that tread Thy holy courts
From light do Thou not banish;
The bodies by Thy body fed
With Thy new life replenish.[2]

A familiar Western name for the Eucharist is Mass, a name that makes a point about commissioning. It comes from the Latin *Missa*, found in the *closing* words: *Ite, missa est* – 'Go, you are dismissed' (or, literally, 'Go, this is the dismissal'). Our word 'Mass' comes from something rather close to 'Off with you! Out you go! You've got work to do!'

Character and names

In the biblical world, character was expressed in a name. Little sense of this remains to most of us in the West, and in this we are poorer. In the sacraments, however, a relation between name and character lives on. This is most familiar in baptism. While baptism is far more than the Christian naming ceremony, it is also that. Immediately before baptizing a child in many liturgies the priest asks for the child's name: 'Name this Child' is the blunt form of words in the Book of Common Prayer. Even more universally, the name is used in the act of baptism itself: '*Andrew Paul*, I baptize you in the name of the Father, and of the Son, and of the Holy Spirit.'

At baptism we give a child a name to mark him or her out as a Christian, a name that signifies something about Christ. This is a *Christian name*, a name the boy or girl can grow into while growing into Christ. Until recently, when cultural sensitivities moved us to the blander alternatives of 'forename' or 'first name', in historically Christian countries we referred to a person's name as his or her 'Christian name'.

By a Christian name we mean one that reveals Christ. Christ is revealed to us in the history of redemption in the Bible and in his saints: those who have most perfectly exhibited his character throughout history. It makes sense to give a Christian child a Christian name in this sense. This might be the name of an Old Testament hero but, since we usually give children more than one name, it similarly makes sense for at least one of their names to be a Christian name in the fullest sense, which usually means the name of a saint: a Christian hero, one in whom the mystery of Christ has come to full fruition.[3]

The other sacraments that impart the character of Christ are each also associated with name taking. In marriage, we do not necessarily find it palatable today for a wife to take her husband's surname but, at best, it bears witness to the new state of common life that the sacrament brings about. We might not like the sense that it subsumes the woman to the man; in more liberal circles, what is of value in the tradition has sometimes been preserved by both parties taking both surnames.[4]

That leaves confirmation and ordination. Here too we find a good and venerable tradition of taking an additional name, although it has largely passed out of use in Anglican circles. Confirmation, with its sense of taking hold of one's Christian identity with both hands, is a good opportunity for name taking. We do not have to amend our birth certificates; we can just ask the bishop (or, often, the priest for Roman Catholics) to add the name at the confirmation.

Character and worship

One intriguing, and profound, angle on sacramental character is that in every case it bears some relation to worship. This link does not simply mean that we should celebrate the sacraments within a context of worship, although certainly we should. The point is that each of the sacraments that bestows the character of Christ calls us to worship God in some particular way. These sacraments make a person a Christian (baptism) or develop that Christian life in a particular way or state (confirmation, marriage and ordination). They are to make the Incarnation bear fruit in us, and it is clear from Christ's conversation with the Samaritan woman that one goal of the Incarnation is that the Father seeks 'worshippers' (John 4.23). Christ is the perfect worshipper of his Father; he is 'the high priest of our confession' (Heb. 3.1). In each of these sacraments we enter in some unique way into Christ's priesthood and the praise he offers to the Father.

Baptism makes us members of the Church, God's new Temple, and a part of the priestly people of God. At confirmation, we take our part in this worshipping community by our own choice and as adults. With confirmation we take on a certain duty to be part of the worshipping community. A confirmed Christian should join with his or her brothers and sisters to celebrate the Lord's resurrection each Sunday, and on certain other principal feasts: Christmas, Epiphany,

Ash Wednesday, Holy Week, the Ascension. The list will differ slightly from church to church. Luther and Calvin soon thought better of momentary laxity over Sunday worship.

That the life of the ordained person is oriented towards worship should be obvious: the bishop is the chief celebrant of the Eucharist in each region; the priest offers the Eucharist in each place, and in most traditions all clergy take on the responsibility to say prayers (the 'offices', such as morning and evening prayer) each day, offering to God the worship and thanksgiving, the penitence and the needs, of the whole Church, and indeed of the whole world.

To say that *marriage* establishes the couple as worshippers may be a strange idea for many of us today, but that makes it both intriguing and promising. The Christian couple begin a life together. The life of the Christian is a life of worship. The couple now enter that together and worship together. Marriage creates a home, and in the Christian home we find worship and all the other sorts of prayer that go along with it: thanksgiving, intercession and penitence. The Roman Catholic Church has an appealing and potent way to express this. It is willing to call each Christian household a 'domestic church'.[5] Aquinas touches on this, saying that within a marriage we bring children up within a setting of worship and to be worshippers themselves.[6] It is also a Protestant idea. An important principle of the Reformation was that the family should provide the day-by-day setting for prayers and Bible reading.

This connection between character and worship (as it used pithily to be expressed, 'the imputation of character is the delegation to cult') is relatively unexplored at present. If we are looking to invigorate a sacramental understanding of the Christian life, thinking through what it might mean for our sacraments of character to establish us as worshippers offers some of the 'easiest gains'.

Indelibility

Sacramental character is indelible. The stamp that God places upon us cannot be rubbed out. Even if we rebel against him to the ultimate degree, even if we choose damnation, we do so as Christians or, for instance, as priests. There are priests in Dante's *Inferno*, and bishops and deacons, married people and many who had embraced mature Christian discipleship. That adds to their tragedy.

Sacramental character is indelible. The churches that follow the ancient tradition of the Church over ordination would never reordain someone (if, for instance, someone wandered away and came back, although he or she might be commissioned afresh for Christian work). A priest can be stripped of every vestige of position and every scrap of authorization but, 'defrocked' or even excommunicated, his or her Eucharist would be a Eucharist (valid although illicit); his or her absolution would be an absolution (likewise illicit but valid).

The Church forged these principles *in extremis*, in face of martyrdom, torture and apostasy. During the horrific persecutions of the early centuries, some clergy forsook their faith and office in face of bloodcurdling threats.[7] That posed a problem especially, as it happens, in North Africa. There, a group grew up of those who had held firm. They rejected priests who had not held firm. For this group, an apostate Christian could not be restored; an apostate priest or bishop retained no vestige of his ordination. This church of super-Christians were called the Donatists (prosaically, after their leader, Donatus, who had remained true under terrible ordeals). Against them stood Augustine, Bishop of Hippo. In this, he earned for himself the title of 'doctor of grace' (as he could have done many times over, on many accounts). Grace is the beginning and end of things for Augustine. No one is a Christian, or indeed a priest, a deacon or a bishop, because he or she deserves to be. We receive these things as gifts, and 'the gifts and the calling of God are irrevocable' (Rom. 11.29). God's grace calls us, and God's grace restores us if and when we fall. Ever the disciple of St Paul, Augustine challenged the Donatists with this, one of Paul's most basic points: we are saved by grace. Rebaptism was heartily condemned, as was reordination. A deacon can be ordained priest, and a priest can be ordained bishop, but a deacon is always a deacon, a priest is always a priest, and a bishop is always a bishop. The tussle with the Donatists, which Augustine won quite spectacularly, also established the helpful principle that 'the unworthiness of the minister' does not invalidate any sacrament that he or she might perform. If I celebrate the Eucharist in a state of great sin, I do myself no good, but it makes no difference to the grace that you obtain at my hand. To think otherwise would place the emphasis on the priest and not on God. As Aquinas says, if the only efficacious sacraments were those performed by good people then we would in a sense be vesting our hope in all that the sacraments bring in that person and his or her righteousness, not the righteousness of Christ; but 'Cursed are those who trust in mere mortals' (Jer. 17.5), as he quotes.[8]

One reason that the sacraments of character are indelible is their wonderful quality of being always ongoing. I was baptized in 1974 and, being a sacrament of character, it made me a-baptized-person, with the grace of baptism always springing up anew. The same applies to my confirmation and my ordinations. I might wander from my vocation as a Christian, or as a deacon and a priest, but if so I do not need to be baptized, or confirmed, or ordained a second time, or a third or fourth time. I simply need to reconnect to what I received (and the sacrament of confession will usually be the best way to do that). The sacraments of character are not like a bucket of water, thrown over someone once, getting him or her very wet at the time, but soon dripping off and evaporating. We do not need a fresh bucket thrown over us. The sacraments of character are like a hose-pipe with the tap permanently turned on. The married couple can wake up every morning and receive the grace of marriage like they did on their wedding day. One or both of them might stand on the hosepipe, impeding its flow. In that case, the lifting of a foot is what is needed.[9]

Marriage also, for the bulk of the Christian tradition, throughout Christian history, has been seen as indelible. Today some Christians recognize remarriage, although not all of them take that to deny the indissolubility of marriage. This is the trickiest of pastoral questions, and we will return to it in the chapter on marriage. Whatever reactions this question provokes in heart or mind, it should not distract us from the value of remembering the centrality of grace and the hosepipe-over-bucket abundance of the sacraments of character. We can daily re-appropriate the grace of our baptism, confirmation, marriage or ordination. This is one of the most immediately useful things we can learn about sacramental theology, and one of the insights that can bring the sacraments alive for us.

4

The Eucharist

(The greatness of baptism is that it incorporates us into the body of Christ. Its link to the Incarnation is to extend the Son's relationship to the Father to human beings, such that we too become children of God. The goal of his dying and rising, to which baptism unites us, writes Paul, was that Christ might become 'the firstborn among many brothers [and sisters]' (Rom. 8.29). Alongside baptism, the Eucharist, Lord's Supper or Holy Communion is the other great sacrament of the body of Christ. Baptism is the once-for-all sacrament of incorporation into Christ; the Eucharist is the sacrament of ongoing incorporation, where Christ takes us to himself by giving us his very self. 'I am the food of the fully grown,' Augustine has Christ say in his *Confessions*; 'grow and you will feed on me. And you will not change me into you, like food that your flesh eats, but you will be changed into me.'[1] As with baptism, the meaning of the Eucharist unfolds in terms of the pattern set in the Incarnation. In the Eucharist, as in his earthly life, Christ comes to be with us and, through his presence, to unite us to God and to one another. He comes to teach us, to be our food, to be our sacrifice, to make us friends of God. All this we find in the Eucharist.

Good Book –

Presence

God was made flesh)to be among us and redeem us from the predicament we have brought upon ourselves through our waywardness, namely estrangement from God. We will turn to the first: to Christ's presence among us. We have the word 'Incarnation' from the beginning of John's Gospel, where we read that the Word was *made flesh* and *dwelt* among us. The Greek for 'dwelt' is quite literally an image of dwelling *with*: it means 'pitched his tent among them'. That theme is taken up at the end of the book of Revelation, another work in the Johannine tradition: 'See, the home of God is among mortals' (Rev.

21.3). The presence of God among his people forms the bookends for the story that falls between his first and second coming, the story of sacrifice and redemption, for which 'being among mortals' was both the precondition and goal. We find a similar theme at the very end of Matthew's Gospel: 'remember, I am with you always, to the end of the age' (Matt. 28.20).

The early Church was clear that Christ's presence with his Church was perpetuated in a particularly remarkable way in the Lord's Supper. A great twentieth-century scholar of early doctrinal history, J. N. D. Kelly, summed this up as follows: 'Eucharistic teaching, it should be understood at the outset, was in general unquestioningly realist, i.e., the consecrated bread and wine were taken to be, and were treated and designated as, the Saviour's body and blood.'[2] It was cheerfully 'realist': Christ is *really* present; we *really* eat and drink his body and blood. About this there was no great dispute in the early Church. In around AD 110, Ignatius of Antioch, a prominent early bishop, soon to be a martyr, wrote to the Christians in Antioch that

> [The heretics] abstain from the Eucharist and from prayer because they do not confess that the Eucharist is the flesh of our Saviour Jesus Christ, flesh which suffered for our sins and which that Father, in his goodness, raised up again.[3]

Ignatius labels those who denied the presence of Christ in the Eucharist at the start of the second century as 'heretics'. Their heresy was Gnosticism: a complex of ideas built around the belief that the material world is the flawed work of an inferior god, from which a purely spiritual Christ can rescue us by secret knowledge (or 'gnosis'). They denied the presence of Christ in bread and wine because they distrusted the whole idea that God, who is Spirit, can act in matter. Irenaeus of Lyons devoted himself to combatting this idea at the end of that century, and again made the most explicit possible link between rejecting this heresy and affirming the presence of Christ's body and blood in the bread and wine.[4] Already by about AD 150, his younger contemporary, Justin Martyr, had written that

> not as common bread nor common drink do we receive these; but since Jesus Christ our Saviour was made incarnate by the word of God and had both flesh and blood for our salvation, so too, as we have been taught, the food which has been made into the Eucharist by the

Eucharistic prayer set down by him, and by the change of which our blood and flesh is nurtured, is both the flesh and the blood of that incarnated Jesus.[5]

Before the early Church had settled on a worked-out doctrine for the Incarnation, or the Trinity, or even completely fixed the canon of the New Testament, the Eucharist was understood to put before us the body and blood of Christ, present with his people. Little more needed to be said by way of precise definition of what was going on.

By the time we come to the high Middle Ages, however, definition was very much on the mind of theologians. We reach an important moment with the Fourth Lateran Council of 1215 and the word 'transubstantiation'. As with Ignatius and Irenaeus, the context for this discussion of sacramental theology seems to have been one of world-hating heresy, in this case that of the Cathars, who represented the Gnostic resurgence of their time. (Gnosticism is forever re-emerging.) Transubstantiation has been dragged through the hedges over the past half-century: for being obscure, for being philosophical, for being mediaeval. The chief crime is employing terminology from Aristotle. Aristotle, however, was one of the most acute thinkers in human history, and his distinction between substance and accidents is one of his most useful insights. It points to a difference between *what* something is (its substance) and *how* it is (its accidents). Something can change in many ways and still be the same individual and kind of thing. I grow up and then grow old; I learn to play the piano and then more or less forget; I change in innumerable ways, but I am still the same person, and that similarity rests in being the same kind of thing throughout: a human being. My *substance* is to be a human being; my accidents are to be this tall, have this colour of skin, know these facts, and so on.

We answer questions such as 'How?' and 'In which ways?' with a string of *accidents*. We answer the question 'What?' with the name of the *substance*. Transubstantiation makes a strong claim about what is going on in the Eucharist. There is a transformation, such that after the consecration of the elements the best answer to the question 'What?' is 'the body of Christ' and 'the blood of Christ', rather than 'bread' and 'wine'.[6] This makes the Eucharist a particularly intense example of the dynamic we have already encountered: that God accommodates his communication to the means we can take in. In the

Eucharist, he communicates his body and blood to us, veiled, under the accidents of bread and wine.

This is not to say that God is deceiving us. What we see in the priest's hands, and then consume, is not something pretending to be bread. As the body and blood of Christ, it is the truest food, the truest drink: 'my flesh is true food and my blood is true drink' (John 6.55). It is appropriate that it should come to us as bread and wine.

The Eastern Church has not sought to define the presence of Christ in the Eucharist in such precise terms. As the *Catechism of St Philaret of Moscow* puts it,

> the word transubstantiation [*metousiosis*] is not to be taken to define the manner in which the bread and wine are changed into the Body and Blood of the Lord; for this none can understand but God; but only this much is signified, that the bread truly, really, and substantially becomes the very true Body of the Lord, and the wine the very Blood of the Lord.[7]

It is not clear that the West has wanted to say more than this.[8]

With the Reformation, debates about the presence of Christ reached fever pitch.[9] Over this, the reformers differed as much among themselves as they did from the received, 'catholic' position. Martin Luther (1483–1546) was closest to the earlier tradition with his doctrine of 'consubstantiation': what we have before us is *substantially* both bread and the body of Christ, both wine and the blood of Christ. This suited Luther's paradoxical turn of mind, since it is axiomatic for the metaphysics of Aristotle, from which this terminology is borrowed, that something is only ever substantially *one* thing. Even a hybrid would be one thing, not two: namely, the hybrid. On this basis, consubstantiation is a noble failure. Nor can we really justify consubstantiation by appeal to the two natures of Christ, which do perfectly overlap. The utter difference of humanity and divinity allows for that overlap, whereas 'body' and 'bread' are similar: they are two different sorts of material substance. If we try to use the human–divine relationship to describe an overlap of bread and body, we are in danger of rendering the body of Christ wholly, and only, divine, when in fact it is as material as any bread.

John Calvin (1509–64) gave a prominent role in his eucharistic theology to the Holy Spirit. He did not believe that the elements of

Holy Communion underwent any substantial change, but that does not imply a particularly 'low' view of the Eucharist. In receiving the bread and wine, the Holy Spirit communicates the *power* or *effect* of the body and blood of Christ to the believer. This is sometimes called 'virtualism', not from a contemporary sense of 'virtuality' but from *virtus*, meaning power or strength. The effect of the sacrament is so significant for Christians that we should not quite say that the elements are quite as they were before. Although 'not changed in themselves', as T. W. Coleman puts it, they 'are set apart to a new and holy use, and are not therefore in all respects the same as before'.[10] Calvin's position makes for a particularly devout reception of Communion but it does not quite pass the test, set out by Ignatius and Irenaeus, that *materiality* matters. The grace of Christ comes to us when we eat and drink, but it is not particularly clear why what goes on in Holy Communion could be described as *eating* Christ's body and *drinking* his blood (as Jesus puts it in John 6 and Calvin wants to uphold, as in *Institutes* IV.17.1) or a *participation* in his body and blood (as Paul puts it in 1 Cor. 10.16), rather than simply a reception of the grace that Christ has won for us. The bread and wine are 'signs'[11] of the body and blood, but the body and blood become themselves signs of something else, namely the nourishment that God provides.[12]

Huldrych Zwingli (1484–1531) went furthest of the mainstream Protestant reformers in shifting the emphasis away from the elements to the faith of the believer. He was insistent that when Christ said 'is' in his declaration 'This *is* my body' (Luke 22.19, emphasis added) he meant 'signifies' rather than the more usual status of the word as the third person singular form of the verb 'to be'. Like the other reformers, Zwingli rewrote the Communion service. For him, it was principally a memorial meal, by which, with the sermon centre stage, our faith can be strengthened. This puts him a long way from the settled faith of the early Church over the Eucharist, and that doctrinal consensus established well before there was clarity over points such as the two natures of Christ and the doctrine of the Trinity.

The Book of Common Prayer of the Church of England is clearly a Reformed rite. It was a work in progress until the enduring form of 1662, and reflects a particularly Anglican desire to retain legitimate latitude. While not affirming the whole of Catholic doctrine, it seems careful not to rule some of it out either. Anglicans of different stripes have been able to use it in a way which was compatible with their particular emphasis. It is a simplified rite compared to those of the Middle Ages, and yet it upholds many aspects of earlier liturgical practice: the celebrant must be a priest;[13] the elements must be bread and wine, and the priest must touch them; the consecrated elements must be devoutly consumed if any remain.

If we were to attribute one position to the Prayer Book, it might be 'receptionism': that in receiving the bread and wine, we receive the body and blood of Christ (in some sense) and (in all surety) their grace. 'Grant', the priest asks, 'that we receiving these thy creatures of bread and wine, according to thy Son our Saviour Jesus Christ's holy institution, in remembrance of his death and passion, may be partakers of his most blessed Body and Blood.'

As a complete scheme for what is going on, receptionism falls short in a similar way to the position of Calvin and even Zwingli. As Coleman, a twentieth-century Free Church writer, put it, going to the heart of the problem, 'These words of the Saviour identify in some way His Body and Blood with the elements ... *Receptionism* breaks this identity: it separates the symbol and the Reality symbolised.'[14] Bread and wine are 'means', not simply 'helps'; 'instruments', not merely 'influences'. They are more than 'memorials' and aids to fellowship.[15] He quotes the 'down-right evangelical Free Churchman' P. T. Forsyth, for whom the Sacraments

> not only suggest Him [Christ], but ... convey [him] to the Church ... They are not accidental suggestions. They are connected with Him much more than by association. They are more than souvenirs, keepsakes. They are bequests. They are conveyances. And what they bring and mean is of the very essence of what He was and is and willed to be to the Church – its Redeemer and Sanctifier.[16]

Receptionism has its strengths, however, if taken as a true but incomplete account. In receiving the bread and wine we do *receive* the body and blood of Christ and their grace. We can say that and leave open the *means* by which it happens. A benefit of a very robust account of Christ's eucharistic presence, such as transubstantiation, is that all the other, less substantial, accounts come with it. If we can say that we receive Christ's body and blood *substantially*, then we can also say whatever else Calvin, Zwingli or the receptionist wants to say. Pope Paul VI pointed to a similar dynamic in relation to his own immediate context in his encyclical *Mysterium Fidei* (1965). Some had proposed that a complete account of the Eucharist could be found simply in saying that what the bread *signifies* had changed or that what it ultimately *leads to* had changed (positions called 'transignification' and 'transfinalization' respectively). Paul VI replied that there is indeed a new significance and a new 'finality', but that this comes *because* of the radical transformation rendered by the true *presence* of Christ in the elements rather than instead of it.

We began this section with a reference to God 'pitching his tent' among us. John was making a reference to the Old Testament tabernacle in which God dwelt with his people and which later found its expression in the holy of holies in the Temple at Jerusalem. That was a focus for prayer for the people of Israel, so much so that they prayed *towards* the place of God's presence (e.g. 1 Kings 8). In many churches, the consecrated bread is stored or 'reserved' so as to be immediately available for the Communion of the sick. It is natural that this 'reserved sacrament' has also become a focus in prayer for the sense of God's abiding presence with his Church.

Reception in both kinds

Christians in the Eastern churches have always received in both the bread and wine ('reception in both kinds'). This was the pattern in the West until the twelfth century, after which it became more and more common for the celebrant alone to receive from the chalice. The argument was that Communion is complete in either kind, so why risk spillage? This *premise* is widely held to be true, but as a *practice*, reception in one kind introduces the unhelpful symbolism of a sharp distinction between the priest and the people, and Holy Communion is for both. When it comes to spillage, precautions can be made, and since Christ was willing to spill his blood upon the ground to redeem us, it seems unduly protective to refrain from communicating that blood to his people on the basis that we risk spilling it.

Communion in both kinds – the restoration of the chalice to the people – was one of the great battles of the Reformation. It was one of the first reforms to be enacted in England, for instance.[17] It was granted for a while during one of the few moments of early practical conciliation between Roman Catholicism and the nascent stirrings of Protestantism on the continent, in what is now the Czech Republic. The story is an ugly one. The leader of this reforming group, Jan Hus, was tricked with a letter of indemnity into giving himself up but was then arrested, tried and burnt at the stake for heresy. To end the wars that arose as a protest, the chalice was extended to communicants by the Council of Basle in 1431, although this was later revoked in 1462.

Since the Second Vatican Council, Communion in both kinds has been restored sporadically in the Roman Catholic Church, since although a full Communion is made through either of the elements, 'Holy Communion has a fuller form as a sign when it is distributed under both kinds.'[18] In practice, the opportunity for lay Christians to receive the chalice has been patchy, and is different from province to province and even from parish to parish.

These were fierce disputes in the Reformation period. Frequently, disputes lead to the clarification of theology, however much they may be deplored on other grounds. One clarification was this sense that the whole of what the Eucharist offers is present in each of the elements, bread or wine. This is called the doctrine of 'concomitance'. The key is the *living* presence of Christ. We are not talking about a crude change of the bread into his body and of the wine into his blood. Rather, in the Eucharist, Christ comes to be present with us. He is present in all that he is in both elements, present, as the phrase goes, in 'body, blood, soul and divinity'.[19] This understanding was upheld in the Church of England by the English Sacrament Act of 1547.[20] Primarily, it stressed the significance of Communion in both kinds. However, it also allowed that the chalice could be withheld if 'necessity otherwise require'. 'Necessity' was said to require suspension of Communion in both kinds during the outbreak of 'swine flu' in 2009.[21] The idea of concomitance also means that someone with coeliac disease can communicate, if necessary, from the chalice alone, and that an alcoholic need not receive from the chalice. It also means that a dying person who has lost the ability to swallow can be communicated with a drop from the chalice.

Catholic and Orthodox Christians have always had a very strong sense of the objective presence of Christ in the Eucharist, a sense that is also preserved in some traditions of Anglicanism and Protestantism. This is sometimes criticized as leading to *reification* – rendering the body and blood of Christ as *things* or objects: what one critic has called 'a sacred object or relic par excellence of Christ's body'.[22] Frederick Bauerschmidt has made a forceful reply:

> only if the Other who is encountered in the Eucharist is not deter-mined by human consciousness, but rather determines human con-sciousness – saturates human consciousness – can the Eucharist be anything other than idolatry and the Eucharistic community anything other than one more human community.[23]

The Eucharist, on this estimation, stands as the very opposite of worship conceived as 'therapeutic liturgy', as it often is today.[24] When I was at theological college, the task for the group planning the main service of the week was often to work out 'what we could make of the Eucharist', as if it were a relatively featureless substrate upon which one could paint significance.[25] Conceived this way, the liturgy becomes a human opportunity for *us* to 'create environments that will foster transformative encounters with God'.[26] This places the emphasis on *us* arranging the conditions for the encounter with God, who on that account could increasingly be redundant. Worship becomes the 'tool' through which we can manipulate our emotions and psyche, and little in the liturgy depends on whether God is present, or even whether God exists. In contrast, robust eucharistic realism puts the emphasis on God, who descends to exceed anything we could imagine. Rather than saying that we can construct something 'very suitable' for our needs, we say that we have gathered to receive a gift that God gives.

If we see nothing more in the Eucharist than symbolism and a change of meaning in the elements, we are, as Bauerschmidt puts it, placing 'the consciousness of the celebrating community' at the centre, as the focus.[27] The objectivity of Christ's presence in the Eucharist is why it weathers the criticism, made by the great German 'master of suspicion' Ludwig Feuerbach, that religion is simply humanity becoming conscious of itself.

Sacrifice

Christ, who came into the world and who comes to us in Holy Com-munion, offered himself upon the cross. That offering exceeds our understanding, on account of which the atonement is an area of Christian theology where a number of overlapping understandings have been in play since the beginning. A prominent strand among them is sacrifice. As we have seen Augustine commenting, Christ offers himself in such a way as to be all four things connected with sacrifice: the sacrifice, the priest, the God to whom sacrifice is offered and, as a human being, one with those for whom sacrifice is offered.[28]

Christ is present in the Eucharist in his risen life, but not so as to efface an emphasis, as in all the sacraments, upon the cross. In the Eucharist and baptism, in particular, we are united to the death of Christ and, *through that,* with his resurrection. Baptism sets us on the path described, and desired, by Paul in Philippians 3: to share in his sufferings, becoming like him in his death, so as to share in his resurrection from the dead. What happens once for all in baptism is recapitulated and developed week by week as we receive Communion. The Eucharist is not one of those sacraments that imparts a once-for-all character, but it is the principal means by which that character of Christ is perfected in us. That necessarily takes the form of joining us to the sacrifice of Christ (in line with Gal. 2.20 and Col. 1.24).

We will turn to Christ's resurrection later. For the moment we consider that Christ is present with us as the one who offers himself to the Father on our behalf. The association of the last supper with sacrifice is present from the start, and is therefore associated with the repetition of that supper when we do it 'in memory' of him. Christ chose bread and wine, which are sacrificial elements, as for instance in Leviticus or, before that, in the offering of Melchizedek. He talks about the supper as sealing a covenant in his blood, and covenants were sealed by sacrifice. Christ was making the closest relation between the events of the evening of Maundy Thursday, in the upper room, and those of the next day, on Golgotha.

Christ is our offering. As he comes to us week by week, or day by day, in the Eucharist he comes as our offering, as the one who now stands for ever before the Father 'to make intercession' for us, on the basis of his offering upon the cross, so that we are able to 'approach God through him' (Heb. 7.25). As with Christ's presence in the Eucharist, from the days of the early Church, even before other doctrines were established, the Eucharist was described as a sacrifice. We find this, for instance, in the writings of Gregory of Nazianzus and in the Liturgy of Serapion (mid fourth century).[29]

In 1897 the Archbishops of Canterbury and York provided a perceptive threefold analysis of what it means for the Eucharist to be a sacrifice:

> first we offer the sacrifice of praise and thanksgiving; then next we plead and represent before the Father the sacrifice of the cross, and by it we confidently entreat remission of sins and all other benefits of the Lord's Passion for all the whole Church; and lastly we offer the sacrifice of ourselves to the Creator of all things which we have already signified by the oblation of His creatures. This whole action, in which the people has necessarily to take its part with the Priest, we are accustomed to call the Eucharistic sacrifice.[30]

John Chrysostom spoke about this in one of his homilies at the end of the fourth century:

> I wish to add something that is plainly awe-inspiring, but do not be astonished or upset. This Sacrifice, no matter who offers it, be it Peter or Paul, is always the same as that which Christ gave His disciples and which priests now offer: The offering of today is in no way inferior to that which Christ offered, because it is not men who sanctify the offering of today; it is the same Christ who sanctified His own. For as the words which God spoke are the very same as those which the priest now speaks, so too the oblation is the very same.[31]

The reformers were more or less as one in either rejecting the idea of the Eucharist as a sacrifice (for Luther the Mass 'stank of oblation'[32]) or seeing it as something entirely spiritual (as in Cranmer's 'this our sacrifice of thanks and praise'). In this they were rejecting a real abuse, which had arisen in the later Middle Ages, of talking about the Eucharist as a 'new sacrifice' (as for instance in the rite used in England, the Sarum Rite) and of putting undue emphasis on the work of the priest.

The patristic, and contemporary Catholic and Orthodox, understandings can seem impossibly distant from that Protestant position. In fact, useful parallels and bridges are close at hand. In the house church I belonged to as a teenager, the elders would talk of 'pleading the blood', which was to say, of praying to God and making petitions *on the basis of the merits of Christ's blood, or sacrifice.* I remember hearing that phrase in the same week that I happened, uncharacteristically, to be helping out the choir of the parish church

I had otherwise left. We sang a short but magnificent eucharistic hymn by William H. H. Jervois:

> Wherefore, O Father, we Thy humble servants
> Here bring before Thee Christ, Thy well belovèd,
> All perfect Offering, Sacrifice immortal,
> Spotless oblation.
>
> See now Thy children, making intercession
> Through Him our Saviour, Son of God incarnate,
> For all Thy people, living and departed,
> Pleading before Thee.[33]

We were 'pleading the blood'. Jervois describes the Eucharist as the Fathers described it: as a means by which the saving death of Christ upon the cross is proclaimed and pleaded. Christ's sacrifice was offered once for all upon the cross, and in that sense, there is no new sacrifice. Christ's death did not, however, stop the rest of his life being an offering to the Father, and ascended to heaven he constantly presents his offering. With the Eucharist, the Church has thought since early days, we are drawn into that offering. The Father places into our hands the greatest of all offerings: Christ's own.

When John and Charles Wesley wanted a doctrinal commentary for their collection *Hymns on the Lord's Supper* (1745) they turned to Daniel Brevint's *The Christian Sacrament and Sacrifice* (1673), from which they included many extracts, among them the following:

> This Sacrament, by our remembrance, becomes a kind of Sacrifice, whereby we present before God the Father that precious Oblation of His Son once offered. And thus do we every day offer unto God the meritorious sufferings of our Lord, as the only sure ground whereon God may give, and we obtain, the blessings we pray for. Now there is no ordinance or mystery that is so blessed an instrument to reach this everlasting Sacrifice, and to set it solemnly forth before the eyes of God, as the Holy Communion is. To men it is a sacred Table where God's minister is ordered to represent from God his Master the Passion of His dear Son, as still fresh, and still powerful for their eternal salvation. And to God it is an Altar whereon men mystically present to Him the same Sacrifice as still bleeding and suing for mercy.

In the Eucharist we acknowledge that we have nothing to offer to the Father that is comparable to the offering of Christ, and yet God gives precisely that offering into our hands. 'The King of king and Lord of lords, Christ our God', as the Liturgy of St James has it, 'comes forth to be our oblation, and to be given for food to the faithful'.[34] Behold 'this *our* sacrifice of thanks and praise,' wrote Cranmer in his Communion service,[35] but 'Father, we remember all that *Jesus did*, in him we plead with confidence *his sacrifice* made once for all upon the cross,' we read in *Common Worship* prayer E.[36] *Common Worship* takes us back towards the theology of the catholic Middle Ages and an emphasis on the offering of Christ, but in precisely the way that accords best with Protestant concerns: indeed on this matter it 'out-Protestants' Protestantism.

Because the Eucharist brings us so close to the offering of Christ, it is the primary occasion for intercession, when 'we call upon God for the common peace of the Churches, for the welfare of the world, for kings, for soldiers and allies, for the sick, for the afflicted; and in summary, we all pray and offer this Sacrifice for all who are in need'.[37] The intercessions of the Eucharist are intentionally *general*. Gathered to unite our prayers with those of Christ, we pray for all people, for others as well as ourselves, for needs of body as well as soul, for those outside the Church as well as those within, for civil matters as well as ecclesiastical. There is an expansiveness to eucharistic intercessions that expresses itself naturally in lists. In the Book of Common Prayer we ask God 'to comfort and succour all them, who in this transitory life are in trouble, sorrow, need, sickness, or any other adversity'. In the ancient Liturgy of St James we pray for Christians who are 'voyaging . . . journeying . . . in foreign lands, in bonds and in prison, captives, exiles, in mines, and in tortures, and bitter slavery . . . [those] in sickness or travail . . . tribulation or distress', for peace and for an end to 'scandals . . . wars . . . and heresies'.[38] Every Christian can come to the Eucharist with one or more matters for prayer on his or her mind, prayers which he or she wishes to unite with the offering of Christ. This is often called one's 'intention' for the Eucharist.

The end of sacrifice

We would be unfaithful to the constant mind of the Church, and to the New Testament, if we were to deny that the Eucharist unites us to the sacrifice of Christ. That makes it all the more important for us to make sure that we understand *how* the sacrifice of Christ is a sacrifice. It is not one more sacrifice among all the sacrifices of Israel, or Greece or Rome, or the Incas, or the slave markets, and so on. Christ offers the sacrifice that *ends* sacrifice (Heb. 9–10). Jesus undid the futile cycle of sacrifice and counter-sacrifice. He makes his death upon the cross a perfect expression of the eternal love of the Trinity, which is without loss, without frustration and without violence. After the cross and resurrection there is no more animal sacrifice, nor can any pragmatic 'sacrifice for the sake of a greater good' sit easily with the Christian: not in politics, not in economics and not in war.

The sacrifice of Christ, upon which we lay hold in the Eucharist, is the sacrifice that fulfils all that sacrifice entailed and strove for, but which also leads to the resurrection. It was not loss for the sake of loss; it was loss for the sake of fullness. It offers this pattern for Christians today. In a world of sin, the love of God is worked out under conditions of sacrifice, and we must be willing to bear our part in this. 'In the sacred mystery of communion', wrote Underhill, 'the Christian accepts membership of the Body which continues in time this sacrificial life of Christ.'[39] However, our hope is of restoration and resurrection. In the eucharistic offering, we offer all that we are in the bread and the wine, but in the confidence that God will give in return. He will not give back exactly what we gave, and in that, our offering has to be without strings attached. We have to be willing, as Irenaeus wrote, to be 'the Church, that poor widow, [who] casts all her life into the treasury of God'.[40] God will, however, give back more than we can imagine: 'a hundredfold . . . [although] with persecutions – and in the age to come eternal life' (Mark 10.30).

Feeding

To say that the Eucharist has the nature of a sacrifice is already to say that it has the nature of a feast, since at a sacrifice the community characteristically both offers and eats. Unlike any other sacrifice, however, it is not the dead body of the victim that we eat in the Eucharist, but the living body of the victim who has become victor, and triumphed over death as well as sin.

John's Gospel devotes a long chapter, chapter 6, to one reason that Christ came. He came to be our food, 'the living bread that came down from heaven'. A related cluster of ideas sees Christ as the tree of life. In the words of an anonymous eighteenth-century poem, Christ is an apple tree:

The tree of life my soul hath seen,
Laden with fruit and always green:
The trees of nature fruitless be
Compared with Christ the apple tree.

His beauty doth all things excel:
By faith I know, but ne'er can tell
The glory which I now can see
In Jesus Christ the apple tree.

For happiness I long have sought,
And pleasure dearly I have bought:
I missed of all; but now I see
'Tis found in Christ the apple tree.

I'm weary with my former toil,
Here I will sit and rest awhile:
Under the shadow I will be,
Of Jesus Christ the apple tree.

This fruit doth make my soul to thrive,
It keeps my dying faith alive;
Which makes my soul in haste to be
With Jesus Christ the apple tree.[41]

The central metaphor comes from the Song of Solomon:

As an apple tree among the trees of the wood,
so is my beloved among young men.
(Song of Sol. 2.3)

In patristic and mediaeval commentary, this imagery was taken up for Christ.[42]

In both of the two parts of the Eucharist, the liturgy of the word and the liturgy of the sacrament, we are fed. In the readings and homily we are fed in our minds. 'My body lives by my soul,' wrote Augustine, 'and my soul lives by thee.'[43] However, human beings are bodily as well as intellectual creatures, and therefore Christ becomes for us not only intellectual bread but also physical bread. With the Eucharist, our soul, which is to say our innermost being and the form of our whole identity, lives 'by God' and, in an inversion characteristic of the Incarnation, here our soul lives by the body (by which we eat and drink the body and blood of Christ), rather than our body living by our soul.

The author of 1 John writes of 'what we have heard, what we have seen with our eyes, what we have looked at and touched with our hands' (1 John 1.1). We can even add, in a very Johannine fashion, 'what our mouths have tasted'. On this note, for the coronation of Elizabeth II, Ralph Vaughan Williams composed an anthem for the moment when she received Communion with the text 'O taste and see that the LORD is good' (Ps. 34.8). The ancient Liturgy of St James makes the same point: 'O taste and see that the Lord is sweet: He that is broken and not divided, distributed to the faithful and not consumed, for the remission of sins and eternal life.'[44]

Unless we are very sick, our desire for food will be one of our strongest desires. We can take this as one reason for Christ's coming to us in bread and wine. With this sacrament he both harnesses and purifies our natural desires, represented by our desire for food and drink. We are taught to desire a good which comes to us from beyond the world by means of the most mundane of goods that comes to us from within the world. We read of a wonderful, instructive misunderstanding along these lines in John's Gospel. Christ offers the crowd bread that 'gives life to the world' (6.33). The people seem to take this in a very physical, mundane way, replying, 'Sir, give us this bread always' (John 6.34)[45] Although they did not understand to the full what Jesus was saying, we can commend them for their direct, earthy wish to apprehend what Christ promises. It is we, with our refined spiritual understanding, who risk coming off the worse from a comparison with the crowd, if we do not desire Christ's gift in the Eucharist *even more* passionately because we understand it more fully. Coming *as food*, Christ accommodates himself, to use a favourite phrase from Calvin, to a way in which our desire runs naturally, in the desire for bread and wine. We might also say that, in this way, Christ captures our attention through elements that naturally capture our attention. Not only is food close to the centre of our daily interests, it is also apprehended by all of our senses. In the readings of the liturgy of the word, Christ is *heard*; in the liturgy of the sacrament the elements are not only *seen* and *touched*; they are also *smelt* and *tasted*. Since our physical and sensual life can be so resistant to the 'Invisible and Supernatural', in the words of Evelyn Underhill, it has pleased God that the invisible and supernatural comes to us through our physical and sensual life: 'the touch and taste of visible food assuring us of the intangible and invisible food'.[46]

Although this natural human desire for food and drink is good in itself, it can also be led astray, and lead us astray. Placing the Eucharist at the centre of the Church's life, Christ opened the way for it to discipline and reform our attitude to food and drink. Paul commented on this just before he gave his own account of Communion and the last supper in 1 Corinthians 11. This sacrament is intimately connected to how we eat and drink. Those who have more must share with those who have less and not eat in luxury while others go hungry. The Eucharist also chastens our excess in that these humble elements provide a feast that surpasses anything that could be bought in any restaurant, at any price. That sense of moderation is also reflected in ancient disciplines of fasting before receiving Communion. For others, the message is not of restraint but of encouragement: the Eucharist draws the solitary person, and the miser, into sharing and hospitality.

The missionary Vincent Donovan recounts the story of the first celebration of the Eucharist among the Masai in Tanzania:

> Masai men had never eaten in the presence of Masai women. In their minds, the status and condition of women were such that the very presence of women at the time of eating was enough to pollute any food that was present.[47]

Donovan held to the principle that the Masai were free to accept the gospel or to reject it, but at its heart stood the Eucharist and a message of equality before Christ. 'They did accept it . . . I don't remember any other pastoral experience in which the "sign of unity" was so real to me.'[48]

With food, as with anything else, the Christian message is that we need not desire *less*, but we should desire *rightly*. The Eucharist is given for the education of our desire. In the Eucharist we learn to desire *more* and *rightly*: 'Lord, you have bewitched me with the spell of desire for you; you have enchanted me with divine love. Consume my sins in a spiritual flame and make me worthy to be filled with your sweetness', runs part of the prayer of St John Chrysostom before Communion.[49]

Our happiness lies in God, but sometimes this is no more obvious to us than a haunting suspicion that things can be better than they are. In the words of Augustine, we seek the happiness that is to be found in God as if 'longing to learn of it as though it were something unknown, which either I had never known or had so completely forgotten as not even to remember that I had forgotten it'.[50] In the Incarnation, God seeks us, so that we might learn to seek him. The Eucharist is the constant reminder, not only of that wedding banquet where our longings will be truly satisfied, but of an even deeper theological point, that if we are to feed we must feed upon God himself. Julian of Norwich asked,

> God, of your goodness, give me yourself . . . you are enough for me, and anything less that I could ask for would not do you full honour. And if I ask anything that is less, I shall always lack something, but in you alone I have everything.[51]

The Eucharist and incorporation

The two greatest sacraments, baptism and Eucharist, the sacraments called 'dominical' or 'of the Lord', and 'generally necessary for salvation', are both sacraments of the body and of incorporation into the body of Christ. The '-corp-' of 'incorporation' is *corpus*. The reality of Christ in the Eucharist points to the reality of Christ in his Church and in our brothers and sisters. 'Eucharistic realism' belongs alongside 'ecclesial realism', and vice versa. In the context of a discussion of the Eucharist, Paul writes, 'Now you are the body of Christ and individually members of it' (1 Cor. 12.27). He urges us to discern 'the body' (1 Cor. 11.29) and it is not quite clear if he meant the presence of Christ in his brothers and sisters or in the eucharistic elements. Given the content of the surrounding passages, it is likely that he meant both.

This link was one of the principal themes of the twentieth-century Jesuit theologian Henri de Lubac. He recognized what it meant for practical Christian life and put it into action, making him one of the unsung theologian heroes of the Second World War. De Lubac made his point through historical analysis in his book *Corpus Mysticum* (1944): as the West stopped seeing the physical as the domain of the spiritual, so Christians shifted to seeing the Eucharist as primarily spiritual rather than physical, and therefore missed its message about the practical needs of their fellow men and women. Inasmuch as anything was recognized as the body of Christ, this became concentrated on the eucharistic elements, not the people. As such, the elements picked up the name 'true body' after about the end of the twelfth century, with the Church relegated to the position of the 'mystical body'. Previously, the terms had been used the other way: the Church was called the 'true body' and the Eucharist (from around the fifth century) was called the 'mystical body'. For de Lubac, recognizing the people as *the body* has political consequences for the social nature of Christianity, its life and hope. He had mapped some of this out in his book *Catholicism: Christ and the Common Destiny of Man* (1938), a book that remains as significant now as when it was first published. According to his diagnosis, a drift in Christian piety towards private interiority had left the French Church weak to resist descent into right-wing sympathies in the later 1930s and early 1940s. A spirituality of 'spiritual things', he thought, had left the Catholic unable properly to resist the Vichy regime. In contrast, de Lubac put forward the idea, then radical, that the individual is united with Christ through being united with the community.[52] After all, the sacraments are not performed by lone individuals; they are rites of the communal Church. He stressed this communality by putting Communion at the heart of the Church: the sacrament that continually makes and remakes the Church by continually uniting us to *Christ*.[53]

The idea that the Eucharist makes the Church became important in twentieth-century theology. It is to say no more than 1 Corinthians 10.17: 'Because there is one bread, we who are many are one body, for we all partake of the one bread.' It suggests that in the Eucharist the Christian stands in a relation of immediacy to the last supper, as the act by which Christ formed his disciples into the body of his Church. The Eucharist makes the Church in a parallel fashion to the way in which the Passover makes the Jewish community, not only at the first Passover, but in every subsequent yearly remembrance. We find a strong parallel in the Jewish Mishnah:

> In every generation a man must so regard himself as if he came forth himself out of Egypt, for it is written, 'And you shall tell your son on that day saying, "It is because of that which the Lord did for me when I came forth out of Egypt."'[54]

The Eucharist builds the Church. One response has been to recognize that *children* are members of the Church, as well as adults. The Orthodox Churches retain an early tradition of communicating even (baptized) babies.[55] In the West this practice died out in the twelfth century. In 1910, Pope Pius X restored Communion to children, if not infants, when he said that all baptized Catholics could receive Communion 'from the age of reason' (which is taken to be around the age of seven). This shifted First Communion to before confirmation. His decree began, in Latin, with the words *Quam singulari* or 'How special':

> How special, we see clearly from the pages of the Gospel, was the love that Christ showed to children when he was upon earth . . . It was his delight to be in their midst . . . At the same time he was not pleased when they would be driven away by the disciples.

There is every reason to extend Communion to children. If they are baptized, they are fully members of Christ's body. The 'age of reason' is chosen as the age at which children are capable of receiving Communion with proper reverence. There is no necessity for a child to be able to understand the intricacies of eucharistic theology. Not only would that bar many adults from receiving, but it would also put the emphasis on our understanding rather than on God's grace. If anything, it is adults who should seek to emulate the faith of children, not children who need to emulate the sophistication of adults.

Eucharistic realism and the limits of Communion

Part of the link between the Eucharist being the body of Christ and the Church being the body of Christ is the association of the Eucharist with unity and universality. From the days of the early Church, the Eucharist was seen as fulfilling the prophecy of Malachi, that a day would come when 'a pure offering' would be presented 'in every place' (Mal. 1.11).[56] We talk of the unity between churches as 'communion' and of churches being 'in communion' with one another. Sadly, we also find churches 'out of communion' with one another, often because of doctrinal differences. Among the most tragic consequences of this is the inability of Christians to receive Communion together, in each other's churches.

Churches tend to take one of two positions towards the imperfect unity of the Church and its relation to the Eucharist. For some, such as Anglicans, the Eucharist transcends our current divisions, being a gift from God. It is a gift from that future when we are fully reconciled to God and to one another. On this basis, the Eucharist is extended to all fellow Christians, not least as medicine in face of our disunity. For others, such as Roman Catholics, eucharistic hospitality must not run ahead of the situation on the ground.[57] Part of the difference here is over how closely the 'workings' of the Eucharist can be defined. Those churches that are less prescriptive about how the Eucharist 'operates' tend, naturally, to be less demanding of other Christians as to the doctrinal tests they must pass in order to be able to receive Communion. Another difference is over understandings of disunity as a sin. For Anglicans, for instance, the disunity of the Church is an offence against God, but the guilt is fairly evenly distributed. It would bar us *all* from Communion if it barred any. For Roman Catholics, the sin of disunity is largely upon the shoulders of those said to have schismatized from the true (Roman) church, although other Christians do not see it that way. This is in itself taken to be enough to block someone from Communion, until he or she has repented and been reconciled.

Another way to address this is to ask where we recognize the Church. Christians do not agree that every Christian denomination or movement is equally an instantiation of the Church. Episcopal churches, in particular, hold that something is lacking in churches that have not preserved episcopal order and authority. All the same, every baptized Christian is in some strong sense 'within the Church', since baptism is the sacrament of incorporation. He or she is a member of Christ's body, even if that connection is not worked out in the institutional or organic way that a particular church might uphold as definitive. If we can recognize someone as a member of Christ's body, then we should be able to communicate him or her (the usual caveats about sin and scandal withstanding). This is simply to live by Augustine's principle:

> If you, therefore, are Christ's body and members, it is your own mystery that is placed on the Lord's table! It is your own mystery that you are receiving! You are saying 'Amen' to what you are: your response is a personal signature, affirming your faith. When you hear 'The body of Christ' you reply 'Amen.' Be a member of Christ's body, then, so that your 'Amen' may ring true![58]

This principle, which argues for a greater degree of inter-communion among Christians, is what prevents the churches containing the vast majority of the world's Christians from communicating the unbaptized. Justin Martyr began his discussion of the Eucharist in his *First Apology* with a discussion of this topic:

> no one is allowed to partake but the man [or woman] who believes that the things which we teach are true, and who has been washed with the washing that is for the remission of sins, and unto regeneration, and who is so living as Christ has enjoined.[59]

This rule seems to have been practised in apostolic times and was spelt out in the *Didache* at the end of the first century: 'Let no one eat and drink of your Eucharist but those baptized in the name of the Lord'.[60]

We should of course accept with joy anyone's aspiration to belong to what the Eucharist also is: the body of Christ. The proper means for joining that body, however, is baptism. Baptism takes up the themes that Justin described in relation to the Eucharist: profession of the Christian faith and turning from what is contrary to the life that Christ 'enjoined'. If someone will accept these, he or she can be baptized, and why would anyone not embrace that saving sacrament? If a person will not accept these, then neither is it appropriate for him or her to receive Communion.

Frequency of Communion and preparation

Over the course of Church history, the frequency with which Christians received Communion has changed. It is possible that Acts 2.46 suggests a daily celebration in the earliest days of the Church: 'Day by day, as they spent much time together in the temple, they broke bread at home and ate their food with glad and generous hearts.' Weekly Communion was stressed from the second century onwards, on Sunday as the day of the resurrection, and on other principal feast days. By the time of the Fourth Lateran Council in 1215, we find a different link to the resurrection: Communion was required at least once *per year*, at Easter. This was a minimal requirement, and it is likely that people communicated a little more regularly than this. On the other hand, the penalties for not receiving at least once per year – being barred from ever entering a church again and from having a Christian burial – suggest that wholesale disengagement from Communion was a real danger. Most Christians were in church much more often than once per year, but we can certainly note a shift from participating in the Eucharist by receiving to participating by being present at the liturgy, increasingly by saying one's own private devotions and by observing the spectacle of the Mass.

Since the Reformation, the Church of England has urged its members to communicate at least three times each year, at Christmas, Easter and Pentecost. At the Restoration, following the Puritan Commonwealth, there was a move towards monthly Communion. Both the Methodist Revival and the Oxford Movement led to even more frequent Communion. The Wesleys are said to have received Communion several times per week. Since the impact of the 'liturgical movement' in the mid twentieth century, the Eucharist has been restored in most parishes as the principal Sunday service and proper celebration of the resurrection. In the Roman Catholic Church, the biggest shift came in 1905 when Pius X recommended frequent Communion. Rather than seeing sinfulness as a bar to Communion, Communion was seen as a remedy for sinfulness (although no one in a state of mortal sin should receive Communion until he or she has first made confession).

Today, in the Church of England, the Eucharist is to be celebrated 'at least' each Sunday in every parish, and on principal feast days, Ash Wednesday and Maundy Thursday.[61] The Eucharist is also celebrated on days of national thanksgiving, including events in the life of the local church such as ordination, confirmation and, normally if not usually, marriage. In the words of Schleiermacher, the greatest Reformed theologian of the century centred round 1800:

> It is pretty clear that Christendom as a whole in its public teaching and practice has from of old regarded the Supper as the climax of public worship. The rounded whole of our united experience in public worship would seem to us incomplete unless at definite points – and most often at the highest and holiest points – the Supper held its place as the most intimate bond of all.[62]

The move to Communion at least weekly, rather than a few times each year, is a wonderful development. Even such a restoration, however, is not without its problems. Communion was infrequent in previous centuries but it was taken very seriously. It was an encounter with one's God and an occasion for careful preparation, including the examination of one's conscience and manner of life. In the eighteenth century, for instance, a century often held (incorrectly) as one of no great piety, the second most popular book, after the Bible, was a manual for preparation for a devout reception of Holy Communion. During the Cambuslang revival in Scotland, of 1742, Christians newly convicted of the truth of their faith spent days in preparation for receiving Communion. Serious preparation was an important part of the birth of the Methodist movement. The Book of Common Prayer set an exhortation both to those who would communicate lightly[63] and to those who would hold back from communicating.[64]

Today, Communion is frequent but it is not necessarily devout. The solution is probably to make it more devout rather than to make it less frequent. A long-established pattern is to set aside an hour beforehand, perhaps immediately beforehand, but not necessarily, for prayer, Bible reading and looking over one's life in penitence, forgiving others and seeking to be forgiven. The benefit of doing this the day before is that we will then have time to make amends with those with whom we are at enmity, or whom we have wronged, if necessary. Preparation does not need to take an hour. Any period is better than nothing, and it will allow us to approach the Eucharist (which means 'thanksgiving') with a sense of what it is we are thankful for, and to take Communion a little more aware of what that means. It also provides an opportunity to bring before God the prayers that we want to unite with Christ's offering.

For most of the life of the Church, communicants fasted on the day they received Communion, until after they had received it. This was one important reason why evening celebrations were rare. This discipline is still observed in the Orthodox Churches. In the Roman Catholic Church this was relaxed in the twentieth century to a fast of an hour before reception. Fasting is an important way to enter into preparation with our bodies, and to rank the food we are about to eat above any other food. (Those who are sick, or have responsibility for the sick, are taken to be exempt from all requirements to fast.) Abstaining from food is only part, however, of putting God first. As the Orthodox hymn for the first Monday in Lent has it, true fasting is also 'estrangement from evil, temperance of tongue, abstinence from anger, separation from desires, slander, falsehood and perjury'.

If we are conscious of grave sin, which can helpfully be characterized as a sin against love or charity, we should not receive Communion until we have put that right with our neighbour and with God, which for many traditions will mean making use of the sacrament of confession. Otherwise, we should receive Communion, with due penitence, as an aid against sin. The converse is that there are limited but real occasions when a priest should refuse Communion to someone who, in the words of the Prayer Book, is in 'malicious and open contention with his neighbours, or other grave and open sin without repentance'. Ideally this is signified in advance, having obtained a decision from the bishop. However, someone may be turned away from Communion at the last moment in the case of 'grave and immediate scandal to the Congregation',[65] which is to say, if a situation has become known to the congregation such that it would present a stumbling block to faith (the Greek is *scandalon*) for the Church to be seen to communicate that person.[66] This is a delicate area. We are all sinners in need of God's grace but, on the other hand, priests, as shepherds, have a duty to defend their flock from causes of stumbling.

We should not, however, end this chapter on such a downbeat note. The Eucharist holds before us the nature of God's best gift: the gift of his own self, in Christ in the manger, upon the cross, resurrected and coming again, and in the humble elements of the Holy Communion. Here presence and sacrifice, nourishment and sacrifice meet. In the words of Evelyn Underhill:

> here the Church, the Mother of Souls, looking towards Calvary, takes up the ancient tokens of sacrifice and lifts them up to Eternity in the name of Christ her high priest, and with them satisfies her children's hunger and thirst. By this unceasing giving and receiving the whole of life is to be eucharistized; this is the Christian task. It is to be offered, blessed, and made the vehicle of that infinite self-giving, of which our small reluctant self-giving is the faint shadow on earth.[67]

5

The anatomy of the sacraments I: signs, matter and form

This chapter is the first of two in this book that will examine the nuts and bolts of sacramental theology. Taking time to think about the aspects of a sacrament is not simply the work of theologians with too little to do, although it can be. It is not necessarily a matter of playing with things until they break, nor is it the sole preserve of Roman Catholic theology, with its strong scholastic heritage. The Church of England's *Catechism* of 1662 includes a section that runs as follows: '*Question*. How many parts are there in a Sacrament? *Answer*. Two: the outward visible sign, and the inward spiritual grace.'

In this chapter we will begin to look at these elements. We will consider the sacraments as *signs* and examine the physical and verbal dimensions: what are called the *matter* and the *form*.

Sacraments as signs

The sacraments are signs that promise and point to salvation. However, they are also more than signs, since they convey that salvation to us. Sacraments both promise and deliver what they promise.[1] Lawrence Mick makes the comparison with a kiss. It signifies love but it is more than a sign: it 'somehow contains the love it expresses, though it does not exhaust that love'.[2]

The Greek word used for 'sacrament' in the Eastern Church is *mysterium*. This has the sense of a clue to something hidden. Jesus used the word when he said that the parables reveal the kingdom of heaven, but not directly: 'to you it has been given to know the *secrets* of the kingdom of heaven' (Matt. 13.11, emphasis added). This prehistory of the word 'mystery' is close to the prehistory of the word that gives us 'sacraments': the Latin *sacramentum*. A *sacramentum* was a visible sign of an invisible relationship. It was the word used, for instance, of the Roman soldier's tattoo, which we encountered in Chapter 1 and which linked him to the (divine) emperor.

Signs can bear a loose relation to what they signify. The numeral 7 does not have much in common with what it represents. Sacraments, however, bear a close material resemblance to the spiritual benefit they promise. Water cleanses; bread and wine sustain and bring joy; reaching out to touch someone is a sign of recognition and support. The material aspect is not arbitrary. The natural meaning is retained but excelled. The Eucharist *is* a meal, for instance, but it is more than any other meal. In the sacraments, God takes something natural, perfects it and makes it the means by which he – who transcends nature, but made it – works in us. The sacraments are signs, and more than signs.

Sacraments are more than signs because of the degree of sureness they bear. If sacraments operated as mere signs then the assurance and comfort that they offer would go no further than our own assurance that we had received what they signify. The sacraments, however, are not underwritten by human confidence but by a divine gift. They rest on the unshakeable faithfulness of God, and therefore deliver what they signify. This surety is one reason that the sacraments work with simple, directly communicative elements: water and washing, bread, wine and feeding. God uses that which is ordinary because it is communicative and straightforward, and because the sacraments address aspects of the human predicament every bit as fundamental as those simple elements and gestures and the needs to which they naturally relate.

This sureness is given a name in Latin, with the phrase *ex opere operato*. The sacraments work 'from the work having worked', which is to say, 'by the very fact that the action has been performed'. The point is to shift the emphasis away from *how* the act was performed: was the water the right temperature? Did the priest have the right tone of voice? Was I in the right mood? Had I prepared properly? Was I good enough? Did I get my theology right? It also shifts the emphasis from the person performing the sacrament and onto the power, goodness and promise of God.[3] Our faith, motives and goodness are only of secondary importance. As with faith in general, our confidence rests not in our own faith but in the faithfulness of God in Christ. That faithfulness has been demonstrated, most of all, in his Passion. The Passion of Christ is the highest expression of the fidelity of God, and the Passion is the source from which the sacraments draw their efficacy.

The Scriptures do not lay out the principle of *ex opere operato* in so many words, but they do make it clear in other ways. The sacraments are presented as having a foundational quality, which requires and implies sureness, such that baptism and 'laying on of hands' are listed among the foundational principles in Hebrews 6.1–2. The simplicity of the sacraments presented to us in the New Testament chimes with this sense of security. Of baptism, Paul writes,

> *all* of us who have been baptized into Christ Jesus were baptized into his death [and] if we have been united with him in a death like his, we will *certainly* be united with him in a resurrection like his.
>
> (Rom. 6.3, 5, emphasis added)

Of the Eucharist he writes, 'The cup of blessing that we bless, is it not a sharing in the blood of Christ? The bread that we break, is it not a sharing in the body of Christ?' (1 Cor. 10.16). Inasmuch as *ex opere operato* shifts the emphasis in thinking about salvation away from our own efforts and onto God, it could not be closer to the message of the New Testament.

Form and matter

Alongside the sign and the thing signified, the other most significant distinction in sacramental theology is between *form* and *matter*. The matter is the stuff-and-gestures of the sacraments; the form is the words that are spoken.[4]

In the sacraments, God communicates with us. More than that, in the sacraments God communicates himself to us. God communicates with us, and to us, in the way in which human beings understand, and we naturally communicate by means of a mixture of words and gestures.[5] These two aspects are present in the sacraments in the form and the matter.

We see the same combination of word and gesture-and-materiality from Jesus when he performs miracles. The Reformed tradition places its own strong emphasis on the sacraments as communicative when it talks about them as a sort of preaching. All Christians could do to learn from this insight, although they are not *only* a sort of preaching or intellectual communication. We are not Gnostics and God is concerned about more than ideas.

Form

Human beings are linguistic animals. For us, culture, language and identity are interwoven with our materiality. When we talk about the sacraments, we tend to stress their materiality. The element of form (the words), however, reminds us that we search in vain for materiality that is devoid of meaning and spiritual significance. The glory of matter is that it is never just matter.

The sacraments involve words as well as matter. Just as Christ dignifies all matter by drawing it into the sacraments (and, before that, into his Incarnation), he dignifies all language by drawing it into the sacraments (and because the eternal Word came among us and communicated in human language). As the Word-Incarnate, God puts his truth not only into the frailty of flesh – our earthenware vessels (2 Cor. 4.7) – but also into the frail vessel of human language. As the poet David Jones put it, Christ 'placed himself in the order of signs'.[6] In doing so, he began to redeem our speaking and thinking.

In the theology of the Middle Ages we can find a tendency to look for the minimum effective form for each sacrament. Minima are hardly of the order of the sacraments, which deal with God's abundance, but the task seemed a useful one as part of a quest for certainty. For that reason, since we are concerned with the certain communication of God's grace, we would not want to risk deviating from what the Church has given us to say. The words that are attached to each sacrament are intentionally short and unconvoluted: unlike a magic spell, they do not rest on us getting something complicated right.

The principal area of contention today in this area is in the use of 'inclusivized' titles for the Trinity at baptism, such as 'in the name of the creator, redeemer and sanctifier'. Most churches – and certainly all of the largest and ancient ones – are emphatically clear that the formula 'I baptize you in the name of the *Father*, and of the *Son*, and of the *Holy Spirit*' (and its Eastern Orthodox equivalent) cannot be changed under any circumstances. The baptized person needs to know that he or she was baptized, and one church has to be able to trust that another has administered baptism in the time-honoured fashion.

The alternative, 'inclusivized' formula poses two principal problems. First, it is not biblical. Matthew closes his Gospel with Jesus telling his disciples to baptize in the name of the Father, Son and Holy Spirit. Baptism and the Eucharist fulfil two of the most direct commands that Jesus ever gave ('Go . . . make disciples . . . baptizing . . .' and 'Do this . . .'; Matt. 28.19; Luke 22.19). We should do what he says.

Second, when we baptize someone in the name of the Trinity, we baptize him or her into the Trinitarian faith, in all of its depth and profundity, as it has been explored over two thousand years. Almost all of that Trinitarian depth is missing from the alternative formula. In particular, 'creator, redeemer and sanctifier' signifies nothing about the relations of the Persons of the Trinity, and yet the doctrine of the Trinity is about nothing if it is not about relations. 'Father' and 'Son' present us with inherently relational names, in a way that 'creator' and 'redeemer' do not. Nor is 'sanctifier' relational, whereas 'Holy Spirit' has been interpreted relationally in the West: just as 'Holy' and 'Spirit' apply also to the Father and the Son, in an analogous way the Spirit proceeds from the Father and the Son as their relation of love.

With the traditional names, we understand God to be three without ceasing to be one. We can express this, for instance, with the idea of 'subsistent relations': the Son makes the Father the Father, and the Father makes the Son the Son. We can then see that the Son is so integral to the Father being the Father, and vice versa (and in a parallel, but mysterious way, with the Spirit), that the Father is not independent of the Son, nor vice versa. With 'creator, redeemer and sanctifier', however, we could quite easily mean three gods, and be tritheist, not Trinitarian. The traditional formula does not in itself rule out tritheism, but with notions such as subsistent relations, which follow directly on from it, we begin to see the difference. The alternative formula also risks the opposite of tritheism, namely 'modalism'. It is perfectly possible to take 'creator, redeemer and sanctifier' to mean the one God in three guises or modes: one God doing three different things, without any sense of a Trinity of Persons at all. By being relational, the traditional names point beyond both tritheism (three gods who might or might not be related) and modalism (an isolated God with three jobs to do).

The alternative formula is usually put forward in the name of gender equality, 'Father' and 'Son' being gendered terms. If so, it is a disappointing victory for the feminist sensibility if it makes the foundational rite of Christianity *less* relational. The restoration of a proper sense of relationality has often been close to the core aims of feminist theology.[7] A different alternative, of 'Parent, Child and Spirit', falls foul of fewer of these doctrinal pitfalls, but it remains unbiblical and without ecumenical acceptance, and is therefore ruled out with the full force of canon law.

Anyone baptized with any form of words that deviates from those laid down by the principal traditions of East or West cannot be considered to be baptized, and should be baptized using the correct formula: not 'baptized again' but baptized for the first time.[8]

Does the form and matter of sacraments change?

In the early Church we see a rare example of the Church changing the form of a sacrament, to the extent that a previously valid form came to be considered as invalid, now not a legitimate option. The example relates to baptism 'in the name of Jesus'. Although the Trinitarian form was by far the most common in the early Church, the Jesus-only formula was considered a valid form for the sacrament because it is found in the book of Acts (2.38; 8.16; 10.48; 19.5; 22.16). There was nothing about baptizing in the name of Jesus that contradicted baptism in the Trinitarian name. Once the person of Christ was under heated debate, however, those who denied the Trinity could take refuge in the Jesus-only formula as a way to deny a Trinitarian understanding of God. After Arius – who denied that Jesus was fully divine – the Jesus-only form no longer made clear that someone was being baptized into the Trinitarian faith of the Church. To guard that faith, it became necessary to insist that only those baptisms were unquestionably valid that were 'in the name of the Father, and of the Son, and of the Holy Spirit'. Today we might occasionally encounter Pentecostal churches that call themselves 'Oneness Pentecostals' or 'One God Pentecostals'. They baptize in the name of Jesus out of concern over the developed doctrine of the Trinity. As with those baptized with an unrecognized Trinitarian formula, anyone baptized solely 'in the name of Jesus' should seek baptism with the accepted form.

Matter

The sacraments are about materiality, and by them the Church makes a strong stand against Gnosticism, with its disparagement of matter. For Christian theology, the flesh sanctifies the soul. In the sacraments, Christianity stands ancient hang-ups about the foulness of the flesh on their head. In the words of Tertullian,

> the flesh is the very condition on which salvation hinges. And since the soul is, in consequence of its salvation, chosen to the service of God, it is the flesh which actually renders it capable of such service. The flesh, indeed, is washed, in order that the soul may be cleansed; the flesh is anointed, that the soul may be consecrated; the flesh is signed (with the cross), that the soul too may be fortified; the flesh is shadowed with the imposition of hands, that the soul also may be illuminated by the Spirit; the flesh feeds on the body and blood of Christ, that the soul likewise may fatten on its God.[9]

The 'matter' of the sacraments is the physicality of the sign, usually in the sense of both the material substance, such as water, and the material gesture, such as pouring. With each sacrament, there is both a central aspect of materiality (such as sharing bread and wine) and a broader material context. This broader context is important without being essential; it is significant without being of the essence of how the sacrament signifies. For instance, there is often a great deal of gesture related to the bread and wine in the Eucharist beyond what might be thought to be strictly *necessary*: the elements might be brought from the congregation by representatives of the people, since with bread and wine we bring to God for blessing and transformation all that we have and are; the priest may raise the elements to God as a gesture of offering; the gestures of blessing and breaking may be made in a pronounced way.[10] All the same, this is strictly secondary. For that reason, only the elements themselves, and the bare minimum of gesture needed to relate them to the last supper, are defined as the *matter* of the sacrament, strictly speaking.

Baptism in the sea poses an intriguing question about matter. Alongside the primary reference of the matter of a sacrament are a host of others. Baptism is primarily about *washing* and sharing in the death of Christ, and therefore in his resurrection. However, the water of baptism also represents the water that Jesus says will quench every thirst (John 4.13–14; 7.37–9). We cannot drink seawater; it causes thirst rather than relieving it. For that reason, we might think that seawater is not proper matter for baptism. In his treatise *On Baptism*, however, Tertullian argued that what is most generic about water, rather than anything specific to a particular type, is what makes it right for baptism. Among his examples of where to baptize someone, he lists 'a sea [*mari*] or a pool, a stream or a fount, a lake or a trough' (§4). Baptisms have been carried out in the sea from early times, and were so widespread that it was expedient to accept them. This is the tradition we inherit, and baptism in the sea cannot be considered invalid. That said, we might still wonder whether it best signifies all that baptism means, if fresh water is also available. After all, salt water is not even a very good symbol of *washing*. Unlike fresh water (if it is clean), when we come out of the sea we would do well to take a shower, and that is not particularly good symbolism when it comes to baptism.

There is occasionally some disagreement between churches as to what counts as the matter (or form) of a sacrament. These are serious disagreements, since they are necessarily disagreements about the efficacy of sacraments in the other tradition. Similarly, it is usually only because of an existing serious lack of recognition and communion between churches that the form or matter of a sacrament has scope to diverge. Confirmation is an example. At the Reformation, the Church of England stopped using oil (the oil of chrism) at confirmations. If the Roman Catholic Church had recognized the Church of England, or if it had particularly mattered to the Church of England at the time that it was not recognized, then it is highly unlikely that this divergence would have occurred. Today, Anglican bishops commonly use the oil of chrism at confirmation, bringing their church back in line with the Roman Catholic and Orthodox Churches (for all we can reasonably hold that the biblical basis for confirmation puts the emphasis on the laying on of hands, making it sufficient matter for the sacrament).

In any case, over the past century, the tendency has been towards understanding the matter of the sacraments in a way that is more, rather than less, generous towards other churches. The Roman Catholic Church accepts the confirmations (or chrismations) of the Eastern Orthodox Church, although there is no laying on of hands distinct from anointing. Alongside confirmation, another example of convergence is in ordination. Whereas Roman Catholic theology used to put considerable emphasis on the delivery of the 'instruments' to the priest (the chalice and paten, or plate, used to celebrate the Eucharist) as the matter for priestly ordination (and defined as such by the Council of Florence),[11] today it defines the matter as only the laying on of hands by the bishop (as revised by Pius XII), which is also the Anglican understanding.[12]

The sign proper to a sacrament must be consistent with what it promised and is given. The Eucharist offers spiritual nourishment, for instance, and so its form is something that gives bodily nourishment. It involves bread, as a staple food, and wine, since it is abundant rather than meagre provision. Our salvation was accomplished by the Incarnation and on the cross, and this bread and wine signify the body and blood of Christ. Pizza and coke would not do this. However much those fast foodstuffs might in all truth represent basic food and abundant life to some today, they could not be the matter of the Eucharist because of their distance from flesh and blood. Christ's Incarnation has to it the *scandal of particularity*. Keeping to the elements he used, the sacraments witness to this.

The matter of baptism is *living water*, which is to say water that flows over us.[13] It has usually been considered appropriate that the water should be poured three times, in conjunction with the Trinitarian formula, but what matters most is that it is poured at all. Pouring is not a heavy requirement, but it needs to be stressed in contrast to *dabbing* or *smearing*. The water of baptism *washes away* sin, and simply to dab a little water is too far from what is signified to count as baptism. Even if one is baptizing a baby in an incubator, enough water should be squeezed through a pipette for it to flow. In many traditions, the water of baptism is blessed before it is used, but this is not by any means essential and is inadvisable in an emergency if time is pressing.

The water not only has to flow at a baptism; it also has to be *water*. That might sound obvious, but quite what counts as water has sometimes been under dispute. In 1241, Pope Gregory IX wrote to Archbishop Sigurdof of Norway to outlaw the use of beer as the matter of baptism. His argument was a sensible one: baptism must be 'from water and the Holy Spirit' (echoing John 3.5) and beer is not water. Those who have studied this question have come to the sensible conclusion that something is water if a sensible and observant person would call it water. If we would call the substance in front of us by another name, then it is not 'water', even if it contains a great deal of water. A glass of water with some salt in it is 'salty water', so it is water, as is water which happens to have a few drops of ink in it. Ink itself, however, is not water, and neither, for instance, is tea or coffee. Archbishop Sigurdof could get away with beery water, but not with watery beer. Technically speaking, we might say that it matters what is the noun and what is the adjective.[14] Less technically, we could call for an eight-year-old child and ask him or her, 'What's this?' and trust the answer.

Heightened sensitivity to medical conditions in the past few decades has raised pastoral questions about the matter of the sacraments, as has alcoholism and the emergence of teetotalism. Intolerance of gluten (a protein-rich component of grains) is among the most common of all food-related conditions in the West. The symptoms are unpleasant and debilitating, and for those who are sensitive, prolonged consumption of gluten-containing foods can cause irreparable damage to the all-important fine structure of the gut. Gluten is plentiful in the wheat flour used for the bread of the Eucharist. The solution is to use bread made from flour without gluten. One option might be to use flour from a source that does not contain gluten at all, such as rice or tapioca. Neither the Church of England, however, nor the Roman Catholic Church, would consider the product suitable matter for the sacrament.[15] It is not *bread*. The arguments for using wheat bread are cumulative rather than decisive: the New Testament abounds in references to wheat, although not all of them are obviously eucharistic. Among the more significant ones are the words of Jesus that link his own death and resurrection, central to the eucharistic celebration, to the death and rebirth of a grain of wheat (John 12.24). However, this is not necessarily an argument for using only wheat; it might be a reason for making wafers, not from rice, but from grains like oats or buckwheat (which are gluten free). The point is of sowing a grain so that it will sprout, not that the grain is wheat in particular. The point about the scandal of particularity remains, however: we do what Jesus did and use what he used.

The knock-down solution is to use 'low-gluten hosts': hosts made from wheat from which almost all of the gluten has been extracted, so much indeed that they qualify as 'gluten free' for food-labelling purposes.[16] The wine must be 'the fermented juice of the grape, good and wholesome'.[17] Grape juice is no substitute, since it is not

64

and never has been wine.[18] That said, we should also remember the doctrine of 'concomitance'. Communion in the body and blood of Christ is complete even when only one of the two elements is received.

These discussions by no means exhaust the range of topics relating to form and matter, but they might serve to illustrate some of the theological underpinnings, and their practical significance. We will return to the anatomy of the sacraments in Chapter 9, when we consider the setting, intention, minister and recipient.

6

How many sacraments?

Christians do not always agree about the sacraments. In particular, they do not all agree as to the number of sacraments. The disagreement is not as serious as it might look; this may simply be a dispute about names: 'A rose by any other name would smell as sweet'.[1] Even those traditions that are unwilling to give the name 'sacrament' to marriage, for instance, value it highly. Few would disagree that it is an 'outward and visible' means of grace. In this chapter, for my part, I will argue that each of the seven rites commonly given the name 'sacrament' is worthy of that name.

Baptism, the Eucharist, confirmation, ordination, marriage, confession and anointing of the sick: no one settled on this list of seven straight away. Although it is *de facto* the list of sacraments or 'mysteries' for the Eastern churches, to this day they do not take that to be a settled matter. The Latin West, however, had agreed on these seven by the thirteenth century, when they were named in the decrees of the Second Council of Lyons in 1274.[2] This seems to be the earliest document with this level of authority to be so definite. The list was repeated at the Council of Florence in 1439 and many times since.

Turning back to only a couple of centuries before the Council of Lyons, Peter Damian (*c.*1007–72) came up with a list of *12* sacraments. He excluded the Eucharist, presumably not out of disregard but because it was in a league of its own, and included the anointing of kings and the dedication of churches, and the making of canons, monks and hermits as three separate sacraments.[3] Hugh of St Victor (died 1141) wrote an authoritative work on sacraments (called simply *De Sacramentis*, 'On the Sacraments'). On the precise question of *how many* he is unclear. He might list 18, or he might list 30, depending on how you count, or maybe somewhere in-between. Taking the more expansive account, he includes the Incarnation and the Church as the body of Christ on the grander end, and on the humbler side, liturgical vestments, sprinkling with holy water, ashing on Ash Wednesday and postures used in prayer. Peter Abelard (1079–1142) lists six, namely the familiar seven minus holy orders.

Aquinas justifies *seven* sacraments by parallel with the features of human life.[4] When it comes to 'bodily life', five things are necessary: first, birth, growth and preservation by nourishment, which relate to baptism, confirmation (growth to full strength) and the Eucharist, and then remedy in face of sickness, which is both moral and physical, giving us confession and anointing. God also wishes that life should be perpetuated, and here two things are necessary. One is the perpetuation of the individual, which is hallowed within marriage, and the other is the perpetuation of society, which is guarded and overseen by leaders, which is the purpose of ordination.

Contrary to popular opinion, the Reformation did not amount to a divide between Catholics who loved sacraments and Protestants who hated them. Both sides held sacraments in high regard. Protestantism in the twentieth century has not always lived up to its beginnings in this regard, but the reformers esteemed sacraments, and so have 'Low Church' Christians in subsequent centuries. There was, however, real dispute at the Reformation over just how many sacraments there are. The Protestant rallying cry was 'two' and the Catholic cry was 'seven'.

The dispute is nothing like as fierce as it was, and the Protestant position was never quite as defined as it might be thought. Plenty of churches with a strongly Reformed tinge said 'two sacraments' in their official polemic but retained an attitude to some of the others that was, in practice, more or less unchanged. The Church of England called marriage a sacrament in the official Book of Homilies,[5] and a 'holy mystery' in the wedding service itself. The English Church, and most of the Churches of Scandinavia and the Baltic, carried on treating ordination in law and practice in an obviously sacramental way. Confirmation continued. The Church of England, among others, kept personal confession with absolution from a priest: there is provision for it in the rite of Visitation of the Sick, with an absolution quite as forceful as anything the mediaeval Church ever knew. Only the anointing of the sick fell out of use, to be widely restored at the opening of the twentieth century.

We can call two different things a sacrament without implying that we mean exactly the same in both cases, and without necessarily putting them on quite the same level. Similarly, *not* to call something

a sacrament – profession as a nun or friar, for instance, or the blessing of a house – is not an insult. There are many things that Christians
do in which we recognize a sacramental quality but which are not
fully fledged sacraments. They are often called 'sacramentals'. Marcus
Donovan produced a readable survey of that field in 1925 with his
book *Sacramentals*.[6]

If there are seven sacraments, there is also a hierarchy within the
seven. The two principal sacraments are baptism and the Eucharist.
These are often called the dominical sacraments, meaning 'of the
Lord'. This term is both useful and well attested: here the Book of
Common Prayer agrees with Thomas Aquinas.

The *Catechism* of 1662 asks, 'How many Sacraments hath Christ
ordained in his Church?' The answer, we are told, is, 'Two only, as
generally necessary to salvation, that is to say, Baptism, and the Supper
of the Lord.' Salvation is a good reason for singling these two sacraments out. They are particularly associated with salvation: 'baptism
now saves you,' we read in 1 Peter 3.21; 'unless you eat the flesh of
the Son of Man and drink his blood, you have no life in you,' says
Jesus in John's Gospel (John 6.53).

In addition to baptism and Holy Communion, the *Thirty-Nine
Articles* list five rites that are 'commonly called Sacraments'. These,
we can infer, are not 'generally necessary to salvation', which is easy
to grant.[7] The article goes on to say that these other five 'partly are
states of life allowed in the Scriptures', which is reasonable, and are
partly a 'corrupt following of the Apostles', a statement both unclear
and true only inasmuch as it points to abuses in then-recent history.
This article also argues that these five differ from baptism and Holy
Communion in that 'they have not any visible sign or ceremony
ordained of God'. We will return to this contention below. As a charge,
it is both inaccurate and requires too much: inaccurate since, for
instance, anointing is found in the Gospels and urged by the Letter
of James, and requiring too much since even in the case of baptism
and Holy Communion there is need for some definition of 'sign' and
'ceremony' by the Church. What counts as bread, for instance? Can
we baptize infants?

John Henry Newman was a famous defender of the 'other five'. He
took the Prayer Book definition at its word in his subtle *Tract Ninety*.
(The subtlety was more than the Church of England could quite bear;
he left soon after.)

If, then, a sacrament be merely an outward sign of an invisible grace under it, the five rites may be sacraments; but if it must be an outward sign ordained by God or Christ, then only Baptism and the Lord's Supper are sacraments.[8]

I will stand my ground even more firmly than Newman, and not so quickly cut the other five loose from Christ. The efficacy of each, whatever they might be, sacrament or no sacrament, comes from Christ and nowhere else: from his life, death and resurrection. Moreover, we find justification for all of them in his life and teaching. Christ instructs us to observe all seven. I will go further, with the outlandish claim that one way or another Christ sets the scene by *receiving* all seven.

Sacraments in the life of Christ: Christ bestows seven

The divine human Jesus did not institute sacraments from scratch. Even with baptism and the Eucharist he took something and transformed it. His baptism builds on the baptism of John, which was not itself without parallels among other groups at that time, or before and since. The institution of Holy Communion built upon the Passover meal. This is not to say that John's baptism was Christ's, or that the Passover was the Eucharist, but it does urge us to think carefully about what it means for these two sacraments to have been 'instituted by Christ'. It does not mean 'without precedent', even for baptism and the Eucharist. Neither, therefore, can we judge whether the other five are sacraments by the measure that they were 'invented from scratch' by Christ. In each case we see a history parallel to that of the two sacraments accepted by all. In each case Christ took something that already existed and incorporated it within the new order of the kingdom of God, within the order of that new community which we call the Church.

As an example, he sent out the Apostles with the command to anoint the sick. The sick had been anointed before: Jesus took an existing observance and made it part of his kingdom and new community. The anointing of the sick is therefore a 'dominical' sacrament, a sacrament of the Lord, in a fashion at least analogous to baptism and the Eucharist. Further, just as both the law and the prophets had called upon the chosen people to repent of their sins, Jesus also made repentance part of the mission of the Apostles. There had been repentance before; now it is repentance because 'the kingdom of heaven is at hand' (Matt. 10.7). Previously it had been repentance with animal sacrifice to secure it; now it is underlined by the authority of the Apostles to absolve people from their sins: 'If you forgive the sins of any, they are forgiven them; if you retain the sins of any, they are retained' (John 20.23). As he proclaimed those words, Christ breathed his Holy Spirit on his disciples, placing repentance and absolution near the heart of the work of his new community. The rest of the New Testament makes it clear that Jesus did not mean by this that absolution should be pronounced into a vacuum. Absolution follows contrition. Jesus had already told them to call people to repentance, and unless people repented, how were the Apostles to know that there were sins to be remitted or retained? The practice of confessing sins 'to one another' is attested in the apostolic writings, in the Letter of James (5.16). In other words, all the basics of the sacrament of confession and absolution are 'of the Lord'.

Anointing and confession belong to the blueprint for the Christian community, inscribed there by Christ himself. When it comes to ordination, we can cheerfully admit that Jesus did not lay hands on the Apostles in the way a bishop lays hands on a candidate for ordination. He could hardly be said to have needed to. The bishop's gesture signifies and creates a physical bond (a 'tactile' bond) that goes back through the line of bishops to the Apostles, and through them to Christ. The Apostles had a 'tactile' enough bond to Christ, without receiving the laying on of hands. Christ lived and worked with the Apostles. He embraced them in friendship; he pulled Peter from the sea; he no doubt occasionally had to shake Andrew to wake him; John reclined against him at the last supper. As 1 John has it, they not only saw him and heard him; they also touched him: 'what we have heard, what we have seen with our eyes, what we have looked at and touched with our hands [this we declare] concerning the word of life' (1 John 1.1). Beyond that, he 'ordained them' to preach the Gospel: two by two, individually (at least in the case of Peter) and as a group at the end of Matthew's Gospel. He explicitly breathed the Holy Spirit upon them, and as we have seen, this is linked in John with the authority to forgive sins.

The link between Christ and confirmation is through baptism. The Church and kingdom of God are a matter of being born of water and of the Holy Spirit (John 3.5). By confirmation we mean an extension and renewal of baptism by the invocation of the Holy Spirit. In the East, confirmation (or chrismation) is part of the baptismal rite.[9] Baptism and confirmation, as a single rite, line up with 'water and the Holy Spirit'. In the West it has become separate. Admittedly, then, among the sacraments confirmation does not fit into this scheme as neatly as the others. However, while *as a separate rite* it may not be instituted by Christ in his earthly life, everything about it was: the baptism out of which it grows, reception of the Holy Spirit as the beginning of Christian discipleship, and growth in the life of the Spirit as its middle and end.

We might think that marriage has the least tangential relationship of all to Christ – if, that is, we are looking for institution from scratch, but we are not. The idea and rite of marriage very much pre-exists the ministry of Jesus, in forms in many ways analogous to what we find in the Church.

Although Christ could speak severely about the demands of marriage in relation to following him, he also gave his blessing upon marriage by attending a wedding and performing his first miracle or 'sign' there, changing water into wine: 'Jesus did this, the first of his signs, in Cana of Galilee, and revealed his glory; and his disciples believed in him' (John 2.11). Such a blessing from Christ is integral to what marks out marriage as a sacrament within the Christian order, and blessing has become an important part of the marriage service itself.

The Church has long seen particular significance in this being his first miracle. It indicates that there is something of marriage and water-into-wine about the whole of what Jesus was about. He went on to talk about his relationship to his disciples in marital terms: they are the bride and he is the bridegroom (Mark 2.18–20; Matt. 9.14–15). The life of the world to come is described as a wedding feast (Matt. 22.1–14; 25.1–13; Rev. 19.6–8). Here we come to the second aspect of what marks out Christian marriage from the background of marriage in general. It is not only blessed by Christ, as we have seen; it is also Christian because it is a symbol of the relation of God to his people in Christ. Marriage is no merely illustrative symbol; it is a lived and living symbol. Christian marriage is shaped just as much by its status as an image of the relationship of Christ to his Church as the nature of that relationship is shaped by our understandings of marriage. Consequently, marriage *as Christian* is emphatically 'instituted by Christ', since it rests on everything that his Incarnation was about.

Christ a recipient of the sacraments

We find the foundation for all *seven* sacraments in the ministry of Christ. The order of grace, however, is one of such interweaving and overlap that we can say – remarkably – that Christ not only instituted the sacraments but also that he in some sense received them.

Christ received and participated in rites of the Old Testament which theologians see as being sacramental or quasi-sacramental;[10] Christ was no stranger to relating to God within a sacramental scheme. Among these are circumcision, the Passover meal and the sacrifices of the old covenant. To deny that Christ related to God through a sacramental order is to risk denying his full humanity. The union of humanity and divinity in Christ made him all the more fully human, not less. It is characteristically human to relate to God through mater-iality, through word and gesture. Christ's humanity was united to God by means of the union of divinity and humanity in his person, but that did not short-circuit his union with God as a human being through all the usual human means. Jesus prayed, for instance: he prayed a great deal.

Alongside the rites of the Old Testament we can explore the sense in which Christ received the sacraments of the new covenant. Certainly, scandalously, he was baptized. As the hymn puts it,

> The sinless one to Jordan came,
> and in the river shared our stain.[11]

Similarly, he ate at the last supper, the first Eucharist. Indeed, as we would wish for any devout Christian, he received the elements – 'true food' and 'true drink' (John 6.55) – immediately before his death. That first Eucharist was Christ's own 'viaticum': food for the journey through the valley of the shadow of death.

By Christ's own interpretation, the Eucharist was not the only rite that prepared him for his death. He was also anointed at Bethany. 'Let her alone,' he says to the disciples concerning the woman who performs this rite; 'she has anointed my body beforehand for its burial' (Mark 14.6–8; cf. Matt. 26.10–12; John 12.7). The emphasis is on burial, but the similarity to the rite of anointing is striking, and movingly so, since it prepared Christ for death, as the sacrament of anointing prepares Christians for their deaths. That Christ shared in death is integral, even definitive, of his sharing in our life for our salvation:

> So, he tasted death for all men,
> he, of all mankind the head,
> sinless one, among the sinful,
> Prince of life, among the dead;
> thus he wrought the full redemption,
> and the captor captive led.[12]

He shared in burial with us, and beforehand, he shared in anointing, being truly our Brother in all things, so that he could also be in all things our Saviour.

Confirmation, as we have seen, takes its place among the sacraments as something related to baptism. Just as Christ was baptized, that baptism meant that the Holy Spirit rested upon him, or anointed him. Moreover, just as he was baptized, then tempted, and was said to be 'strengthened' by the Holy Spirit, Christians in the episcopal traditions of the West are baptized and then later receive the prayer of a bishop that they may be confirmed – which is to say *strengthened* – by the Holy Spirit.

Christ is certainly 'ordained' by God for his work. If he is the 'Lamb slain from the foundation of the world' (Rev. 13.8 AV)[13] then he is equally *ordained* from before the foundation of the world. We might particularly associate the baptism with Christ's 'ordination', which is reflected in his quotation from Isaiah at the beginning of his ministry: 'the Spirit of the Lord is upon me . . .' (Luke 4.18, quoting Isa. 61.1). In his humility, Christ even receives a commission to his ministry from others, in parallel with later ordinations: from John the Baptist (John 1.29) and before that from the priest Simeon and the prophetess Anna (Luke 2.22–38). Simeon even 'lays hands' upon Christ in that he takes the infant Jesus into his arms, saying, 'This child is destined for the falling and the rising of many in Israel, and to be a sign that will be opposed.' Pushing even further back, Christ is hailed as 'Lord' in his mother's womb by Elizabeth (Luke 1.41–45) and could even be said to be commissioned by the archangel Gabriel to his work as Saviour at the very moment of his conception (Luke 1.26–38).

As to marriage, the life and work of Christ was to be bridegroom to the bride which is the Church. In this sense, Christ came to be married and marriage is the whole of his work. As for penance, an important strand of thinking about the atonement sees Christ as making vicarious penance for the sins of his brothers and sisters. This is one way in which we can say that Christ's relation to us is one of 'substitution': as a matter of solidarity, not as if substitution and solidarity stood against one another. As with other sacraments that Christ 'receives', this substitution of penance finds its roots in his baptism. Here we see Christ entering into a solidarity of penitence, in 'a baptism of repentance', which he made his not as an isolated individual and for sin of his own (he 'knew no sin', 2 Cor. 5.21) but as the most fully human being, in the water as our representative:

> The Lamb of God is manifest
> again in Jordan's water blest,
> and he who sin had never known
> by washing hath our sins undone.[14]

Conclusion

The purpose of this chapter has been to defend the proposition that those five rites 'commonly called sacraments' are commonly so called because they are, indeed, sacraments. Fighting for the title is not of the first importance, but it can be done.

Precise definition of the number of the sacraments might fall to a future general, or ecumenical, council. Other than from the Roman Catholic position (which considers its own councils ecumenical), there has not been one of those since the eighth century. The position of the Orthodox Churches on the number of the sacraments therefore seems sensible: these seven *are* sacraments, or mysteries. They are hallowed by time and it is hard to imagine that any will be demoted. The future might bring developments, but for now, and perhaps while time remains, we have seven: enough, as Aquinas said, for all that Christian life requires to flourish and reproduce.

7

Confirmation

Confirmation is the sacrament of Christian maturity, at least in the West, where it is separate from baptism. At confirmation, people take up with particular seriousness the vocation given to them at baptism, and respond to God's call to enter into the work of his kingdom. This was expressed particularly clearly at the Second Vatican Council in the 'Constitution on the Church'. Christians

> are [yet] more perfectly bound to the Church by the sacrament of Confirmation, and the Holy Spirit endows them with special strength so that they are more strictly obliged to spread and defend the faith, both by word and by deed, as true witnesses of Christ.[1]

Each of the sacraments is the domain of the Holy Spirit but this is particularly stressed in confirmation, which is built around a prayer that God would 'confirm' the Christian 'with the Holy Spirit'. It is accompanied with laying on of hands and, in its most typical form, with anointing with fragrant oil: the oil of chrism. Confirmation puts both the Holy Spirit and the Church at the heart of the life of each adult Christian and this is one good reason, among many, to be thankful for it. The conjunction of Spirit and Church here is helpful, illustrating that what is divine comes to us by human means, and that the gifts of the Spirit, even at their most charismatic and startling, belong alongside the more mundane work of the Spirit in animating the ongoing life of the Church. /

Theology of the laity

The sacrament of confirmation languishes in the twenty-first century. Numerically, not only are fewer people being baptized, but fewer of the baptized are proceeding to confirmation. Ideologically, confirmation is not favoured by those liturgists and sacramental theologians who seek for a tidy, minimal vision: for them, confirmation seems all but dispensable. These are not its only problems, however. Confirmation is a great sacrament of the laity – it is the sacrament of the work of the mature member of the Christian people or *laos* – and the Church has often only a weak theology of the laity and a weak practical sense of their role. Not the least part of recovering confirmation as a lively part of Church life would be to recover the theology and practice of the laity.

All of that deserves a fuller treatment than it can receive here. Suffice, perhaps, to say that while a theology of the laity should be fully ecclesiological – rooted in the sense that the people of God find their home in his Church – that sense of the Church needs to be wider than it usually is at present. When, and if, we talk about the mission of the laity today, we more often than not cast it in terms of some church function: leading worship or children's work, serving at the Eucharist or keeping the accounts. All of these are incredibly valuable roles, but they are not the heart of the lay vocation, which is to be Christians in the world: at work, in the home, in wider culture. For many people, for instance, confirmation demands to be held alongside marriage, since married life and a household is the primary setting for the fulfilment of the Christian vocation and mission, which is *confirmed* at confirmation.

Sometimes a link is made between confirmation and ordination, as if confirmation were 'ordination for the laity'. This approach has come in for some criticism in recent decades but the link is there and is a useful one. Like ordination, confirmation is a matter of growing into something bestowed in baptism. Like ordination, but in a different fashion, confirmation confers a new authority and role within the body of Christ and commissions us for our part in the work of the Church. Christ is not only priest, however. Within an ancient sense of his 'threefold office' he is also prophet and king. These too belong to the whole Church, and the individual Christian enters into all three in a new and more profound way at confirmation. In the words of the Second Vatican Council: 'the laity, too, share in Christ's priestly, prophetic and royal office and so have their own part to play in the mission of the whole People of God in the Church and in the world'.[2] At confirmation the Christian takes up this dignity and responsibility with a specific intention: to witness to the faith like a prophet, to pray like a priest, and to serve and to take responsibility like a king.

Sacrament of maturity

For those who have received baptism as a child, confirmation is typic-ally celebrated in adolescence, making it the sacrament of maturity. Others receive the sacrament later, if for instance someone was baptized as an infant but wandered from the faith. Returning perhaps in middle age, confirmation is the rite through which he or she lays hold to that faith as an adult. The sacraments involve sharing in the mystery of Christ and Luke refers to Christ *growing up*: 'The child grew and became strong, filled with wisdom; and the favour of God was upon him . . . And Jesus increased in wisdom and in years, and in divine and human favour' (Luke 2.40, 52). Between these two sentences Luke recounts an event in the life of Jesus at 12 years of age, the only incident recorded in the Gospels to have taken place between Christ's infancy and adulthood: the 'finding in the Temple' or 'Christ among the doctors' (Luke 2.42–51). We do not know whether this visit to the Temple is singled out because it fell at a particularly significant time in the life of Christ, but it is possible that it bore some relation to the slightly later practice of the Jewish bar mitzvah, for boys around this age. They enter into the responsi-bilities of their faith in a fashion that directly parallels confirmation. The term 'bar mitzvah' is not found in Judaism until later, but indica-tions from the Mishnah suggest an earlier sense that a new degree of responsibility came to Jewish boys at around this age.

The very aspect of confirmation that some Christians find diffi-cult – that it fulfils a rite of passage in the natural life cycle of a human being – is quite possibly attested to in the life of Christ itself. We cannot deny something sociological or anthropological is at work in the sacrament of confirmation, nor should we be afraid of that. God's grace always reaches us as we are, and takes human life as its starting point. One of the ultimate maxims of Christian theology is that grace does not undo nature but, rather, perfects it.[3] The work of the Holy Spirit is to build up: the link is made in Jude 1.20 and it is also to be found in Paul's letters. The very name 'confirmation' bears witness to this: it is the sacrament where the Spirit 'makes firm'. If society and psychology call for a solemn moment when we accept the joys and responsibilities of adulthood, then it is good for this to take place in a context where they can be understood in terms of mature Christian discipleship, and for it to take place within the church, with the community gathered to pray, and with the bishop asking for the strengthening of the Holy Spirit. We need only add that the link between grace and nature does not *collapse* this or any sacrament into a rite of passage. The Holy Spirit works with that which is natural, but he does not leave nature where it is.

Work and salvation

We are not saved by our works (Eph. 2.8–9), but our salvation is not abstract: it is 'worked out', in the words of Paul (cf. Phil. 2.12). God is in the business of transforming us, and there is little more effective on that front than practical involvement with others and their needs. Confirmation is the sacrament when each Christian is drafted into the *work* of the kingdom of God. Christ described his own mission in terms of entering into the 'works' of his Father: 'My Father is still working, and I also am working' (John 5.17). He then extends that sharing in his Father's works to his disciples: 'Very truly, I tell you, the one who believes in me will also do the works that I do and, in fact, will do greater works than these, because I am going to the Father' (John 14.12). Confirmation in particular is the moment when our share in this work comes to us.

Another central theological maxim is that what God could do without us he chooses to do with us. This is part of what it means for his salvation to work itself out in us: that he draws us into the work of salvation itself.[4] In confirmation, God blesses human agency and activity. He makes us 'fellow workers' with Christ (1 Cor. 3.9 RSV).[5]

One dimension of this motif is that confirmation is the sacrament of strength. As we have seen, this is found in the name itself: con-*firm*-ation. It asks of God what Psalm 80.17 also asks:

> But let your hand be upon the one at your right hand,
> the one whom you made strong for yourself.

Confirmation enlists us as God's 'right-hand men and women'. The psalm has been read by Christians as bearing witness to Christ. Confirmation calls us, not to anything in isolation, but to take our place alongside Jesus. The word, we might point out, is not *firmation*, simply making firm, but *con*-firmation: the Spirit strengthens us by being with (the Latin '*con*') us. The reference to 'hand' in this psalm is also significant. It bears witness to the association throughout history of the laying on of a hand as a sign of recognition and investiture of authority. When the bishop (or priest in some traditions) lays a hand on a candidate for confirmation, he or she is a proxy for God, who is laying a hand upon 'the man or woman of his right hand'.

Relation of this sacrament to baptism

The principal theological question facing us over confirmation is its relation to baptism. We have already seen something of this in our discussion of *seven* sacraments. The other six have a more direct foundation in the life of Christ. Confirmation had to stand, to a significant degree, as extrapolated from baptism, and that is how it evolved.

As far as we can tell, a rite of anointing, as a prayer for the reception of the Holy Spirit, first grew up as a component of baptism. Only later, and only in the West, was it separated so as to become the sacrament of confirmation, administered at a later stage. That development parallels another, in the sacrament of orders, which we will turn to below. As the Church became more rural and far-flung, bishops were joined by another order, the presbyterate or priesthood. Anointing at baptism had been an episcopal rite, but in the East it was taken up by priests, who were more widely dispersed and increasingly performed baptisms rather than the bishop. In the West, anointing and prayer for the gifts of the Holy Spirit remained an episcopal function. For that reason it had to be detached from baptism (now performed by priests), to be performed by the bishop when he happened to come to a particular parish on a visitation.

The Anglican churches have retained that absolute link between confirmation and the bishop. Indeed, for those churches this is one of the principal merits of confirmation: these churches are episcopally ordered and confirmation means that every Christian meets the bishop at least once, although ideally more often than that, and on at least one occasion receives prayer and the laying on of hands from those who are counted as the successors to the Apostles.

The Roman Catholic Church maintains a position somewhere between the Orthodox and Anglican approaches. The bishop is the 'ordinary' (which is to say 'archetypal' or 'originatory') minister of confirmation. Thomas Aquinas, for instance, is ambiguous in the *Summa Theologiae*: by and large he reserved confirmation to bishops, but he admits that it has sometimes been delegated to priests in the past.[6] That practice has become more and more common. Today, confirmation is still considered episcopal in its character, but the bishop's authority is routinely delegated to priests.[7] The link to the bishop is by legal delegation and also through the oil of chrism, used in confirmation, which is only consecrated by a bishop.[8] In summary, in the Roman Catholic Church, priests can confirm, as with the Orthodox but unlike Anglicans, but confirmation remains a separate sacrament from baptism, as with the Anglican pattern.

The theological question is 'What does confirmation add?' Eastern priests confirm (or 'chrismate') babies at their baptism. The West does not chrismate at baptism, but it does not think that its baptisms are any less than those of the Orthodox East. This raises the question of whether our confirmation is therefore superfluous. For this reason, some Western theologians and liturgists run confirmation down. This is perhaps a result of an overly tidy frame of mind. We have no reason to suppose that the Western development of confirmation is illegitimate and there is every reason to suppose that this real and distinct sacrament is *usefully* distinct. We have already seen the role that it can and does play as a rite of Christian maturity.

In any case, it is unhelpful to think of Christian initiation as something that is *complete* at an early stage, simply because Christian initiation is *never complete* in this life. Baptism, certainly, has a once-for-all, character-conferring quality. It does not, however, leave us in a state of completion as Christians. Baptism inducts us into a *life* of growth into Christ, into a life of initiation. The Eucharist, in this sense, is a great sacrament of initiation: the week-by-week sacrament of our continuing incorporation into Christ. Within that perspective, with induction stretching out beyond the first weeks of someone's life, confirmation can be conferred in someone's early teens, if that is what fits best within a pattern of developing discipleship. Churches in the West have thought that it does. Part of what is at stake here is accepting that there can be legitimately different patterns when it comes to the sacraments, a point that has already been made in considering form and matter.[9]

The relation of confirmation to baptism comes into sharpest relief in relation to the reception of the Holy Spirit: since the Christian receives the Holy Spirit in baptism, how can he or she receive the Holy Spirit 'again' in confirmation? This need not be the conundrum that it is sometimes presented as being. The Christian becomes a temple of the Holy Spirit in baptism. That is the great and foundational reception of the Spirit.[10] Having received the Spirit in baptism does not, however, prevent the Spirit from coming afresh later on: with new work to do within us and new gifts to bestow. Baptism opens the way for many visitations of the Spirit, as Pentecostal Christians are quick to stress. Confirmation is not unusual here, since *each one* of the sacraments is the work of the Holy Spirit (see Chapter 13), as also is the prompting that comes through prayer or Bible study. Reception of the Spirit in baptism does not prevent the specific gifts of the Spirit associated with the sacraments of ordination or marriage, nor does it prevent the specific gifts associated with confirmation.

8

Ordination

Ordination is simply the sacrament of 'order' It recognizes the importance of good leadership in the Church. It also recognizes how demanding that is. The New Testament itself gives the sense that exercising
the ministry of oversight in the Church, and related tasks, calls for
a certain special gift of God, which is bestowed by the 'laying on of
hands' (1 Tim. 4.14, and see Heb. 6.2).

The Church receives its pattern from the incarnate Christ. In the case
of ordination, this involves a relation to features such as worship, justice
and particularity. Christ came to offer worship to the Father and to
draw us into that worship. This is a primary function of the ordained
ministry: the bishop, and others who receive orders, lives to offer worship and to draw others – by mission – into the community that worships
God. This mission is not an individual task) The bishop receives a
commission for the sake of enabling others to do this work. The point
about justice may seem more oblique, but it helps us to be unashamed
of ordained ministry. Christ came to reconcile: to restore justice to the
cosmos. Justice in this sense is no cold or abstract statute laid down
from on high; justice is order and right relationship. Christ restores
justice in its deepest sense: he restores a right relationship, and order,
both of the world to God and of the world to itself. The Church is
ordered by God as a beginning and instrument for the right ordering
of all things. This tells us something important about ordination: it
must always work for forging and restoring relationships. Finally, Christ
was among us as a 'scandal of particularity'. God was incarnate as
this person for the sake of all. Something of this 'scandal' is reproduced
with ordination, with its strong sense of representative ministry.

The necessity of order

Today, the background for any discussion of order has to be our
highly individualistic culture, where the emphasis in the Church

is often on the relationship of the individual to Christ] That may place a question mark for some against whether the Church needs to be ordered at all.]The answer is both pragmatic and profound: it is both about 'getting things done' and about the nature of the human being as a social animal.

Observation will confirm that order and leadership are human necessities. Every congregation, however free and informal, will have leadership, and even the most independent of churches operates in some sense of an ordered relation to others. Even those evangelical churches in the United Kingdom with the strongest sense of being individual congregations have the Fellowship of Independent Evangelical Churches as an umbrella body.

In the *Institutes* Calvin had a strong sense of the necessity of a recognized order: 'for neither are the light and heat of the sun, nor meat and drink, so necessary to sustain and cherish this present life, as is the apostolical and pastoral office to preserve a church on the earth'.[1] The Church is intrinsically ordered, and has been from the start. There was neither order first, without a community, nor an order-less Church that adopted an order later. Rather, 'from the first, there was a fellowship of believers, finding its unity in the Twelve'.[2] Soon after, deacons were appointed.

The purpose of orders

The Church has an ordered ministry for several reasons. One is to teach and preserve the faith] Timothy, a young elder or bishop, could trust the Christian faith he had received because he knew those from whom he learned it, namely Paul and perhaps other apostles and their delegates: 'continue in what you have learned and firmly believed, knowing from whom you learned it' (2 Tim. 3.14). Timothy then faced the task of entrusting the faith to others in turn: 'what you have heard from me through many witnesses entrust to faithful people who will be able to teach others as well' (2 Tim. 2.2). Teaching is a vital part of the ministry of the Church. Since the ordained minister takes a place in a wider whole, this ministry is exercised with accountability, so that the faith can not only be propagated but be propagated faithfully, and therefore preserved]

In the early Church, the teaching role of the bishop developed in clear contrast to the Gnostic cults that were also taking form. While the Gnostics taught secret, esoteric knowledge to the enlightened few (the root is in *gnōsis*, Greek for 'knowledge'), the Christian bishop taught in public, seated where all could see him in the cathedral (from *cathedra*, Latin for 'seat'). To this day a list of the succession of bishops is displayed in a cathedral to show that we know 'those from whom [we] learned' the faith.

The sacrament of orders involves investiture with authority and the concern that, like teaching, such authority should be exercised with care and accountability. In part, the authority given is authority to celebrate the sacraments discussed in this book in the name of the whole Church. Preaching and teaching, however, are also in view, as is pastoral care. Within an ordered church, people can be tested and prepared for these roles, and held accountable for any abuses.

In his book *The Country Parson*, George Herbert stresses that the clergyman (as it was in his day) should be a learned person, not perhaps in the sense of specialized academic learning, although a scholarly training in theology was vital, but in the sense of wisdom and wider knowledge. The parson, in Herbert's vision, would be someone to whom anyone in the village might resort for advice on a wide range of topics. Nothing that had an impact on human life falls outside the concern of the local church and its ministers, including health and law. The name 'parson' seems to come from 'person': you were the village ecclesiastical 'person', to whom anyone might turn. Although the setting has changed, the clergy today similarly find themselves accompanying people from their parish through many spheres of life that may be outside their primary specialism: through medical treatment, asylum claims, legal proceedings or dealings with the council housing office, for instance.

The sacrament of orders is sometimes cast in terms of receiving 'power' to do certain things. This is not completely wrongheaded, but 'authority' is a more helpful word than 'power'. There are two opposing dangers here. One is to attribute powers to the priest understood separately from God; the other is to remove human agency from the picture. All of Christian theology helps us guard against the first danger. Sacramental ministry is held within a vision of reality where nothing is seen as separate or abstracted from God. Everything receives what it is from God as a gift: the electron and the jaguar, the saint and the priest, to take four examples. Beyond that, the prayers at the various sacraments are just that: prayers, full of invocation, and in particular invocation of the work of the Holy Spirit. The Spirit is the principal agent; Christ is the principal agent. This is one reason why the authority to administer a sacrament does not rest upon the moral state of the minister.

The opposite danger is *occasionalism*, which is the idea that the priest does nothing and is simply providing an 'occasion' during which God acts, with no reference to human agency at all. This danger *has* sometimes been flirted with. Some later mediaevals more or less separated the action of God in the sacraments from the actions of the human priest.[3]

Between these two mistakes we find a middle way in the idea of 'instrumental causation'. This stresses that God is the author of all that happens in the Eucharist, for instance, and also that he chooses to work *through* human beings. (As we have noted, it is often the case that what God could do without us, he chooses to do with us.) With this idea of 'instrumental causation', we can put the emphasis on what the priest *is* (a priest) rather than on some power that the priest *has*. Being a priest is not something that you grasp but something you are, just as a rake (which is the instrumental cause of raking) does not primarily *possess* its instrumental causality but simply does what it does, in the hands of the gardener, by *being* a rake.[4] Putting the emphasis on what the priest *is* rather than what the priest *does* also helps us to see ministerial development in terms of character and virtue, which relates to being properly what we are, rather than in terms of skills, important as they are, since someone can exercise skills without being transformed.

From early times, as we will see below, the sense was that this authority is given by God as an irrevocable gift. A priest is always a priest. This is part of a strong commitment to saying that authority is invested in a person. However, it is also important to say that this authority ultimately finds its source and completion within the wider Church. With this in mind, we can make a distinction between celebrating a *valid* and celebrating a *licit* sacrament. Any priest can celebrate the Eucharist *validly*, for instance. He or she is 'in orders'; it is a Eucharist. Those orders only mean what they are supposed to mean, however, when they are properly held in bonds of relation, and when the priest's authority finds its place in the larger, organic whole. For that reason, only those who are currently licensed by the local bishop would celebrate that Eucharist *licitly*. The same distinction applies to other sacraments. This emphasis on ordaining people to a place within a whole is the reason why no one is ordained, in the Church of England at least, to an order in general without also being ordained to a place in particular. Curates are ordained to a particular parish or mission initiative; bishops are ordained to be the bishop of a particular place (or 'see').

When ordinations happen outside a proper order, we have a particularly destructive failure to let a sacrament achieve all that it is supposed to achieve. The sacrament of ordination becomes an occasion for disorder and fragmentation. Sadly, over the course of Christian history, and perhaps particularly in recent centuries, a fixation with *validity* has led some to seek orders *illicitly*: I will know that I am *really* a priest when I've been ordained in orders from the Syrian Orthodox Church as well as from the Church of England, and so on. When bishops are consecrated outside proper order we see the worst splintering of the Church. Bishops so consecrated inevitably found their own, tiny, churches. Without the commitment to maintain unity that comes from proper order, breakaway groups usually break apart themselves, leaving churches with more bishops (often called *episcopi vagantes* – 'wandering bishops') than laity. Peter Anson detailed some of this history in gruesome but fascinating detail in his book *Bishops at Large.*[5]

That presents us with the situation of bishops without a church. We might also ask about churches without bishops. This calls for both ecumenical sensitivity and clarity of conviction. From the theological perspective that stresses episcopal order, a perspective that goes back to the Fathers, something important is lacking where episcopal ordination is lacking. A deficiency, however, means just that: some important aspect is missing but much that is good remains.

Often, mutual recognition between churches across this divide, or between ministers, is easier than it might seem at first. Free Church pastors likely consider themselves to have an authority to minister that comes from the recognition and appointment of the local or national church, without a sense of this coming by means of a link to the Apostles, passed on by the laying on of hands. They are not likely to claim a priestly function or 'character', nor to be God's instrumental cause to make Christ substantially present at the Eucharist. Someone from the patristic, episcopal perspective can concur with this account of both the source and form of their authority to minister quite exactly. Conversely, even if Christians of a Free Church perspective see no particular value in episcopal succession, they can recognize episcopally ordained ministers as everything they would want an ordained minister to be: they are recognized and appointed by the local or national church, even if the involvement of figures called 'bishops' seems unnecessary.

Turning from ministers to sacraments, from the perspective of the theology of the episcopal traditions, the rites of the non-episcopal churches are not all that they could be. That does not mean that such celebrations are without value or grace. A baptism, in particular, is recognized as fully a baptism, as long as it is carried out with water and the Trinitarian formula. There would be 'eucharistic' elements in even a lay celebration of the Lord's Supper: for instance, a remembrance of the Passion and communal sharing. It would not be *fully* eucharistic, but it would be something of value. Precisely because the Eucharist is so significant, however, the episcopal traditions would nonetheless want to see the Eucharist in what they hold to be its proper context. For the Anglican, Roman Catholic and Orthodox Churches, and others such as the Scandinavian and Baltic Lutheran Churches and the Old Catholics, that proper context and guarantee of sureness comes from episcopal orders. To say this, unpopular though it may be, is simply to hold fast to the teaching of the early Church.

Representation

Alongside authority as a purpose of ordination belongs the idea of representation. Through this sacrament, a Christian becomes a representative of the Church in a new and public way; through this, he or she becomes a particular representative of the gospel and of Christ. As a representative role, we will only understand the priesthood of the ordained properly if we understand it in relation to the 'royal priesthood' of all Christians (1 Pet. 2.9 – although we sometimes read about the 'priesthood of all believers', the better, biblical, image is of a *royal* priesthood). The Church will stand or fall with the work of its lay members. One important role of the priest, and part of all that he or she does, is to further the work of the people of God. The orders of ministry are each an elaboration, for that person and in a particular way, of the vocation conferred in baptism and strengthened at confirmation. Priestly orders are conferred so that this person can help all of God's people fulfil their vocation as a priestly people.

The Church has certain roles and offices as a whole: to serve, to teach, to counsel, to lead, to be a royal priesthood, and so on. This is nurtured, not overturned, when what belongs to the Church as a whole is passed on to certain of its members in a particular way. The Church as a whole teaches, and some members teach in particular; the whole Church is prophetic, but some are called to be prophets; likewise, the whole people of God are priestly, and some in particular are called to the office of priest. The Epistles are full of lists which emphasize this differentiation of roles within the Church.[6] Part of the task here, which is very necessary for a renewed theology of the laity, is not to confuse either 'vocation' or 'ministry' with 'ordination': alongside the ministry of the ordained clergy are a great many ministries that belong to other members of the Church, ministries that are as much focused on the world, work, the family, and so on, as on the Church. All Christians have a vocation on account of their baptism, even if not all have a vocation to ordination.

One of the principal theological tasks of our age is to reclaim the term 'religion' from its use as a term of abuse. An even harder task would be to retrieve the word 'cult' (bound up as it is with 'cults' and even 'the occult'). The word may be lost for ever, but the idea it signifies is important and worth retrieving, even if under a different name: the 'cult' of the Church is its *culture of praise*. A central role of the priest is to lead the whole people in worship precisely as a people. This gives us an approach to worship that is larger than the isolated actions of individuals, performed only here and there, only now and then. The worship that the priest sustains forms a whole in which the parts become more than they would be by themselves. The priesthood sustains a cultural enterprise dedicated to the worship of God. Our parish churches, cathedrals and college chapels, to name three examples, are precisely this: cultures of praise, an approach to worship that is larger than the actions of individuals at particular times. The priest is someone placed at the centre of a culture of praise. In this sense, the priests of the Church of England are *particularly priestly*, particularly concerned to uphold a culture of praise. This Church sustains a culture of praise that has been among the finest creations – spiritually as much as aesthetically – of Christian history.

Order from the bishop

The churches that most explicitly wish to pattern their orders of ministry after that of the patristic period – among them the Roman Catholic Church, the Orthodox Churches and the churches of the Anglican Communion – stress that the Church is ordered to and from the bishop. This finds its expression in many ways, from elements of liturgy at its most symbolic to church organization at its most practical. The mother church of a diocese, for instance, is called a *cathedral* because the seat (or *cathedra*) of the bishop is there. The bishop, and the bishop's office, have a leading role in all matters relating to finance, land and appointments.

Most fundamental of all is the role of the bishop in the sacramental order. In John Macquarrie's helpful phrase, it is upon the bishop that 'the fulness of ordination' rests.[7] A bishop, if present, might be expected to be the principal celebrant of the Eucharist, and even if not, to pronounce the absolution or give the blessing. That is because the priest functions in a place only as a delegate of the bishop. The 'fulness of ordination' rests with the bishop, as the figure carrying on the work of the Apostles, and from him (and in most churches it is still a man rather than a woman) this is passed on in a delegated sense to priests and deacons by ordination. Bishops alone, however, can ordain.[8]

Through the bishops, unity is established through time and across place. The geographical communion of the Church is maintained by communion between bishops; the agony of its lack of unity is expressed in a lack of communion between them. The Anglican Communion, for instance, is called a 'communion' because within this group of churches there is full mutual recognition and communion between bishops (almost, and for the moment). Continuity over time finds its expression through the ordination of one bishop by another, in a lineage that is claimed as going back to the Apostles themselves. For the sake of both security in time and fellowship in space, many bishops take part in the consecration of any new bishop. The involvement of bishops who neighbour the vacant diocese was stressed in the *Apostolic Tradition* of Hippolytus in the third century. The Council of Nicaea required all the bishops in a province to participate, with three or more laying on hands and the rest showing agreement at least by letter.[9]

The bishops are the principal representatives of the Church, and for that reason it is important that they are consecrated to their office with the consent of the Church. This was stressed as early as the time of the *First Letter of Clement* (late first or early second century AD) and was pithily summarized by Leo the Great with the words 'the one who is to preside over all should be elected by all'.[10] Different churches have different schemes for their appointment.

A threefold order

The model of order that comes down to us from the patristic period is of bishops, priests and deacons. The preface of the rites for ordination in the Book of Common Prayer (the 'ordinal')[11] begins: 'It is evident unto all men diligently reading holy Scripture and ancient Authors, that from the Apostles' time there have been these Orders of Ministers in Christ's Church; Bishops, Priests, and Deacons.' We do indeed read about bishops (or 'elders'), priests (or 'presbyters') and deacons in the New Testament, but the relation between the first two is a matter of debate, even of conjecture. This in no way weakens the sense of sacramental order laid out in the ordinal or held by other churches with a threefold ministry. Within a century or two of the writing of the New Testament it is clear that the Church had bishops, priests and deacons. That pattern of ministry and sacramental order was established well before other matters were settled which today we hold as being inviolable: before, for instance, the Church defined the doctrines of Christ's human and divine nature or the doctrine of the Trinity. The fluidity in the first century or two was over whether priesthood was a separate order. It is likely that 'elder' and 'presbyter' were used somewhat interchangeably at first, reflecting a twofold order of bishop and deacon. The Church was relatively small and, crucially, largely urban. It sufficed for each metropolis to have a bishop who celebrated the Eucharist, taught, and led the community, and to have deacons who assisted him. Even today, bishops are still associated with cities. In the United Kingdom every place with a cathedral counts as a city, almost by definition, no matter how small it is. Plenty of towns are larger than Ely or Wells, but having a cathedral and bishop, they are both cities. Archbishops who preside over a province of dioceses, as well as a diocese of their own, are known as *metropolitans*, which has a deliberately urban ring.

As the Church grew, bishops proliferated. This could only proceed so far, especially as the Church took off in rural areas. It was no longer possible for the bishops, even with many of them, to preside over every local community. This seems to be the origin of the distinction between bishops and priests. The bishops ordained representatives to minister in far-flung places, conferring upon them much of their authority, but retaining to themselves the authority to ordain anyone else. A twofold order, of bishop and deacon, was augmented by the distinction between bishops, in whom the fullness of priesthood rested, and people called 'presbyters', with an attenuated and delegated share in their authority or *episcope*. Our English word 'priest' comes from 'presbyter' via intermediate forms such as 'prester'. 'Priest', we can note, is a Christian word.

The deacon has been associated from the earliest days of the Church with its servant ministry: the Greek word *diakonos* means 'servant'. The order of deacons, or *diaconate*, was instituted by the Apostles, as recorded in Acts 6, so that there could be a division of labour between the Apostles, who focused on prayer and preaching, and the deacon, who focused on practical arrangements, not least in care of the poor.

Deacons cannot celebrate the Eucharist themselves, but certain parts of the liturgy traditionally belong to them, if one is present, including reading the Gospel and leading the intercessions. Casting deacons as the practical servants does not mean that the life of a present-day bishop is free from a focus on practical arrangements, far from it. One task for the Church in the present time is to find ways to free bishops for a renewed focus on prayer and preaching, alongside other forms of teaching, and pastoral care, especially of the clergy, while retaining the sense that practical matters have spiritual significance and need to be overseen by the bishop. Similarly, most parish priests find themselves at an intersection of roles that take in administration, service, preaching and leading worship. This conjunction can be messy, but it is not inappropriate. Almost all priests were made deacons first, and they retain the diaconal emphasis on practical service to the local church and community.[12] Similarly, the whole character of priesthood is one of devolved oversight from the bishop, and that will take in elements of administration as well as sacramental authority and a ministry of teaching.

Coming to us from the early Church we also have a number of 'minor orders', which do not participate in the authority of the bishop to the same degree and are not as central to the life of the Church. Indeed, many have largely died out as living ministries, or been taken up by those in major orders. Among these minor orders were doorkeepers, lectors, exorcists, acolytes, and subdeacons. In the Roman Catholic Church the minor orders were suppressed by Paul VI by an apostolic letter in 1972. 'Reader' and 'acolyte' were retained, but as 'ministries' rather than as 'orders'. Whereas a candidate for the priesthood used to advance through each of these minor orders, there is now only one preparatory stage for ordination as a deacon, called 'candidature'. Many minor orders, however, remain in Orthodox rites. The twentieth century saw the revival of the ministry of 'reader' in many Anglican churches. Today that is joined by a variety of licensed lay ministries.

Communities of 'religious' – monks, nuns, friars, canons regular, and so on – play an important part in the life of many churches. Their solemn vows or 'profession' are not seen as a sacrament, although they are not any less of a remarkable undertaking for that. For the sake of completeness we can also note that alongside major and minor orders we also have the idea of 'orders without sacramental distinction'. These designate differentiated *roles* (or are sometimes simply honorific) without designating a differentiation of sacramental *character*. Among them we could list the role of archbishop or pope, rural dean or archdeacon, monsignor or cardinal, archimandrite or archpriest. Similarly, we should make a distinction between a set of words that describe what a person *is* (deacon, priest, bishop, lay person) and what a person *does* (rector, vicar, chaplain).

Consecration

Alongside a differentiated life within the Church goes the idea of consecration. The Latin word for 'priest' is *sacerdos*. Its root, *sacer*, means consecrated, sacred, set aside and, in a remarkable way, both blessed and cursed. This language of consecration runs through the Christian tradition. We find it in high moral expectations, and also in titles (or, strictly, 'styles') such as 'The Reverend' and 'The Right Reverend'. R. C. Moberly provided a particularly acute account of consecration within ordained ministry in his book *Ministerial Priesthood* (1897):

There are not only priestly functions and prerogatives; there is also a priestly spirit and a priestly heart – more vital to the reality of the priesthood than any merely priestly functions. Now the priestly spirit is not the exclusive possession of the ordained ministry; it is the spirit of the priestly church. But those who are ordained priests are bound to be eminently leaders and representatives of this priestly spirit.[13]

A bishop recently surveyed the ways in which diocesan statements in the Church of England describe ministry, and summarized them in a list of the nine most common. Nothing along the lines of consecration appeared on the list. This is remarkable, since a note of offering and consecration is clearly present in the ordination services, and it seems undeniable that those who offer themselves for ordination mean it as a consecration, in a parallel sense to the way in which Christians instinctively see offering themselves in marriage as a form of consecration. Indeed, a connection is often made between ordination and marriage. The *Catechism of the Catholic Church* notes this:

Those who receive the sacrament of Holy Orders are consecrated in Christ's name 'to feed the Church by the word and grace of God.' On their part, 'Christian spouses are fortified and, as it were, consecrated for the duties and dignity of their state by a special sacrament.'[14]

The sense of consecration attached to ordination (and to marriage), inchoate as it might be, deserves to be supported by the Church. This suggests that as much as we need to attend to the theology and practice of priesthood, we also need to attend to the spirituality of priesthood. The same would go for marriage.

Priestly character

As we have seen, the once-for-all sacraments are once for all because they impress the character of Christ. The Western tradition has wanted to stress that *worship* is an important element of what any of the sacraments involve that impart character. This is particularly obvious with ordination, where leading the church in worship is a particularly central aspect.

The once-for-all quality of ordination is often called 'indelibility'. Like many topics in theology, the mind of the Church on this matter was worked out in the fires of dispute, in this case following the persecution of Christians in northern Africa under Diocletian (AD 303–5), as we have seen. In response to the 'Donatists', Augustine developed a sacramental theology with an emphasis on God's grace rather than human worthiness or conduct. With this went an account of sacramental character that is not erased even by heresy, schism or denying the faith. Augustine spelt this out, for instance, in his *Letter against Parmenian*:

> Both of these, Baptism and Orders, are Sacraments . . . therefore, it is not permitted to repeat either of these Sacraments. For . . . even their leaders [leaders of the Donatists], when they come over to us from among the schismatics . . . are not ordained again, but, just as with their Baptism so too their ordination remains whole, because the defect was in their separation, which is corrected by the peace that comes of unity, and not in the Sacraments, which, everywhere they are found, are the same.[15]

A couple of centuries later, for instance, in AD 601, we find Gregory the Great writing to the bishops of Georgia, teaching that 'without any doubt', ordination is ordination, even if received irregularly, and that it should not be repeated.

Indelibility is held absolutely by the Roman Catholic Church[16] and the Church of England, among others: 'No person who has been admitted to the order of bishop, priest, or deacon can ever be divested of the character of his order,' reads the law of the Church of England.[17] It is nonetheless possible, although exceptional and inherently tragic, to relieve someone in orders from the permission to exercise them, and of the responsibilities that go with them. As the canon goes on: 'a minister may either by legal process voluntarily relinquish the exercise of his orders and use himself as a layman, or may by legal and canonical process be deprived of the exercise of his orders or deposed therefrom'.[18]

Conclusion

Like the other sacraments, the sacrament of order is all about the Church carrying on the work that the incarnate Christ handed to his body. It confers upon certain Christians a particular representative office and character. It is not given 'in spite' of the vocation of all

Christians, but so that the vocation of all Christians can be nurtured and encouraged.

Bishops, priests and deacons share in the work of Christ as overseer, since he is the 'shepherd and guardian [*episcopon*, the AV has 'bishop'] of your souls' (1 Pet. 2.25), as priest, since he is the 'great high priest' (Heb. 4.14), the one who instituted the Eucharist and gave himself on the cross as priest and victim, and as servant, or deacon, who came 'not to be served but to serve' (Matt. 20.28) and who was among us 'as one who serves' (Luke 22.27).

9

The anatomy of the sacraments II: setting, intention, minister and recipient

Setting

The sacraments are such significant means for the encounter with God that it is worth paying some attention to the setting in which they are performed. Having said that, that encounter with God lies at the heart of the sacraments, so while questions of setting are important they are also secondary. The sacraments are inherently simple, since relation to God does not rest on anything complicated that we might do. While *magic* depends on technique (doing something just as the sun rises over the hill; reciting the words perfectly), sacraments, in contrast, depend on grace.

Grace does not come by frills, music, superstar preaching or the right vestments, or for that matter by virtue of our faith, or morals, or the probity of the minister. The *Thirty-Nine Articles* of the Church of England summarize an ancient tradition when they say that 'the unworthiness of the ministers . . . hindereth not the effects of the sacraments'.[1] As surely as this is water poured with certain simple words, we have a baptism and the grace of rebirth. As surely as this is bread and wine offered by a priest with the words of Jesus, we have the Eucharist and receive the body and blood of Christ.[2] We could perform a baptism in 15 seconds, with no frills, in an emergency. The requirements are minimal ones, sensibly associated with being sure that this *is* a baptism, that this *is* a marriage.

Setting is not definitive, but as long as we are not in extreme circumstances, the sacraments deserve to be undertaken in a way that observes their dignity and draws out their meaning. Ultimately, when we talk about the setting of a sacrament, the touchstone is not what is *necessary* for the sacrament to function, but what is

most *appropriate*. As a summary, each sacrament should be celebrated within the context of the Christian community, worshipping
together, reading the Bible and engaged in ongoing pastoral care.
Stripped of this setting, the sacraments begin to look like magic, and
to be cheapened.

One way or another, all the sacraments are sacraments of the body
of Christ, the Church, so it is right that they should be celebrated pub-
licly, within that body. Many people can be present, or few; the setting
can be a cathedral or a small village church or, for that matter, a
prison camp. Private and privatized celebrations of the sacraments
are a departure from this rule, and should only be an exception for
exceptional circumstances, for instance in time of persecution. Taking
baptism as an example, the Book of Common Prayer urges 'the
Curates of every Parish', here meaning the incumbent, to 'warn the
people that without great cause and necessity they procure not their
children to be baptized at home in their houses'.[3]

Such a gathering of the Church calls for worship, which is an important part of the setting of the sacraments. They are all about God,
and when we come face to face with God worship is the appropriate
response. The presence of God reminds us of our waywardness,
and so there should be an element of confession. The sacraments are
wonderful gifts, and so we should thank him. The Church challenges
us to pray for those who are in need, near and far, so it is fitting for
us to offer intercessions.

A reading from the Bible is always appropriate, and possibly more
than one. The officiant or someone else would ideally offer reflections
on the reading, to teach a little about the sacrament in question, and
relate the celebration to both the local context and the faith of the
Church. The Second Vatican Council addressed these points about
the setting of the sacraments in the Constitution on the Sacred
Liturgy:

> The purpose of the sacraments is to sanctify men [and women], to
> build up the body of Christ, and, finally, to give worship to God; because
> they are signs they also instruct. They not only presuppose faith,
> but by words and objects they also nourish, strengthen, and express it;
> that is why they are called 'sacraments of faith'. They do indeed impart
> grace, but, in addition, the very act of celebrating them most effec-
> tively disposes the faithful to receive this grace in a fruitful manner, to
> worship God duly, and to practice charity.[4]

Intention

The innermost part of the setting of a sacrament is the *intention* of the celebrant and others who are involved. Since, however, the principal agent in the sacraments is God, this makes our intention secondary to God's 'intention', which is salvation (1 Tim. 2.4). Our principal duty is to approach a sacrament seriously. As a bare minimum, that means approaching it *as a sacrament*. A confession would not be a confession if our only purpose were to find out how the priest would react to mention of a particularly salacious sin. A play script that arranged for an unbaptized actor to have water poured over his head with the correct Trinitarian formula would not cause him to be baptized in the process. Seriousness, on the other hand, does not rest on us having anything like full understanding of what is going on: not for nothing are the sacraments also called 'mysteries'. Among phrases that might express the proper balance, an attractive option is to say that the participant should at least wish salvation. To receive from the sacraments, we must come with some desire for grace, however inchoate.

Another succinct expression of the proper minimal intention is that the minister of the sacrament must intend to do what the Church intends to do by that sacrament.[5] With that idea in place we can see why the Western Church has been inclined to accept baptisms performed by non-Christians. A Muslim nurse might notice in the middle of the night that the young child of Christian parents is very sick, and indeed is going to die very soon. He might know that the parents would ardently desire their child to be baptized before she dies. The nurse could baptize the child, even though he does not accept the faith himself, because in doing so he intends for the sacrament to be what a Christian would want it to be.[6]

Alongside intention belongs *preparation*. It is appropriate that we should seek to prepare ourselves seriously before we receive a sacrament, while remembering that we do not and cannot make ourselves worthy to receive the grace of the sacraments. In the case of the indelible, one-off sacraments, an element of instruction will always be part of proper preparation, whether that is ordination training, marriage preparation, or catechesis before baptism or confirmation. This can hardly be taken too seriously. Preparation for baptism, confirmation and marriage can and perhaps should be a major part of the ministry and mission of any parish church or other Christian community. Accompanying such a sacrament should also be some element of reordering the pattern of our lives around the demands of the Christian faith. The adult about to be baptized, for instance, may have to change the conduct of a sexual relationship, or to transfer investments from unethical funds.

Often, one sacrament is an appropriate, or necessary, preparation for another. Baptism is the gateway to the other sacraments. It is therefore necessary preparation for the others.[7] Confirmation is either necessary preparation for ordination, or in any case so eminently suitable that someone to be ordained would always be confirmed first. The sacrament of confession is an exceptionally good preparation for the reception of other sacraments, and is to be commended with all seriousness to those who are to be married or ordained, and to all but the youngest people being confirmed. Roman Catholics and the Orthodox see the Eucharist as the proper setting for Christian marriage; Anglicans concur, to the extent of saying (in the Book of Common Prayer) that if the service is not, in fact, eucharistic, then the couple should receive Communion together as soon as is possible or 'convenient'. The Eucharist has, similarly, either always been, or near universally become, the proper setting for confirmations and ordinations. Anyone receiving the sacrament of anointing for healing would always do well to receive Communion as soon as possible afterwards. While anointing and confession should not be so closely associated as to suggest that illness is a direct result of particular sins on the part of the sick person, these two sacraments certainly belong side by side, and alongside Communion, when someone is in danger of death.

With the question of the proper *recipient* of the various sacraments we find ourselves confronted with many of the most contentious contemporary debates in sacramental theology. As we have already seen, baptism is necessary for the reception of subsequent sacraments. In some local churches in the twenty-first century this is experienced as an unacceptable restriction, not least when it comes to Communion. This question was discussed on pp. 49–51.

Several other contentious questions remain. Over marriage, one question is whether people who have been divorced can be a recipient of the sacrament of marriage a subsequent time. The Roman Catholic Church thinks not; the Church of England and the Orthodox Churches think that they can. This is not to say that a subsequent marriage is commendable in every case, irrespective of the circumstances. This is discussed on pp. 114–15. Another question is whether two people of the same sex could be recipients of the sacrament of marriage. The sense among many theologians is both that this question deserves to be asked and that we have not got very far yet in investigating it. A greater number would be in favour of blessings for same-sex relationships than of same-sex marriage. (See pp. 115–19.)

Over the reception of baptism, the only major difference of opinion is whether infants can be recipients of baptism. The unswerving position from early times has been that they can: a position taking in Protestants as well as Catholics, Orthodox and Anglicans. A more divisive question is *which* children should be baptized. (See pp. 19–20.) Some traditions will baptize only the children of committed Christians. All people who live in England have a right to have their children baptized by the Church of England, in the parish church of the parish in which they live. While the rector or vicar can reasonably require the parents to attend a programme of preparation, he or she cannot – in that or any other way – erect a barrier to baptism for that child.[8] For Anglicans, at least, the parents' desire to have their child baptized should be respected. As a corollary, so should their desire *not* to have their children baptized. This topic was thrashed out in the Middle Ages in the context of the shameful question of whether to baptize Jewish children by force against the wishes of their parents. Duns Scotus was a prominent exponent of this practice, whereas Thomas Aquinas stands among those who opposed it.[9] Over the course of time, Aquinas's position has rightly won out. We do not baptize children against the wishes of their parents out of respect for the role of parents in making decisions about the formation of the children.

With ordination, the principal question for the worldwide Church in our time is whether women, alongside men, can be recipients of the orders of deacon, priest and bishop. Different churches take different lines on this question. There is no agreement among those churches that have maintained this threefold order. The Roman Catholic and Orthodox Churches presently answer that they cannot. Many Anglican and Lutheran churches with episcopal orders have decided that they can, as have Old Catholics. The fact that popes have had to ban discussion of this question in their church suggests that scholarly and popular opinion is far more divided on the ground than it is in the Vatican. Several arguments might be given, among them that Paul calls Junia an apostle (Rom. 16.7 – the plain meaning of the Greek, although it is not always translated this way) and calls Phoebe a deacon (Rom. 16.1); ordination is an elaboration of a ministry given to all Christians in baptism; these are roles where Christ is represented, and Christ assumed humanity in such a way as to share it not only with men but also with women.[10]

We have already discussed some dimensions of who the proper minister is for various sacraments. In the West we tend to be more permissive than the East, so baptism can be administered validly by any layperson.[11] While the 'ordinary minister' of baptism is a priest or bishop, since these are the orders that most particularly represent the Church, a deacon, layperson or even a non-Christian (as we have seen) might nevertheless be called upon to baptize in the absence of a priest. It is appropriate that the minister of baptism should be the priest with pastoral responsibility for the baptized person and, in the case of an infant, his or her parents.[12] In the East, baptism is even more closely associated with priests and bishops because the (priestly) rite of chrismation is so integral. Similarly, in the East the minister of the sacrament of marriage is considered to be the priest; in the West it is the couple.

It is worth noting that in the struggles between more catholic-minded and more Protestant-minded leaders for the soul of the Church of England around the turn of the seventeenth century, the Protestant sympathizers were the clericalists who wanted to restrict baptizing to the clergy, whereas the Catholic sympathizers stressed the ability of all the faithful to baptize. As Protestant figures gained power, 'administration by women and lay persons' was frowned upon, although midwives continued to be instructed about their duty to baptize in cases of necessity.[13]

10

Marriage

The theme of this book is that the sacraments follow the pattern of the Incarnation. The Incarnation is God's loving response to the world, by which he shares his life with us, and we share his. Marriage mirrors this, in one responding to the other and the sharing of lives. As with the Incarnation, the emphasis is not on love as misty-eyed romance, although there is an element of a grand Romance about both, but on practical service: the couple follow the example of the Son of Man, who came 'not to be served but to serve' (Mark 10.45; Matt. 20.28). For most people, marriage is their closest entry into the pattern that Christ set, of giving his life for others, as that saying from Mark and Matthew continues. The 'sacrament of matrimony knitteth man and wife in perpetual love,' we read in the First Book of Homilies, and as such it is an image of the Incarnation, where God 'knitteth' himself to us 'in perpetual love'.[1]

According to John's Gospel, Christ performed his first miracle at a wedding. Theologians have seen this as more than accidental. The setting underlines the fact that Christ's mission was to bring joy and fullness of life, and that it was for the sake of a marriage: a marriage in which he was the bridegroom and the Church was his bride (John 3.29). Similarly, his parables compare the end of the age to a wedding banquet (Matt. 22.1–14; 25.1–13).[2] Marriage is a recurring theme in biblical literature. As the *Catechism of the Catholic Church* points out, 'Sacred Scripture begins with the creation of man and woman in the image and likeness of God and concludes with a vision of "the wedding-feast of the Lamb".'[3] In the prophets, the relationship between God and his people is described in terms of marriage, in Hosea for instance. The other key passage is from the Letter to the Ephesians, which interprets the Incarnation in terms of marriage imagery. We think that we are reading about the marriage of a man and woman, but the author, Paul or whoever, catches us unawares, shifting in midflow and then tipping us off that he has really been talking about Christ and the Church (Eph. 5.28–30).

In Ephesians 5.32, marriage is called a 'mystery'. The Greek word, *mysterion*, is the standard word later employed to mean 'sacrament'. Although the Reformers were generally not enthusiastic about giving the name 'sacrament' to anything other than baptism and the Euch-arist, the Church of England slipped its guard over marriage, as we have just seen, in one of the authoritative homilies in the Book of Homilies, the official companion volume of sermons to go alongside the Book of Common Prayer.[4]

Marriage and blessing

In the West, the idea of blessing is centre stage at a wedding service. Blessing has several dimensions, each of which finds its place within a wedding.

Twentieth-century liturgical theology has recovered one of the primary senses of blessing in the Bible, namely as praise and thanks-giving. Frequently we are encouraged in the Scripture to 'bless the Lord'. That does not mean to *make* God holy but rather to *recognize* his holiness. To bless God in this sense is to praise him, and to bless *something* is to recognize that it comes from God, to recognize it as sacred, and to praise him for it.

Another aspect is that a blessing takes something that already exists rather than creating something new. We find a strong sense of this in a wedding service, since a marriage is always a recognition and a response. It blesses a relationship that is likely to stretch back for months, or even years. Because of this sense of working with some-thing that is already real, the free consent of the couple is essential for marriage within the Christian tradition.

The idea that marriage blesses and witnesses something, rather than creating it, is reflected in the proper title of the marriage service in the Book of Common Prayer. We do not read 'Holy Matrimony' but the 'Solemnization of Holy Matrimony'. This chimes with the sense, at least in Western theology, that the 'minister' of the sacrament of marriage is not the priest presiding (or bishop or deacon) but the couple themselves.[5] The role of the priest and congregation is to 'solemnize' something that the couple are doing. A minister witnesses and blesses; he or she does not 'marry' the couple. The service is also called 'solemnization' because of the necessity of consummation. In that sense, at a wedding the Church is blessing in the church building something that will be finalized elsewhere.

The principle of blessing, rather than creating from scratch, applies, beyond any particular wedding, to the very idea of marriage. Here too, the Church took up something that already existed. It blessed an institution that already existed, rather than creating something from nothing. Marriage is a primordial gift of God in creation. As Anglican marriage rites like to say, it is 'a gift of God in creation and a means of his grace'.[6] Here, 'in creation' means 'in the order of creation itself'; it is a gift received from God via the created order. It is also a gift 'in creation' in that it is a gift of sharing in the business of creating. Out of the unions that human beings naturally form, children are born. In this we can see an image, in the created order, of the Son's coming forth from the Father. For this reason, many traditions of theology argue that marriage does not achieve its full significance unless the couple are at least open to the possibility of bearing children.

With marriage, the Church blesses and gives thanks for something that it did not create: either at the level of the individual relationship or at the level of the institution itself. This is an aspect of what we might wish to teach at a wedding, and one of the ways in which a marriage can be evangelistic. A wedding is an opportunity to recognize that love, and every good aspect of human society, is a gift from God. Marriage can be understood theologically not by means of some theological overlay but because when we arrive at a marriage we find that much that is most significant in theology is already present. Marriage is theological without us having to impose theology upon it. We no more need to work to make *eros* spiritual than we have to work on Shakespeare to make his plays good literature.

As well as praise and the recognition of a gift from God, blessing entails offering back to God what we have received from him. This is the root of what we mean by making something holy or sacred. The words for 'holy' in both Hebrew and Latin have a strong sense of setting something apart for God. At a Christian wedding, the couple pledge themselves, as a couple and as an incipient family, to put their love and common life at God's disposal.

Offering is at the heart of marriage. As the *Catechism of the Catholic Church* puts it, the unimpeded and total offering of one person to another is the essence of marriage: it is precisely the free offering of oneself to the other which is the 'the indispensable element that "makes the marriage"'.[7] In marriage we offer ourselves, our fidelity and all that we possess ('my body', 'my worldly goods', and so on) to another and in this we offer them to God. Marriage stands as a particularly clear example of the overlaps at work in the sacraments: what we offer to another, we offer to God, and what we offer to God, we offer to another; what we receive from another, we receive from God, and what we receive from God, we receive from another.

Blessing also has the sense of protecting, strengthening and making good. With marriage we recognize that all that is best about human love is also what can be most dangerous, and most ruinous when it goes wrong. This theme underlines one of the 'goods' of marriage, to which we now turn.

The three goods of marriage

Marriage has traditionally been said to have three 'goods'. The goods were summarized by Thomas Aquinas (following Peter Damian) as 'faith, offspring and sacrament'.[8] The Council of Florence provides a helpful gloss, although not in the same order:

> These advantages are to be ascribed to marriage: first, the begetting of children and their bringing up in the worship of the Lord; secondly, the fidelity that husband and wife should each maintain toward the other; thirdly the indissoluble character of marriage, for this typifies the indissoluble union of Christ and the Church.

'Sacrament', for this tradition stretching back to Augustine, means something rather narrow at this point: it means conferring indissolubility.

The tradition that marriage has certain defined 'goods' will be familiar to many readers from the preface of the wedding service in the Book of Common Prayer. These words were penned by Thomas Cranmer in 1549 and were carried into the 1662 version of the Prayer Book, which is still in use. They have found slightly more colloquial formulation in the later liturgies that take the Prayer Book preface as their template. The 'good' of something is the reason why you do it. Cranmer wrote of the 'causes' of marriage, in the sense of what would 'cause' God to have instituted marriage. They become, in turn, the reasons why two people would want to be married.

First, It [marriage] was ordained for the procreation of children, to be brought up in the fear and nurture of the Lord, and to the praise of his holy Name. Secondly, It was ordained for a remedy against sin, and to avoid fornication; that such persons as have not the gift of continency, might marry, and keep themselves undefiled members of Christ's body. Thirdly, It was ordained for the mutual society, help, and comfort, that the one ought to have of the other, both in prosperity, and adversity.[9]

These 'causes' or 'goods' line up with the list in contemporary Roman Catholic canon law, that the 'primary end of marriage is the procreation and education of children; the secondary end is as a mutual support and remedy for concupiscence [lust]'.[10]

Mutual society

As Aristotle beautifully put it, human beings are social animals. The Bible bears witness to the same truth at its very beginning: Adam was lonely, even incomplete, by himself. Plato was also onto this, telling a myth in which human beings were created from another sort of being, chopped in two. Ever since, we have literally been searching for our 'other half'.[11] The great twentieth-century Protestant theologian Karl Barth even went so far as to say that the image of God is only fully realized when people are in relationship with one another. God, as Trinity, says, 'Let us make humankind in our image' (Gen. 1.26). The plural is important: the plurality within the unity of God is only fully realized in people when they move beyond their individuality into community. Just as the life of the Trinity is sometimes described in active terms, almost like a dance, so the image of the Trinity in the love of a couple is worked out in action. While the life of God unfolds without impediment, the human business of love sometimes requires a great deal of bearing with one another. As a consequence, finding a way to work things out is one of the joys of a human relationship.

This is a good reason for talking about marriage as a sacrament. A sacrament is a rite that, to a heightened degree, is more than it seems. A sacrament is a mystery: not in the sense of something obscure, or something about which we would rather not have much to say, but a mystery in the sense of something that points beyond itself to God and our relation to God, something which gives without running out, and that creates a bond between what is seen and what is not. Marriage is a 'holy mystery', as the liturgy has it, in each of these senses.

Marriage is the sacrament most doubted as a sacrament by those not otherwise out to strip the number down to two. That is rather odd, since marriage deals with that which for many people comes nearest to the nature of a sacrament in nature itself. Love, sex and human relationships are a better candidate than almost any other facet of human life for recognition as 'an outward and visible sign of an inward and invisible grace'. A glance through any pop 'top 20', or the contents of any book of folk songs, will confirm that we sing about love and relationships, and what do we sing about, if not the situations where we find grace, the situations we find sacramental?

Raising children

Having a baby is about as practical a matter as can be imagined: all nurseries and nappies. It is also one of the most profoundly metaphysical and theological events in which a human being can be involved. The theologian can say that this event is extraordinary because of its participation in the very nature of God as Trinity. When Aquinas discusses the image of God in human beings (and, in this passage, in angels) he notes a way in which we bear the image more profoundly than the angels: we can observe 'a certain imitation of God' in human beings in the fact that 'a human being proceeds from human beings, as God proceeds from God'.[12] He has in mind here the eternal coming forth, or procession, of the Son from the Father.

The French feminist theorist Luce Irigaray saw love at its most erotic as always already beginning to open out upon that which is generative. As a person opens up to another, both are on new territory: there is a shared element of going beyond oneself, which can be said to be orientated beyond the couple, beyond even 'duality in closeness', to something creative.[13] As Sarah Coakley puts it, 'As each goes out to the other in mutual abandonment and attentiveness, so it becomes clear that a third is at play – the irreducibility of a "shared transcendence".'[14]

What for Irigaray is the experience of a shared transcendence, Coakley sees as an intimation of God. First, because it is from God that the good qualities come that we desire in the other person. Second, because from God as Trinity comes that fundamental relationality whereby the couple can be described in Irigaray's words not only as themselves but also as 'ourself in us'. Third, because love is always an imitation of God, who *is* love. Irigaray describes this 'shared transcendence' as 'prior to any child'. The Church goes beyond this to say that it normally finds its fullest expression in the conception of a child.

Love, of its nature, 'triangulates' itself, and marriage, as the paradigmatic example of human love, bears this stamp. The two bring forth a third (and perhaps fourth and fifth). This is an image of God, whose very nature is to be generative: God the Father eternally begets the Son and they eternally bring forth a third, the Holy Spirit. In practice, this language of 'two' and 'three' has to be held as an underlying principle or structure, rather than as a rule: we find plenty of single-parent families without fault and couples without children. There can be good psychological reasons why some couples may not think that it would be appropriate for them to raise a family, or one might wish not to pass on a recessive and debilitating genetic disease. Procreation and marriage are closely aligned, but the Church does not make procreation an unswerving condition for marriage, at least in that it celebrates marriages between those who are past childbearing age.

While celebrating the birth and nurture of children, we can recognize that the principle of bearing and raising children has a wider application than physical generation, although that will usually, and normally, be its principal form of expression. According to notes from Aquinas, collated after his death, the good of marriage that he calls 'offspring' takes in not only 'the begetting of children but also their education'. With this common end in mind, the couple engage in a much wider programme of 'shared works'. That dynamic, of common participation in shared and communal activities, stretches beyond rearing children. As Thomas's note takers recount, Paul uses this image for his own apostolic labour, comparing himself in 2 Corinthians 12.14 to a parent laying up for his children. Parents set us the most widespread example of a common life, lived for the good of others: what Aristotle called the sharing of a common life for the sake of shared work.[15] That should characterize every healthy marriage, whether before children are born, or after they have left the home, or if children do not arrive. Similarly, a family *with* children can fail to live out to the full what the 'good of offspring' means, if they fail to allow that child to be a genuine 'third', and perhaps – to extend the Trinitarian metaphor – if that third is stifled in his or her own creativity, so as not to become a 'giver of life', as the Holy Spirit is called in the Creed.

Holding this good of marriage before us can be a helpful reminder that raising a family, and wider work to build the human community, is not a distraction from Christian work. The evangelistic work of mission is central to the life of the Church, but it is not everything, and the first priority of parents is to bring their own children up as Christians.

Avoidance of sin

The third good of marriage is a negative good, which is to say it is about preventing an evil. Given the particular moral dangers around relationships – and the closer the relationship, the greater the danger – there is a commendable note of realism in claiming one out of three goods as a guard against sin. Paul offered a real endorsement of marriage, if at that moment seemingly a slightly half-hearted one, when we wrote that 'it is better to marry than to be aflame with passion'.[16]

The primary focus of this 'good' is on sexual desire, or lust. Part of the old Prayer Book introduction to marriage, which has not made it into the twenty-first-century rites, is the comment that 'men' are liable to want to satisfy their 'carnal lusts and appetites, like brute beasts that have no understanding'. (Although we might take 'men' to mean male human beings, a mediaeval tendency to see *women* as the sensual sex may suggest that either men or women could be in view here.)

Passages such as this might raise a snigger today, but if so it is in part because they provoke a nervous recognition of the truth about ourselves. Human nature is constitutively 'after' certain things. These are desires, urges or – to use a technical theological word – 'passions'. There is no denying this. Nor are these passions sinful in themselves. The danger is that the passions become out of kilter with each other and with our reason.

The moral task is not to repress our desires but to channel them aright. That involves educating ourselves about their proper ends:

what a human life is for, and how our desires play their part. It is then about orienting our desires within that larger picture, rather than allowing them to be distracted by an immediate wish for satisfaction. This applies as much, for instance, to eating food and drinking as anything else. The best safeguard is growth in good character (or 'virtue'). Also important is placing ourselves in the sort of situations and structures by which the proper outworking of our desires is made easier and following their worst excesses is made harder. In business, for instance, good management practices make the better easier and the worse less likely to happen. In the realm of human sexual relationships, this is also precisely part of what marriage is about.

The 'remedy against sin' calls for the virtue of temperance or restraint. Another virtue is also in view here, however, which is the virtue of courage. Temperance dissuades us from giving in to what is outside marriage. It holds us back when we need to be held back. Courage, however, urges us on when we are wrongly tempted to hold back. Courage dissuades us from giving up on what is inside marriage. Courage, as much as temperance, is a virtue sought within and through marriage.

The Epistles urges us to turn our back on a life lived 'according to the flesh' (for instance in Rom. 8). That is no denigration of the flesh; it is simply to say that 'flesh', taken as an end, is a very poor end indeed. Taken as something ultimate, it will always disappoint us. However, just as those who give up fields and parents and brothers and sisters in the Gospels get them back a hundredfold, although differently (Mark 10.30), when we give up on the flesh as an end in itself, we get it back, not least with the general resurrection. Promising to be faithful to one person, 'forsaking all others', is part of this remedy against sin. As with anything marked by the grace of God, the element of precautionary safeguard is far outstripped by a gift going beyond any mere precaution. Translate sexual relations out of take-it-when-you-can laxity, and they become something far *more*, since the flesh now expresses a complete gift of one person to another.

G. K. Chesterton held that the price of keeping himself to one woman (he and his wife had a long and warm marriage) was a very small price to pay for the possibility of having her as his *wife* at all.[17] We have already seen that the Incarnation involves a 'scandal of particularity': that God came as just this person, at just this time, in just this place, within just this culture, and through that particularity won redemption for all. In that the sacraments are always encounters between one person and another, there is also always an element of particularity about them: sacraments cannot be generic; they cannot come as a blanket offer; they cannot be celebrated at a distance or over the internet. We see an image of the scandal of Christ's particularity in ordination (*this* person, for all his or her faults, is your priest, your bishop, your deacon). We also see the scandal of particularity in marriage; indeed, we see it most of all in marriage.

When we say that marriage is a holy mystery given *in creation* we recognize that these three 'goods of marriage' are goods in themselves. Marriage *seeks* these goods; it does not *make* them good, although it is uniquely well placed to nurture them. As with confirmation as a rite for adolescence, sacramental theology should see no problem in the idea that marriage has an anthropological purpose. Something can be holy as well as useful; it can be a sacrament and have its own logic and good sense. Aquinas stresses this in a particularly creative way in his *Commentary on Ephesians*. Why, he wonders, does the command to love one's father and mother come with a promise attached ('so that it may be well with you and you may live long on the earth')?[18] The promise was attached, he argued, precisely because loving parents is *natural* and usually quite easy. Nothing is *less* moral, right or good for being easy and natural: the promise is attached 'lest anyone imagine that honouring one's parents was not meritorious because it is natural'.[19]

Eros and *agape*

Christian marriage is not about sickly sweet romance and sentimental self-indulgence, nor is it about masochistic self-sacrifice, which seeks only service, and sees service only as misery. Christian marriage does not even stand midway between the two. Rather, it outwits the assumption of a disparity between joy and service, between self-fulfilment and the offering of oneself to another.

Marriage is not self-indulgent or sentimental. As I once heard in a wedding sermon, we approach its heart more directly through unloading the dishwasher than we do by watching the film *Titanic*. For most people, as we have noted, marriage is the principal means by which they can learn to lose their lives in order to find them: it is, we should note, about both *losing* our lives and *finding* them. Marriage is about *agape*, the self-giving love of God, but it is not about *agape* in such a way as to cease to be about *eros*, the love of passion and desire. Christian marriage denies sentimentality, but it does not say that delight in the other is anything less than delight.

The Christian tradition has often said that any desire for anything worthy is ultimately a desire for God. Sarah Coakley makes the important point, on this basis, that the way to begin the right ordering of human erotic desire is not to cover it up but to uncover its relation to God. We must 'turn Freud on his head', as she puts it. Instead of

> thinking of 'God' language as really being about sex (Freud's reductive ploy), we need to understand sex as really about God, and about the deep desire that we feel for God – the clue that is woven into our existence about the final and ultimate union that we seek.[20]

Ultimately, we need to understand our desire, even our desire for God, in terms of God's desire for us. This, as Coakley points out, is how Pseudo-Dionysius understands Paul's exclamation that it 'is no longer I who live, but it is Christ who lives in me' (Gal. 2.20): divine *ekstasis* and the yearning of God for creation are forever 'catching up our human yearning into itself'.[21] As Pseudo-Dionysius put it, 'Paul was clearly a lover and, as he says, he was beside himself for God'.[22]

The root of 'ecstasy' is the Greek *ek-stasis*: coming to stand outside oneself. Here, marriage at its most sexual aligns with marriage at its most practical: letting the focus of one's being stand outside one's own ego. The task is to see the sexual or romantic aspect of marriage as true service, and the practical and humdrum aspect of marriage as the 24-hour embodiment of a true union of heart and body. A puritanical elevation of routine over romance or service over sex strikes at the heart of marriage as surely as a liberal elevation of romance over routine and sex over service. Taken together, the sexual dimension of marriage need not be evaded, and therefore approached only by way of winks and nudges, nor should living for another be anything other than one of marriage's chief recommendations. Practically, as it were 'empirically', it is simply not the case that self-fulfilment stands in contradiction to living for others. For most people, and in the most abundant cases, fulfilment is found in relation to others. This certainly involves self-denial in the details, but the purpose of marriage is a new orientation by which this no longer amounts to self-denial overall, since the structure of one's life is now understood in relation to the other person and to goods that cannot be achieved alone.[23]

Seeking what is good and just involves self-denial in relation to what is called 'the old self' in Ephesians, but not in relation to what it goes on to call the 'new self'.[24] Marriage is one of the best analogies we have to this; 'religious' or monastic life is another. A sharp distinction between *agape* and *eros* ignores this link because it thinks with the logic of an unredeemed life.

The Church wants to place marriage outside both cheap sensuality and miserable self-denial, and because of this marriage has traditionally been celebrated within a Eucharist. This is the normal context for Roman Catholics today. If it is far less common among Anglicans, that is a deviation from the recommendation of the Prayer Book, as we have seen, where the marriage service ends with the rubric that it is 'convenient', in this context meaning 'appropriate', 'that the new-married persons should receive the holy Communion at the time of their Marriage, or at the first opportunity after their Marriage'. The Eucharist is the place where we encounter the perfect *sacrifice* of Christ in the context of his *risen and joyful* presence.

In marriage, as in each of the sacraments, we see that materiality is spiritual and the spiritual is material. Terry Eagleton wrote in *After Theory* that the intellectual culture of our time is 'shamefaced about morality . . . embarrassed about love, biology, religion and revolution, largely silent about evil, reticent about death and suffering . . . [which, on his estimation] is rather a large slice of human existence to fall down on'.[25]

This is all the more remarkable given, as he also notes, this same culture's obsession with the body: 'Among students of culture, the body is an immensely fashionable topic, but it is usually the erotic body, not the famished one. There is a keen interest in coupling bodies, but not in labouring ones.'[26] A theological account of marriage shows that it is possible to be concerned with both the 'erotic' body and the 'famished' one, even if that is simply by placing a common meal, at the end of the working day, at the centre of family life.

When it comes to the body, the Church beats the world at its own game, putting the body centre stage in a far more remarkable way than our culture can offer. Marriage makes this clear, as should the Eucharist and each of the other sacraments. They put the body forward as fully material and, in that, always spiritual and always morally significant.

From all of this it follows that marriage is a demanding business. For that reason, the Church places considerable emphasis on preparing couples for marriage: combining encouragement and wise practical advice, theological instruction and a challenge to think through, and crucially to *talk through*, what lies ahead. Important at this stage is negotiating the transition from a primary loyalty to one's existing family and friends to a primary loyalty to one's spouse, such that nothing is entirely undone of what was known before, nor entirely left the same.

Form and matter

Marriage poses a challenge for us in terms of sacramental theology because it is not clear quite what *action* it involves (what we have called the *matter*). This is something of a red herring. We need not doubt that marriage involves an action. Ask a couple on the morning of their wedding if they are about to *do* something, and they will leave you in no doubt that they are. We can point to various parts of the service that might count as the 'matter' – the giving and receiving of rings, or the joining of hands, for instance – but the bigger point is that marriage *as a whole* has character enough as an action. It is among the most profound actions that many people will perform in their entire lives.

Indissolubility

If Christians have sometimes shied away from calling marriage a sacrament, not least in the twentieth century, that is perhaps because they have been alarmed by the indissolubility that the sacramental quality has been understood to bring. This question took on important, political, consequences in England at the time of the Reformation. A century later, John Milton wrote in favour of divorce and, like Henry VIII, this was not without personal resonances.

Ask a group of ten theologically literate and reflective Christians about divorce and remarriage, and you will probably get three or four different answers. The ancient Western view is that marriage cannot be dissolved. Roman Catholics, officially, hold this view, although it is balanced by a willingness, far beyond that of other Christians, to say that certain marriages never took hold in the first place. In that case, the marriage is not dissolved but annulled: not *made* to be null but *recognized* as null. Other Christians will say that marriages can die or be undone. The Eastern Orthodox Churches allow remarriage, although with a certain penitential mood. It is also possible to hold that marriage is indissoluble but to allow remarriage as a sort of sanctified polygamy.

Divorce and remarriage are clearly already not ideal. We want marriages to work, which is why marriage preparation is so important. Many Christians, however, at least in the Church of England, think that remarriage may be pastorally licit since, as the book of Genesis puts it, 'It is not good that . . . man [or woman] should be alone' (Gen. 2.18).

Singleness and same-sex marriage

Marriage must be central to the vocation of a married Christian, which is to say, to his or her calling. Paul sums up an extended practical discussion of marriage with the words 'let each of you lead the life that the Lord has assigned, to which God called you' (1 Cor. 7.17). Not everyone, however, is married and discussion of marriage should therefore invite us to think about those who are not married.

Some of these people will be in long-term relationships. Our task in relation to them is primarily to commend marriage, rather than to judge their arrangements. Some of these partnerships are between people of the same sex. We will discuss that below. For the moment, we will consider those who are single.

Pope John Paul II made the striking claim that single people are 'particularly close to the Heart of Christ'.[27] If that is so, they have not always had a particularly valued place within Christ's Church. The Pope recognized that the isolation of single people is a particular problem in the contemporary world and argued that this should not be the case within the Church. Particularly vulnerable and isolated, he thought, are the poor:

For those who have no natural family the doors of the great family which is the Church – the Church which finds concrete expression in the diocesan and the parish family, in ecclesial basic communities and in movements of the apostolate – must be opened even wider. No one is without a family in this world: the Church is a home and family for everyone, especially those who 'labour and are heavy laden'.[28]

Some people abstain from marriage for the sake of a greater good, most of all for the sake of Christ. Since early Christian times some in the Church have found a vocation to singleness as a state of life consecrated to God. In the Gospels we read Jesus saying 'there are eunuchs who have made themselves eunuchs for the sake of the kingdom of heaven' (Matt. 19.12). Properly understood, an elevated understanding of marriage and of virginity should reinforce one another. John Chrysostom put this well:

Whoever denigrates marriage also diminishes the glory of virginity. Whoever praises it makes virginity more admirable and resplendent. What appears good only in comparison with evil would not be truly good. The most excellent good is something even better than what is admitted to be good.[29]

It is not uncommon, however, to encounter an emphasis on marriage in churches, over and against singleness, which can reach an almost hysterical pitch. This is a strange position for Christians, if we read Paul's Epistles (and often these are churches that spend a great deal of time reading Paul). Throughout 1 Corinthians 7, Paul weaves together two threads, turning to one and then the other. On the one hand he upholds the good of marriage and the freedom of the Christian to follow a call of life, including marriage. On the other, he turns to the urgency of the gospel call. The relation between the two is difficult, and this is reflected in Paul's unusual decision in these passages to preface many of his remarks with the comment that they represent his opinion, not Christ's.

Paul's conclusion is that 'he who marries his fiancée does well; and he who refrains from marriage will do better' (1 Cor. 7.38), on the basis that the unmarried person can be more thoroughly devoted to the cause of the gospel (1 Cor. 7.32–35). The context is important. Paul is writing in the expectation of the imminent return of Christ: 'the appointed time has grown short ... For the present form of this world is passing away' (1 Cor. 7.29, 31). Even those who are married ('who have wives') should behave as if they did not. The Church embraced marriage more wholeheartedly once the sense of the imminent return of Christ no longer dominated the Christian vision quite so fully. We do, however, still live in expectation of Christ's return, and whether or not Christ returns in our lifetime, Christian eschatology reminds us of the urgency with which we need to attend to the work of his kingdom. On that basis, we cannot put Paul's strictures too far behind us.

Important, however, is the sense here that marriage is not simply an indulgence or a concession towards lust. Marriage is *salutary*. For many, even most people, it is the ideal context in which to work out their salvation (Phil. 2.12). The Christian life is a war with sin, and at the heart of sin lies pride and selfishness. Marriage places before us, as we have seen, an opportunity for living for another and not simply for our self that is unparalleled, other than by religious profession, with which marriage is not accidentally paired. All that Paul writes in 1 Corinthians 7 stands, but to it we might add the sense, developed down the centuries, and not alien to the Scriptures, that marriage is a supreme 'moral gymnasium'.

For most people throughout Christian history, then, marriage has been the context in which they have learned to live beyond themselves. This is the ideal jumping-off point from which to consider perhaps the most hotly debated topic in relation to marriage in our time, namely the admission of same-sex couples to this institution.

In his encyclical *Familiaris Consortio*, John Paul II wrote that 'Christian revelation recognizes two specific ways of realizing the vocation of the human person, in its entirety, to love: marriage and virginity or celibacy.'[30] For those who see relationships between people of the same sex as intrinsically good, for all they can go wrong (as heterosexual relationships can), the Pope's idea argues in the opposite direction from that in which he no doubt intended: towards opening marriage to same-sex couples. Whether one *does* recognize such value in same-sex relationships is, of course, the underlying question. For those who do not, marriage will probably be out of the question. It is not the place of this book to rehearse the arguments about same-sex relationships, other than to say that as every year progresses the 'sense of the faithful' over this matter shifts further towards celebrating what they represent, and that this position is already that of a significant majority of theologians, at least within the Anglican tradition from which I write.[31] Whichever line we take, we should note that devout and learned Christians take opposing positions in this debate.

We might consider two angles on this question. One is whether marriage could be extended as an institution while leaving open the question of sacramentality. The Roman Catholic tradition, in particular, makes a distinction between 'natural' and 'sacramental' marriage, not least in that the former pre-dates the Church, and only Christians (and only then in certain circumstances) can enter into the latter. In some legal jurisdictions a sharp distinction is made between the state and the Church, and between a legal dimension to marriage and a sacramental dimension. This applies, for instance, in the United States. In that situation the extension of *natural* marriage, as an institution, can be considered separately from the extension of *sacramental* marriage.

In other countries, that sharp distinction between the legal and the theological is more difficult to maintain. The United Kingdom is a good example, where the establishment of the Church means that the legal meaning of marriage is more closely bound up with the theological position of Christians, and of the Church of England in particular. In debating how to react to same-sex marriage in such situations, the distinction between natural and sacramental marriage may, however, still be a useful one. The state would expand the scope of an institution; the Church must subsequently determine the bounds of sacramentality.

The other angle is to enquire whether same-sex marriages should be seen as indeed sacramental. One approach would be to consider the three goods of marriage. The 'mutual comfort' element is embraced by same-sex unions clearly enough, as also is the avoidance of sin, both in terms of holding sexual desire within a relationship that is permanent and faithful and, beyond that, in avoidance of selfishness, and other, similar moral benefits of marriage.[32]

With the other good of marriage, nurturing children, those arguing for the sacramentality of same-sex marriage find themselves with more work. For some theologians, who are otherwise in favour of same-sex relationships, and would call upon the Church to bless civil partnerships, we are reminded here of an essential difference in kind between heterosexual and homosexual relationships, which rules out same-sex relationships as *sacramental* marriage.[33] Others wish to ask whether this good is *necessary* for sacramentality in every case, for all it might be constitutive of our understanding of marriage as a whole, and how widely it can be interpreted. We marry people who cannot conceive children, and consider those marriages to be sacramental. This third good, in any case, extends to more than *conceiving* children: it runs to sharing in the upbringing of the next generation and their education, as Aquinas has it, and what he calls the larger, social programme of 'shared works'. Beyond the question of gay couples bringing up adopted children, or children who are the natural offspring of one partner and not the other, it is clear that same-sex couples often take an exemplary part in the 'shared work' of the community, to which this good of marriage belongs, in relation to the care and education of children, certainly, but also in many other ways. Inasmuch as this good of marriage is about having an 'outward-facing' dimension to the relationship, and taking up a role of nurture within the community, this good is not only possible for same-sex couples, but even *necessary*, if their relationships are to be fully Christian.

With the call for civil partnerships, and now for marriage, we see an important shift. A culture that has sometimes been more concerned with *conjugality* than *nuptuality* (at least among gay men) has come to embrace the latter.[34] In reaching out for marriage, gay couples are reaching out for something of the highest theological significance. A dismissal with short shrift is a wasted opportunity. However the Church responds, it should be with the recognition that public enthusiasm for same-sex marriage could be recognized and nurtured as what it is: a remarkable return to, and valuation of, marriage as such.

These questions will not be settled for many years to come. Whatever our response to the controversies of our day, marriage stands as one of the principal overarching images with which we can understand God's dealings with men and women. It is a reminder, in the words of the *Catechism of the Catholic Church*, that love is 'the fundamental and innate vocation of every human being. For man [and woman] is created in the image and likeness of God who is himself love.'[35]

11

Anointing

Anointing is the rediscovered sacrament. For some Christian traditions that is true in an absolute sense. It is the one sacrament, for instance, that was completely eclipsed in the Church of England following the Reformation.[1] For Roman Catholics, the rediscovery was to see this sacrament as belonging to all those who are seriously sick, and not simply for those who are at the very door of death. For yet others, such as charismatics, the discovery was that something that was already very important to them – prayer for healing – had an ancient *sacramental* form.

What does this sacrament promise?

Christians believe that God heals the sick. Jesus gave healing as one indication of what he was about, and who he was, when asked by John the Baptist from prison (Matt. 11.4–5; Luke 7.22). We also accept that he does not always heal the sick miraculously, and even that miraculous healings are rare. God is not going to heal everyone, all the time: Christ did not come to save us from death but to transform death, so that it could be the door to eternal life; sooner or later, we are going to die.

Aquinas was a strong believer in God's supernatural involvement in the world. He was a member of a religious order, the Dominicans, who were in the first flush of their founding zeal. He would have come of age as a friar among stories of recent martyrdoms, and of the miracles that God wrought at the hands of holy Dominican men and women. All the same, he was firmly realistic that prayer for healing, even the sacrament of healing, does not always remove infirmity, since 'the restoration of bodily health – even in those who receive the sacrament worthily – sometimes is not useful for salvation'.[2] The sacraments, like the Incarnation, are concerned with salvation: salvation begun and salvation brought to completion. Bodily healing can be part of this, but the brutal truth is that our salvation is not, eventually, going to be completed by living, but by dying, just as, by death, Christ completed the salvation he was winning for us by his life. Aquinas saw the most likely results of anointing as providing bodily strength (rather than full recovery) and fortification against evil. Perhaps rather creatively, he read the words 'and the Lord shall raise him [or her] up' (Jas. 5.15 AV), as referring to the Christian being raised to Christ after death without impediment. There are always sins that we commit in the business of living, and from these we ought to be washed before we go to God. The whole of the Christian journey is one of healing, and this sacrament stands at the earthly end of this process: it 'consummates the entire spiritual healing', in which the other sacraments have also played their role.[3]

Sometimes the role of this sacrament is described as 'hallowing suffering'. This chimes with Paul's desire in Philippians, not to be spared suffering or death, but that in both he should come to share with Christ, who had suffered and died for him (Phil. 3.7–15). 'Christ' means 'anointed one', and suffering and death were part of what that meant for him and means for us. At the start of our Christian life, in baptism, we are 'Christened': conformed to Christ. At the end of our life, or towards the end, we are anointed, making clear what it means to share in Christ *right to the end*, not least in terms of sharing in baptism to the end: what it means to 'be baptized with the baptism [he is] baptized with' and 'to drink the cup that [he is to] drink' (Mark 10.38–39). All the same, great care has to be used in talking about 'hallowing suffering'. Nothing glib should be allowed to enter, nor any suggestion that suffering holds any ultimate part in God's plan. God drew near to suffering in Christ, not to wallow in it, or to celebrate it, but to defeat it. Some things we hallow because they are good, like marriage; others are hallowed in spite of being evil, such as suffering.

Form, matter and recipient

Anointing the sick is a sacrament not only of healing but also of forgiveness. That is to say, it is a sacrament of healing for the whole person. The association with forgiveness is attested by, and subsequently based on, the Letter of James. By the Middle Ages, the element of forgiveness had expanded to become primary, even dominant.

The Council of Florence summed this shift up when, in 1439, it put the emphasis strongly on the forgiveness of sins. Anointing was called 'extreme unction': an anointing ('unction') to be given *in extremis* – in face of death. For the Council of Florence (1439), danger of death was a prerequisite: 'This sacrament shall not be given to any except the sick who are in fear of death.'[4] The Roman Catholic Church changed this in 1972, when the recipients of the sacrament were defined as 'those who are dangerously ill'.[5]

The *form*, that is to say the accompanying words, used to be pronouncing forgiveness of the sins associated with different parts of the body as they were each, sequentially, anointed.[6] With the emphasis now more strongly on healing, the form for Roman Catholics today has become these theologically pregnant phrases: 'Through this holy anointing may the Lord in his love and mercy help you with the grace of the Holy Spirit. May the Lord who frees you from sin save you and raise you up.' It is similar in the Church of England. With this shift, anointing has regained its place as a sacrament of its own, rather than as 'the completion of penance'.

The earlier association with the end of life came, in part, from the assumption that a person could only receive this anointing once. That idea is now thoroughly discredited. Even by the thirteenth century, Aquinas – for all he reserved this sacrament to 'those who seem in their weakness to be approaching the end' – held that if someone recovers he or she can receive it again just, he says, as we might repeat the use of a healing medicine.[7]

Having discussed the form, we might mention that the *matter* is usually olive oil. The oil refers both to medical ointment and to Christ as the anointed one. We can be relaxed about the use of other sorts of oil of vegetable origin, if olive oil is difficult to obtain.[8] The sick person is anointed on the forehead, and often also on the hands, or elsewhere if the forehead cannot be anointed for medical reasons.

When we anoint the sick it is worth praying for all who are sick, and for the needs of the world more generally. That takes up the theme of forgiveness and overcoming evil already present in this sacrament and helps us to raise our eyes to remember sickness in the 'body politic'. Focus on the communal dimension is part of what it means for the Church to 'weep with those who weep' (Rom. 12.15) and to recognize that if one part of the body suffers, we all suffer

(1 Cor. 12.26). We should also pray for those who treat and those who care for those whom we anoint.

The sacraments belong together, and whenever we seek anointing it is right for us also to confess our sins and receive Communion. These three sacraments go together all the more forcefully at the end of life. This is at the heart of what it might mean to die 'a good death'. We only die once; we should wish to do it well. These three sacraments are among the principal means that the Church affords, but they should not stand on their own. We should also ensure, as much as possible, that people die knowing that they are in the company of the Church: through prayer, certainly, but also through physical company as much as that is possible. This is simply to expand upon a maxim of the desert father, St Anthony of Egypt: 'my life and my death are with my neighbour'.[9] The contrasting sense, that in death *everyone* is alone, even if in physical company, is one of the ultimate horrors of secularity. With this in mind, Dame Cicely Saunders OM, a devout Christian, founded the modern hospice movement.[10] One of the principal acts of charity that a Christian can perform is to accompany someone to death, bearing witness to his or her place in the company of the redeemed. There are a handful of classic prayers for use at a deathbed which it would be wise for every Christian to have to hand, if not to know by heart. An example is this one, *Proficere, anima Christiana*:

> Go forth upon your journey from this world, O Christian soul;
> in the name of God the Father who created you. Amen.
> In the name of Jesus Christ who suffered for you. Amen.
> In the name of the Holy Spirit who strengthens you. Amen.
> In communion with all the blessed saints;
> with the angels and archangels and all the heavenly host. Amen.
> May your portion this day be in peace
> and your dwelling in the city of God. Amen.[11]

For those who are *not* in perilous danger of death, but seriously sick, there is a question of balance over when and whether to receive anointing. That balance has helpfully shifted in the last 50 years towards a less cautious use of anointing, but today it can swing too far and make the sacrament somewhat frivolous. The decision lies with individual conscience and the priest who is anointing. As an indication, we should not seek to be anointed because we have caught a common cold in the usual run of things, or perhaps even if we have a clean break to a bone for which there is every expectation of a full recovery. We should receive the sacrament if we catch a cold on top of pleurisy or for a nasty break, or if a clean break develops serious complications.

Finally, although it would be unpopular to say so among some, we cannot and therefore should not receive anointing for another person – absolutely and unequivocally – any more than we can be baptized, married, ordained or confirmed for someone else, or make a confession for them or receive Communion for them. If someone is sick, we can pray for them and we can encourage them to receive the sacrament of anointing. To receive anointing 'for them', apart from being impossible from the perspective of sacramental theology, also robs the sick person of the associated benefits of the sacrament, such as teaching, fellowship or ongoing pastoral care. It even fails to communicate the natural and physical good upon which the sacrament builds, namely the warmth of physical contact. An attempt to receive anointing for others, in other words, risks reducing the sacrament to something like magic.

In the Roman Catholic tradition, children are not anointed before the age of reason. Some argue that this is because the sacrament is connected with the remission of sin and before the age of reason a baptized child has not committed any sins. Others put the emphasis on joining one's suffering to the Passion of Christ, which a child cannot do before those terms make sense to him or her. Here, perhaps, Christians from other traditions would feel more comfortable anointing even a very sick small child, on the basis that this is a sacrament of healing.

Natural and supernatural

The sacraments are about salvation, and *healing* plays an important role among the various angles we have on what salvation means. God is concerned with healing both the individual and the world from the effects of sin. Healing of the body is not the only dimension to that work, but within the Christian emphasis on the general resurrection it is a vital part. The healing of the body can serve, from time to time, as a foretaste of that complete healing of all things.

The Christian tradition is careful both to stress the possibility of miraculous healing and not to divorce that work of God from the wider work of healing through medicine, which is also 'God's work'. 'Honour physicians for their services, for the Lord created them,' we read in the book of Ecclesiasticus (in the Apocrypha for some Christians, but still to be held in high honour),[12] since 'their gift of healing comes from the Most High' (Ecclus 38.1–2). The sacrament of anointing very obviously extends the work of the Incarnation, but so does the work of medicine, not least when carried out in a Christian context: natural and supernatural are not in competition. The Christian should not neglect to pray just because he or she is receiving modern Western medical care, nor is anointing a substitute for the work of doctors and nurses. In the words of Aquinas, if Christians were to 'neglect human assistance without any useful or urgent motive, they would be tempting God'.[13] He quotes Augustine, who noted that Paul fled from harm when he could, 'not through ceasing to believe in God, but lest he should tempt God, were he not to flee when he had the means of flight'.[14]

Ezekiel, Isaiah, Christ and the author of the Revelation to St John all envisaged medicinal use of plants and oil (Ezek. 47.12; Isa. 1.6; 38.21; Luke 10.34; Rev. 22.2) and Timothy is urged to make medicinal use of wine (1 Tim. 5.23). Ecclesiasticus makes specific reference to medicine and pharmacy:

> The Lord created medicines out of the earth,
>   and the sensible will not despise them.
> Was not water made sweet with a tree
>   in order that its power might be known?
> And he gave skill to human beings
>   that he might be glorified in his marvellous works.
> By them the physician heals and takes away pain;
>   the pharmacist makes a mixture from them.
> God's works will never be finished;
>   and from him health spreads over all the earth.
>
> (Ecclus 38.4–8)

If the author had reason to be grateful for medicines in the early second century BC, how much more do we in the twenty-first century, when a packet of ibuprofen costs very little money, or when certain deadly diseases can be banished with drugs, including bubonic plague and leprosy, and vaccination has eliminated others. There is nothing biblical about despising whatever can be done naturally to aid healing. Ecclesiasticus urges us both to make use of God's provision in nature and to turn to God in prayer (38.9–14).

Saints are recorded throughout history who worked miraculous cures; just as many are revered for 'natural' medical work, carried out with supernatural devotion. For every John of Beverley (died 721), whose legends associate him with many healings, there is a Damien of Molokai (1840–89), who cared for lepers for 16 years on a quarantine island, before succumbing to the disease himself.

Sacraments and making safe

I remember standing in as celebrant of a Eucharist, followed by the anointing of the sick. On that occasion, I anointed those who came forward but did not offer the associated rite of laying on of hands. I will think differently in future, but at the time I followed the truncated logic that since the sacramentality lies in the anointing, that would suffice. Afterwards, someone commented plaintively, 'When Fr Fred [the vicar, not his real name] takes the service, he always *puts his hands on us.*' Fr Fred, I am convinced, conducted himself with nothing but the highest probity, and I am sure that the plaintive tone reflected only a human desire for the warmth of contact. The incident made me aware of both the tremendous power for good of this sacrament, even on a natural level, but also of what charged territory it occupies.

The sacraments start with what is natural and expand it. In another sense, they start with what is natural and limit it, in the sense of rendering it safe. We see this with marriage (with respect to sexual love) and ordination (with respect to leadership), and in a sense with confirmation (with respect to adolescence). This dynamic is also important when it comes to the sacrament of the sick.

As with the Incarnation, the sacraments meet us in our vulnerability, and never more so in sacramental provision for the sick. Abuse, where there is abuse, will most likely occur in relation to those who are less able to defend themselves. This sacrament, again like the Incarnation, is a matter of the body: of the body in its sickness and the body as the instrument of God's love. Rites of healing – anointing, the laying on of hands – have tipped into abuse in every age. As with all of the sacraments, and indeed with ministry more generally, a good rule is that priests can rejoice in the good they can do while guarding carefully against approaching what they do primarily for their own sake or sense of need.

The healing ministry of the Church is for all Christians, but this sacrament is administered only by priests and bishops.[15] This ensures that ministry to the sick at its most intense, and in the moments of greatest need and vulnerability, is properly supervised. Performed by one's parish priest, it also associates healing with proper training, not only in the rite in question, but also in the care of souls and bodies more widely. Its liturgical setting ensures that healing is placed within the larger picture of Bible readings, Christian teaching and prayer for others in need.[16] Beyond concerns for pastoral care and good order, the association with the priest comes through the bishops, as successors of the Apostles. The ministry of anointing was entrusted to the Apostles, and their successors share this commission with priests at their ordinations.

In some traditions, the wider service of healing may also include a time of more informal prayer with the laying on of hands. Sometimes, lay people are involved in this element, which is permissible and can be very helpful. All the same, they should always be perceptive people of good character, and have received appropriate training.

In one city where I have worked, it was not uncommon on a Saturday morning to see that one of the charismatic churches had set up a stall in the main pedestrianized street, offering prayer for healing to passing shoppers. I commend their faith, and their desire to take that faith into the public sphere, but I worried that this approach leaves the ministry to the sick unhelpfully disconnected. It is insufficiently linked to teaching, so that the wider picture can be explored, beyond the hope of miraculous cures; it is insufficiently linked, at least on the face of it, with an ongoing pastoral relationship, and such a pastoral relationship belongs at the heart of that healing ministry. Moreover, since we are all ultimately destined to die (if the second coming is delayed), preparing people for death has ultimately got to be even more vital than the ministry of healing.

After anointing

Now that anointing has been restored as a sacramental response to serious *but not necessarily life-threatening* illnesses, many Christians find themselves recovered, or largely recovered, after a bout of sickness, as recipients of this sacrament. Illness, anointing and recovery should constitute a step on the journey to the completion of our salvation. Life should not therefore go back to the way it was before.

The sacrament of anointing helps us to place sickness in a theological context, within the life of the Church and within the drama of God's purposes for us. As a consequence, it also places recovery from sickness in that renewed context. Restored to health and, all the more, restored to health as those who have given ourselves over to God through anointing, we should pledge to rededicate ourselves, in our recovered strength, to a new resolve in serving Christ, and living for him, others and the Church. This does not necessarily mean commitment to frantic activity. Indeed, an encounter with sickness might be taken as a providential indication to find a new simplicity.

12

Confession

For perhaps three years, Christ had the ministry of a travelling preacher, moving from town to town with a simple message: Repent, for the kingdom of God is at hand (Mark 1.15; Matt. 3.2, 4.17). These years of journeying and preaching were no mere interlude before the Passion. This activity of Christ, and its message, is the template for all that would come after. Now, he has bequeathed it to the Church. Preaching repentance and fostering reconciliation forms a vital part of what it means for the Church to continue the work of the Incarnation. After the Ascension, in the time of the Church, the message becomes, 'Repent, and be baptized' (Acts 2.38). The sacrament of confession takes both repentance and baptism seriously and reminds us that baptism is a 'baptism of repentance for the forgiveness of sins' (Luke 3.3). We should not be baptized unless we are repentant. In turn, baptism deals with the effects of our sins, being a participation in the death and resurrection of Christ.

In an important sense, baptism fulfils repentance. In another sense, with baptism repentance has only just begun. The Greek word for repentance is *metanoia*, meaning changing one's mind, or conversion. Baptism is a conversion, but it also welcomes us into a life of conversion. Baptism is our great turning around but, having turned round, we can wander and, if we do, we need to come back on course. Confession, or whatever we choose to call it, is the sacrament of ongoing conversion and ongoing repentance. The 'ministry of reconciliation', entrusted by the Church to its priests, is 'an extension of Jesus' own ministry', as the Church of England puts it, and 'lies at the heart of this [priestly] vocation'.[1]

The question of the name of this sacrament is a tricky one. There is little doubt what the sacrament of confession *is*. Nor, being among the more nerve-wracking sacraments, is there much doubt when one is involved with it. It is easy to point to, but difficult to name. Call it 'confession' and we downplay absolution; call it 'absolution' and we downplay confession. Call it 'penance' and it seems to revolve too much around our act of contrition; avoid this too virulently, perhaps by referring to it only as 'the sacrament of reconciliation', and we forget that something does rest on us, for all that response is a response to grace: this is a sacrament of repentance, and repentance, in one good definition, is being sorry enough to stop.[2] As with the Eucharist, which also has its synonyms, any of the titles for this sacrament will do, as long as we hold the other dimensions in view.

Whatever we call this sacrament, we have it because people sin after baptism. Confession is a thoroughly realistic sacrament, not launching us on something new but restoring us to newness when we fail. It takes seriously the sentiment of a collect from the Prayer Book: 'by frailty of our mortal nature we cannot always stand upright'.

From time to time over the history of the Church, unrepresentative Christians have held that sin after baptism is impossible, or that it is impossible to sin after someone has 'received the Holy Spirit' (which was unhelpfully separated from baptism). Such people would have little place for the sacrament of confession. Their position, however, is thoroughly unconvincing, both on the grounds of the Bible ('If we say that we have no sin, we deceive ourselves', we find addressed to a community of mature Christians in 1 John 1.8) and the evidence of our own eyes.

Other Christians, again unrepresentative, would not have room for this sacrament for the opposite reason: they thought it was impossible for a Christian who *does* sin ever to be forgiven and restored. The New Testament as a whole stands against this position, although those who advance it find the occasional isolated passage on which to base their argument.[3] If Peter was to forgive 77 times, or 70 times 7, it is unlikely that God is less generous.

Baptism is the primary sacrament of forgiveness. Confession takes second place. No unbaptized person should or could ever receive this sacrament; they should receive baptism. Confession comes after baptism, but it does not improve on baptism. Rather, it renews baptism's effect. Approached from the opposite angle, baptism does not undo the need for confession; it makes the effect of that sacrament possible. Confession is one of the most profound ways in which we can take the Christian moral life seriously. As a way to take stock of where we stand, and reach out urgently to God for grace to make progress on the way to the perfect likeness of Christ, confession is the ideal way to reconnect to baptism. By it, we submit to God's salvation taking the fullest possible hold upon us.

Forgiveness and the Church

We have already considered the occasion when Jesus told the paralytic man that his sins were forgiven and the teachers of the law replied that Christ was blaspheming, for who can forgive sins but God alone (Mark 2.7). The crowd, however, came to a different conclusion. After Christ had healed the paralytic, and the man had walked off, 'they glorified God, who had given such authority to human beings' (from the parallel passage, Matt. 9.8). Christ the divine Son forgives sins, but he does so as a human being, every bit as human as you or I. Christ's divinity does not make him any less human. In Christ we see that God has given the power to forgive sins into human hands. In the ministry of the Church that scandalous delegation is carried on. At the end of John's Gospel, Christ commissions the Apostles, saying, 'Receive the Holy Spirit. If you forgive the sins of any, they are forgiven them; if you retain the sins of any, they are retained' (John 20.22–23).

For the early Church, this meant both that Christ had entrusted this authority to the Church as a whole and that he had entrusted that authority to the Church principally in the figures of the Apostles. They in turn handed that authority on to subsequent generations, and they did that by handing it on principally to their successors. These successors were the 'bishops'. That understanding of authority is preserved in all of the ancient episcopal churches.

Both of these elements should be upheld: forgiveness is the work of the whole Church, in all situations, in all times and places, in every conceivable way; the solemn absolution of sins is the work of those to whom it is entrusted by the bishops as successors to the Apostles, namely to priests at their ordination. This mirrors the sense in which the anointing of the sick is the work of bishops and priests, as those entrusted with this authority and responsibility in ordination, within a healing ministry that belongs to the whole Church.

While the ministry of forgiveness also belongs to the whole Church, there are at least two reasons why it finds its culmination in a sacrament only ever conducted by a priest or bishop. First, the sacraments operate with a cast-iron sense of security. This is one of their distinguishing features. They offer a degree of confidence which rests upon, and reveals, the surety of the grace of God. The effects of sin are as grievous upon us as sinners as upon those whom we sin against. As sinners, we need help and we need to know that we are forgiven. The sacrament of confession embodies the sureness with which we can know that all who turn to Christ will not be turned away (John 6.37). In this sacrament we find a direct connection, through the priest and the bishop, to the Apostles to whom the authority was given.

The sacraments do not exhaust the possibilities of the Christian life. If that life is a building, the sacraments are pillars around which it can be built; if it is a garden, the sacraments are fountains around which it can grow. To see how profoundly this is true, consider that the sacraments do not monopolize even the area to which they most closely belong. Anointing is the sacrament of healing; it belongs alongside every possible legitimate medical intervention, alongside intercessory prayer for the sick, alongside pastoral care, alongside preaching and teaching. The Eucharist is our common meal; it must stand as the basis for feasting together, and feeding the hungry, rather than as a substitute. Similarly, the sacrament of reconciliation is the basis for a thoroughgoing practical commitment to reconciliation in every form, not its substitute or conclusion.

We have already seen a parallel between confession and anointing, and we have noted delicate pastoral considerations to the ministry to the sick. Reserving anointing and absolution to priests and bishops is part of making sure that they are held within a wider structure of training and pastoral care, teaching and accountability.

The rites of the Church of England forge a close bond between the ministry of absolution and the ministry of theological teaching (a person in this ministry is referred to as a 'discreet and learned Minister of God's Word'), as two facets of a priest's work. Any priest, newly ordained, should have received sufficient training to be ready to anoint the sick. Hearing confessions, however, and giving advice and pronouncing absolution is normally reserved for those who have received further supervision and have additional years of pastoral experience behind them. Priests are also held to account and under discipline. In particular, they are under discipline not to divulge anything they hear in the process of performing this sacrament. As an example of how seriously this discipline is taken, we can consider the revision of the canons of the Church of England, its Church law, in the 1960s. The entire code was rewritten, albeit in conformity and continuity with what had gone before. To allow this, the previous code, from 1603, was repealed, with the exception of one item. This concerned the 'seal of confession'.[4] No one was sure that parliament, which ratifies the canon law of the Church of England, would ever again pass a form of words strong enough to satisfy the theological and pastoral requirements for this sacrament. The provision from 1603 was therefore retained and the new canons, in a sense, built around it. We will return to the seal below.

The sacrament of confession and absolution is preserved for priests, but the work of forgiving sins, and of reconciliation, is entrusted to the whole Church. It lies at the heart of the vocation of every Christian. It is not hard to imagine extreme but, sadly, not unknown situations where this lay ministry might look quite like the sacrament itself. There are stories from Soviet times when the single priest in a labour camp would hear the confession of a succession of lay people and, having done that, would make his own confession to a member of the laity. Even in less straitened times, as a parallel to the sacrament although not as its substitute, a small group of Christians, who are committed to one another out of a desire to live an 'intentional' Christian life, may choose to offer a degree of accountability by which they discuss their wrongdoings. We can see this, for instance, in the early Methodist 'class meetings'.

Alongside being forgiven stands forgiving. Christ came to call us to repentance; he also came to teach us to forgive. It is important to be forgiven; it is also important to forgive. Throughout the Gospels, the two points are related; they become inseparable upon the cross, where Christ's death not only reveals the depths of our estrangement from God, and provides its remedy, but also provides the perfect example of forgiveness in his *first* words from the cross: 'Father, forgive them; for they do not know what they are doing' (Luke 23.34).

In the Lord's Prayer, the relation takes the form of a promise that we make to God: 'forgive us our trespasses, as we forgive those who trespass against us' (Luke 11.4, *Common Worship* translation). In Ephesians, it takes on the character of a moral injunction: 'be kind to one another, tender-hearted, forgiving one another, as God

133

in Christ has forgiven you' (Eph. 4.32). In Matthew it finds its most serious formulation of all, when Christ tells us that if we do not forgive others, then God will not forgive us (Matt. 6.14–15). There is little more important to the mission of the Church than forgiveness. This plays out on every level, from its work on an international stage to the day-by-day small details of every Christian's life. It applies as much to life within the Church as without. Hardly anything could more profitably occupy us as Christians as we learn and reflect upon our faith in our local communities than forgiveness: in sermons, study groups and private reading.

Forgiving can be difficult. Some people have suffered wrongs that they are unable to forgive, at least completely, in this life. We entrust such situations to God and the promise that his love will ultimately wipe away every tear. In the meantime we each seek, as much as is within our power, to forgive, and seek to grow beyond those limits, as recipients of the grace of God. Each of the sacraments is a means of that grace to forgive. This is an important part, for instance, of what it would mean for marriage to be a means of God's grace.

'It is in forgiving that we are forgiven,' we sing in the canticle associated with St Francis. The converse is also true: it is in being forgiven that we learn to forgive. There is no better school for learning to forgive than regular use of the sacrament of confession and absolution. Nor is there much in the Christian life that more perfectly introduces us to the radical *newness* that the grace of God brings. 'Behold, I will do a new thing,' announces God through Isaiah (Isa. 43.19 AV); 'Behold, I make all things new,' he promises in the Apocalypse of John (Rev. 21.5 AV). *Nova! Nova!* begins a mediaeval English Christmas carol: New things! New things![5]

As we saw in Chapter 2, the Incarnation was an irruption, the arrival of something new: 'How can anyone be born after having grown old?' asks Nicodemus (John 3.4). 'Can one enter a second time into the mother's womb and be born?' Indeed, but how can the eternal Son of God be born of a woman *at all*? How can he enter *a first time* into a mother's womb? This impossible event is a new beginning: as seemingly impossible as Almighty God, who is already *all*, creating a world, and directly comparable as an act of his self-communication founded purely upon grace. Its only parallel is the other great new event, the resurrection, which is also a matter of forgiveness. Outside any expected order of things, God raises his

Son to life rather than punishing us for his death: God, Paul says, who raises the dead and calls into being that which does not exist (Rom. 4.17). Then there is also birth from a virgin. Out of the many direct connections between the sacrament of reconciliation and the Incarnation, few are as potent as this sense of *newness* – the newness that follows when the grace of God comes into the world.

Anyone who has made a confession will attest that it is profoundly a sacrament of renewal or newness. We leave the confessional with a spring in our step. In my own experience, everything about the world seems brighter, and everything about myself seems less complicated or constrained. Confession of sin, in this case, turns into a wider confession: our confession of praise to God and the confession of our faith, newly renewed within us, to those around us.

Venial and mortal sins

Part of the background for confession lies with the distinction, made by the Christian tradition from early times, between two kinds of sin: venial and mortal. Venial sins degrade us and the world. They impede our growth in holiness and they harm others. They do not, however, entirely ruin us. In contrast, mortal sins do not simply impede our progress on the 'hard' way that leads to life; they set us on the other direction, on the road that leads to destruction (Matt. 7.13).

This is no scholastic embellishment on the biblical faith. We find it in the Fathers and, before that, in the New Testament itself: 'All wrongdoing is sin, but there is sin that is not mortal' (1 John 5.17). Even if the terms 'mortal' and 'venial' sin seem antiquated, or are not part of your tradition, we can still single out certain sins as being 'grave'. We do not rebel against God in the same way by stealing a bar of chocolate as by murdering someone. That is not to say that a demarcation is always easy, and venial sins certainly matter.

The Christian should regularly confess everything on his or her conscience; we should also educate our consciences as to what demands the most attention. Neglecting to educate our conscience is itself a sin: a 'sin of omission'. At the Reformation the idea gained currency that the only grave sin was the sin against faith. Since we are 'saved by faith', the only real disaster would be to waver in our belief. This is not convincing for a number of reasons. First, we are not so much saved 'by faith' as '*by grace* . . . through faith' (Eph. 2.8, emphasis added). If our situation rests too much on our state of faith, or lack of it, as if that were all that really matters, then we risk turning the individual's faith into a work, which is precisely what the Reformers at their best would not have wanted. Another reason why faith may not have pride of place, making sins against faith the worst, is the general primacy given to love in the New Testament: 'faith, hope, and love abide, these three; and the greatest of these is love' (1 Cor. 13.13). On the very serious consequences of turning against *love*, Paul, John and James very much agree (1 Cor. 13; 1 John 2.10–11; 3.17; Jas. 1.27; 2.15–16). In the parable of the Sheep and the Goats, belief does not clinch it; practical acts of charity or love are what count (Matt. 25.31–45). If the essence of a mortal sin rests in anything, it is as a sin against love rather than as a sin against faith.[6] A mortal sin is one that kills the life of God in us, and 'God is love' (1 John 4.8), not faith. It is most of all in rejecting love that we also reject God.

If we sense that we have committed a mortal sin, we should deal with it as soon as possible. We should express our sorrow to God. The greater part of the Christian tradition down the centuries would also urge us, with utmost seriousness, to make our confession to a priest and receive absolution. Nothing is more serious than our salvation; nothing is more debilitating than to be unsure of one's salvation; nothing is more objective than confessing our sins to someone entrusted with that ministry by the Church; nothing is more reassuring than to hear the words, spoken on behalf of Christ and on behalf of all his people, 'Go in peace; your sins have been forgiven.'

To mention the peril of mortal sin is not to say that *venial* sins fail to deserve our attention. We are called to be 'perfect . . . as [our] heavenly Father is perfect' (Matt. 5.48). This is a tall order, and God will not finish his work of salvation until he has turned us from every sin, however minor or venial. The sacrament of confession provides an unrivalled opportunity to take stock of our moral life. There is no better prelude for being 'sorry enough to stop' than being sorry enough to put our sins into words in front of another human being.

The value of this sacrament

Two charges are sometimes laid against this sacrament: that it is unnecessary and that it is unwholesome. On the first point, Christian traditions disagree on the necessity of personal confession and absolution. Even those, however, which do not *insist* upon it, stress its value. The position of the Church of England, for instance, is often taken to be that 'all may, none must, some should'. The canon on 'the ministry of absolution' enjoins all to live lives of self-examination and repentance.[7] Within this, confession to a priest is encouraged for any for whom 'further comfort or counsel' is useful, leading to 'the benefit of absolution', 'quieting' of conscience and 'avoiding of all scruple and doubtfulness'. The sick are then encouraged 'in particular' to make use of confession to a priest with absolution.[8]

The question 'What is *necessary*?' can too easily come down to the question 'What can I *get away without*?' This is to look at things the wrong way, living as we do within an order in which God provides for us with 'grace upon grace' (John 1.16). In the drama of a person's salvation, asking, 'What can I get away without?' is the wrong question. With salvation in view, who would wish to tread the line of the bare minimum? The sense of the wider Western tradition is that Christians should *always* make a confession to a priest if they are conscious of a mortal sin.[9] The Orthodox Churches are fiercer still, requiring confession whenever one approaches God in Holy Communion.

The other accusation is that this sacrament is somehow unwholesome. This might be because of the sense that a gloomy emphasis on wrongdoing breeds an obsession with sin. Two replies are in order. The first is that 'sin *is* serious and we should take it seriously. This argues, for instance, against omitting a general confession in the run of weekly services on the grounds that it is 'off-putting' to newcomers. Taking sin seriously is part of what we *offer* newcomers. Beyond this, while the sacrament of confession takes sin seriously, it is the very opposite of being gloomy. The penitent entirely typically leaves the encounter radiant, perhaps even feeling and looking a little bit younger. Far from breeding an obsession with sin, it is entirely about putting sin behind us.

Related to this is the accusation that the sacrament is unhealthy because it involves entrusting our most personal information, about our shortcomings, to someone else. This is a strange charge, given that we are instructed by Paul in Galatians to 'Bear one another's burdens, and in this way you will fulfil the law of Christ' (Gal. 6.2).[10] James urges us to 'confess [our] sins to one another' (Jas. 5.16). The injunction to the Apostles to forgive sins almost certainly envisages that those sins have first of all been confessed.

The ministry of confession has possibilities for abuse – that which is most good can fall the furthest – but it is hedged around with many safeguards. Priests take the seal of the confessional very seriously. For some critics, it is precisely those safeguards that are unwholesome, and in particular the absolute seal of the confessional.[11] Invariably, a single situation is cited, that of the confession of the abuse of children or vulnerable adults. In fact, this confession is not frequently encountered. We might wish, and indeed should wish, that those who are guilty of such sins would bring them to a priest for confession as a matter of urgency. All the same, even in such a case, or in the case of murder, in the words of the Church of England: even if 'a penitent's behaviour gravely threatens his or her well-being or that of others, the priest, while advising action on the penitent's part, must still keep the confidence'.[12] The point is that, without the unbreakable promise of the seal, there would be no confession in the first place. Only because of that unbreakable promise not to pass on what a priest hears would anyone guilty of a serious crime bring it to the priest at all. Without the seal, the contact would not be made; with the seal, a conversation begins: responsibilities are faced; advice is given. No priest is under an obligation to give absolution and in such situations it might be withheld and some 'appropriate action of contrition and reparation ... required before absolution is given'.[13] In the case of abuse, 'the priest should urge the person to report his or her behaviour to the police or social services, and should make this a condition of absolution, or withhold absolution until this evidence of repentance has been demonstrated'.[14] Without the seal, that journey would not have begun.

It is worth adding that the seal of confession simply requires priests not to act upon the information *so imparted*: they must act as if the confession had not been made. If they subsequently hear of a particular wrongdoing another way, they can proceed as they would otherwise have done at that point, had no confession been made, and act upon the information received outside confession.

A note: more on the anatomy of sin

With the distinction between mortal and venial sins we have introduced some terminology. We might usefully take this a little further.

A *mortal* sin is clearly *deadly*, but 'mortal' is not what we mean by what get called 'deadly sins' in English. A so-called 'deadly sin' is distinguished not by its severity but by its tendency to lead to other sins. The traditional seven 'deadly sins' have a better, but less familiar, name as the seven 'capital sins'. A sin is *capital* if it stands as the source or 'head' *(caput)* of others. (From *caput* we get capital: the 'head' city of a country or the architectural feature at the top, or 'head', of a column.) The usual contemporary list of deadly or capital sins runs to pride, envy, anger, sloth, greed, gluttony and lust.

A sin might be capital in one of at least two ways. On the one hand, capital sins are those most likely to *weaken our defences* against other sins, as anger might pave the way for murder, or drunkenness might leave us more prone to commit adultery. On the other hand, the capital sins might lure us to commit other sins as our *goal*, as we might lie about an illness in order to be slothful, or bump off a great-aunt in order to inherit her wealth. When a capital sin weakens us, it comes first, paving the way for others, such as anger leading to murder. When it is the goal, the capital sin comes after the others, serving as a lure, such as covetousness provoking us to murder.

When we make a confession, it is worth paying particular attention to capital sins. The seven 'capital' or 'deadly' sins were singled out over the course of Christian history precisely in the context of hearing confessions and giving spiritual counsel. The list of these sins is the fruit of discernment of human behaviour and a sense of what is particularly likely to bear bad fruit. Grub up these particular weeds before they scatter too many seeds and the garden will soon be much the better for it.

One more point to make, before we move on, is the idea that a mortal sin includes both 'grave matter' and 'deliberate intent'. As with all such distinctions, this can seem clinical and cold, but used wisely it can be immensely helpful. For a sin to have 'grave matter' is for there to be something *objectively* very serious about it: the murder as opposed to the theft of the chocolate bar. The other aspect, 'deliberate intent', reflects the *subjective* side of sin. Something can be objectively very wrong, but it will not necessarily destroy the life of God in us if we commit it in a state of madness, or under compulsion, or in a state of ignorance. For this reason, some of the most objectively serious sins might not be the most likely to damn us. Suicide, for instance, is objectively gravely serious: life is the greatest gift we are given and it is not to be cast aside. However, for the very reason that casting life aside is gravely unnatural, we might assume that very few who take their own lives are acting in their right minds. In that case, there may be grave matter but there is not 'deliberate intent' in the sense it is meant here. A seemingly arcane distinction urges us not to judge with restrictive severity, but to act with imaginative compassion.

Form and matter

The *form* or verbal component of the sacrament of reconciliation is not difficult to describe. It is whatever words of absolution are laid down by a church for this purpose. Identifying the 'form' with the words of the priest rather than the words of the penitent helps us to keep the focus on the grace of God rather than on our litany of sins. As an example, the Book of Common Prayer stipulates this form of absolution following confession in the rite for the Visitation of the Sick:

> Our Lord Jesus Christ, who hath left power to his Church to absolve all sinners who truly repent and believe in him, of his great mercy forgive thee thine offences; And by his authority, committed to me, I absolve thee from all thy sins, In the Name of the Father, and of the Son, and of the Holy Ghost. Amen.[15]

The situation seems to be more complicated when we come to the *matter* or physical element of this sacrament, just as we saw that marriage can pose a challenge for a tidy-minded sacramental theologian on the same point: it is not clear what absolutely specific and inalienable *action* marriage has to involve, for all it includes many actions. The same applies to penance, and even more so, since penance does not include even gesture in the way that marriage does (such as the exchange of rings or the joining of hands), never mind a physical substance, such as bread, wine, oil or water.

Comparison with marriage is helpful here. Wherever we might look for the precise *matter*, any married couple will confirm that marriage is an *action*. It is probably the most solemn and purposeful action that most married people have ever undertaken. Ask anyone who has made a confession, and he or she is likely to confirm that here too is an action-and-a-half, an action that takes far more strength of purpose than any common or garden activity. The sacrament of confession is physical and material because it is visceral. Unless you are a remarkably unusual Christian, you will take yourself to confession with a beating heart, a little out of breath. Unless you are that remarkably unusual Christian, you will come away from confession with an almost euphoric happiness that is every bit as bodily as the 'runner's high'. The journey to the priest, and making a clean breast of one's wrongdoings, is action enough to count as 'matter'.[16]

13

The sacraments and the Holy Spirit

At several points in this book we have related the sacraments to Christ. They are means, or instruments, by which God works out, in particular, the salvation brought in Christ. In Galatians, Paul pointed out that a second sending follows from the sending of Christ: from the coming of Christ follows the coming of the Holy Spirit.

> God sent his Son, born of a woman . . . to redeem those who were under the law, so that we might receive adoption as children. And because you are children, God has sent the Spirit of his Son into our hearts. (Gal. 4.4–6)

Christ explained that, having come to bestow the Spirit, he must depart in order that the Spirit might be sent (John 16.7).

When it comes to the doctrine of the Holy Spirit, we are never too far from the point if we say that the Spirit bears witness to Christ. In this sense, the Spirit often works under the form of a certain self-effacement. Conversely, however, we would not be true to the message of Christ if we did not see the Incarnation as pointing to the bestowal of the Holy Spirit. What began with the Holy Spirit overshadowing Mary (Luke 1.35) leads to each Christian, analogously, overshadowed by the same Spirit (not for the sake of a new Incarnation but that we may, all the same, bear Christ in the world).[1]

In John's Gospel, Jesus describes his purpose as coming 'that they may have life, and have it abundantly' (John 10.10), which might remind us of the Nicene Creed, where the Holy Spirit is described as the 'Lord and Giver of Life'. We will therefore continue our discussion of the sacraments and the Incarnation by considering the sacraments as the domain of the Holy Spirit ('domain', from *Dominus* – the word for 'Lord' in the Latin of the Creed) and of his work (which is to be 'giver of life').

In the sacraments, as at the beginning of creation, the Holy Spirit overshadows, or broods, over matter (Gen. 1.2). Similarly, the connection of the Spirit with the sacraments is natural in that they are the supreme acts of the Church, and the Spirit is the very life of the Church: its 'soul' to quote Augustine of Hippo.[2] To see the sacraments in relation to the Holy Spirit is also to remember that they have a place within *mission*, both in the sense of evangelism and in the search for justice and well-being for all. When Jesus quoted, 'The Spirit of the Lord is upon me', he went on to quote what Isaiah explained that to mean:

> he has anointed me
> to bring good news to the poor.
> He has sent me to proclaim release to the captives
> and recovery of sight to the blind,
> to let the oppressed go free,
> to proclaim the year of the Lord's favour.
> (Luke 4.18–19, quoting Isa. 61.1–2)

Baptism

In the twenty-first century, we are likely to put the reception of the Holy Spirit at the centre of what baptism is about. That is a happy but reasonably recent adjustment of emphasis. When the American Anglican Francis Hall covered the sacraments in volume nine of his exhaustive (and not un-orthodox) *Dogmatic Theology*, he placed the 'operation and gift of the Holy Spirit' in the section on baptism entitled 'Incidental matters' and not, for instance, the section entitled 'Benefits'. His comment that 'it is practically impossible, in view of the general effects of Baptism described in the New Testament, to suppose that the Spirit is in no sense bestowed in Baptism' is an understatement of almost preposterous proportions.[3]

Hall does, however, make some good points: 'To His operation,' he writes of the Holy Spirit, 'is due the efficacy of this and of every Christian sacrament.'[4] The gift of the Holy Spirit distinguishes Christian baptism from the baptism of John: as John says, 'I baptize you with water for repentance, but . . . He [Jesus] will baptize you with the Holy Spirit and fire' (Matt. 3.11).[5]

Among the Fathers, Basil provided one of the principal foundations for later thought about the Holy Spirit in his treatise *On the Holy Spirit*. Here Basil described two purposes or achievements of baptism: the death of sin, and life in the Spirit with sanctification. Baptism is by water and the Spirit: he links water to the dying, and the tomb, and the Spirit to life: 'the Spirit is the source of the quickening power, by renewing our souls and bringing them from the deadness of sin into the life that was originally theirs'.[6] This is reflected in liturgical practice. When the priest blessed the water of baptism in earlier rites, he used to breathe upon it to symbolize the descent of the Spirit. The prayers for blessing the water, to this day, are full of references to the Holy Spirit.

Baptism is the foundational sacrament to impart the character of Christ. The theological tradition of both East and West has stressed the idea that this 'conforming to the image of the Son' (cf. Rom. 8.29) is the particular work of the Holy Spirit. 'The Spirit by his power of sanctification conforms us perfectly to Christ,' wrote Clement of Alexandria, 'for He is, so to speak, the form of Christ our Saviour, and by His very person, He impresses upon us the divine image'.[7] Elsewhere Clement wrote that, being 'made partakers of the Holy Spirit, we are being restored to the primitive beauty of our nature; the image which we bore at the first is engraved afresh upon our spiritual life, for Christ is formed in us through the Spirit'.[8] A few centuries later, John of Damascus grounded this in the idea that the Spirit's work is to bear witness to Christ, and reveal him, just as it is the Son's work to bear witness to the Father and reveal him: 'He [the Spirit] is the image of the Son, as the Son is of the Father; through him Christ dwells in the human being, and gives conformity to the image of God.'[9]

Eucharist

The association of the Eucharist with the Spirit is a topic of great ecumenical agreement. Calvin, for instance, built his doctrine of Communion around the Spirit, writing that 'the secret efficacy of the Spirit' is what leads us to 'enjoy Christ and all his blessings' in this sacrament.[10] On this point, the Reformed tradition aligns with that of the Orthodox East. The Syrian 'Liturgy of St James' is extreme, but in its way characteristic, when it offers the following gloss in the words of Institution:

> In the same way, after supper, he took the cup, made a mixture of wine and water, raised his eyes to heaven, presented it to you, his God and Father, gave thanks, consecrated it and blessed it, *filled it with the Holy Spirit* and gave it to his holy and blessed disciples, saying . . .'[11]

A similar association with the Spirit is made concerning the bread. There is a Syrian tradition going back at least to AD 475 of communicating someone saying, 'the Body of Jesus Christ, the Holy Spirit, for the healing of soul and body'.[12]

The Holy Spirit is typically invoked in contemporary eucharistic liturgies in the West, as he has been invoked in the East since early times. The word for this is *epiclesis* (from the Greek for to 'invoke' or 'call upon'). It is mentioned in the early third century by the *Apostolic Tradition* of Hippolytus. Early Christians seem to have been all the more enthusiastic to stress the role of the Spirit in the Eucharist in response to those who denied his divinity.[13] From these early times, the invocation of the Spirit on the elements has been associated with a parallel invocation of the Spirit upon the congregation.[14]

For all this, the invocation of the Holy Spirit was found in the mediaeval rites of the West only in the private (although prescribed) prayers of the priest. It was introduced to main eucharistic prayers by the Roman Catholic Church in the revisions following Vatican II. In Britain, the first Book of Common Prayer (1549) asked,

> Heare us (O merciful father) we besech thee; and with thy holy spirite and worde, vouchsafe to blesse and sanctifie these thy gyftes, and creatures of bread and wyne, that they maie be unto us the bodye and bloude of thy moste derely beloved sonne Jesus Christe.

The epiclesis was removed in the 1552 Prayer Book, which set the pattern for 1559 and 1662. The Nonjurors (Anglicans who split from the Church of England in the late seventeenth century) reintroduced an epiclesis into their liturgy. The Scottish Episcopal Church followed their example in their 1637 rite. The proposed prayer book of 1928 would have restored the epiclesis in England. As it happened, we had to wait until the liturgical reforms of the later twentieth century. Today, however, the role of the Spirit in the consecration of the elements is made clear.

Confirmation

Our discussion of confirmation has already stressed the role of the Holy Spirit. Thornton and Lécuyer made the helpful suggestion that we might think of the relation between confirmation and baptism as being like the relation between Pentecost and Easter.[15] One of the glories of the rite of confirmation is that it places the Holy Spirit at the centre of the Christian life for each Christian as he or she enters upon faith as an adult.

Marriage

In the East the crowning moment of marriage is, in fact, a crowning. This represents the descent of the Holy Spirit on the couple.[16] Western wedding liturgies do not make much of the role of the Holy Spirit, but the preacher could: 'fellowship' is the Holy Spirit's business (2 Cor. 13.13); doctrinally, for Western Christians, the Spirit is the *bond of love* (between the Father and the Son: he is their love *as a Person*); marriage bestows 'character', which is the Holy Spirit's work; it is a consecration (a 'making sacred' or *holy*) and a school (or perhaps 'orchard') for the Spirit's fruits (Gal. 5.22–23). Through marriage the couple find a paradoxical freedom through commitment, and freedom is associated with the Spirit in the Epistles (2 Cor. 3.17).

Ordination

The Holy Spirit works in ordination as a sacrament of character, and in as much as ordained ministers are ministers of the sacraments, they are brought to live and work in what we have called a domain of the Holy Spirit. The *form* of ordination typically involves a direct invocation of the Spirit.[17] The words of the ordination rite in the Book of Common Prayer, for instance, draw upon John 20.19–23 and the reception of the Spirit for the forgiving (and retaining) of sins. The laying on of hands may be accompanied by anointing as a particular symbol of the gift of the Spirit. Bishops, priests and deacons are also ministers of the Word, which the Holy Spirit inspired at its writing and by means of which he inspires hearers today. For centuries, the hymn *Veni Creator* ('Come Holy Ghost, our souls inspire . . .') has been sung as part of the ordination liturgy. To minister in Christ's Church is first and foremost to commend oneself to the Holy Spirit and his work.

Anointing of the sick

The healing for which we pray with the anointing of the sick is every bit as much the work of the Holy Spirit as is the charismatic gift of healing, listed as one of the nine gifts of the Holy Spirit in 1 Corinthians 12. We can see this sacrament as bringing the sick person into particular communion with the Spirit as both Lord and Giver of Life: 'giver of life' in the prayer for healing and 'Lord' in the act of commending someone to God, his providence and good care, whatever may befall. This sacrament also places the sick person, *in his or her sickness*, within the specific embrace of the Church, of which the Holy Spirit is the 'soul'. The sacrament of anointing also seeks to renew the bond with the Spirit's sacraments of 'initiation', which lie at the beginning of the Christian life, as someone comes to its earthly close.

Penance

As with marriage, the role of the Holy Spirit in the sacrament of confession is not always as clearly presented as it might be. That someone has gone to a priest for this purpose, however, already shows the work of the Spirit, who stirs our consciences to awareness of sin. Just as the Spirit is at work in this sacrament even before its beginning, its results are also very much the Spirit's: freedom, which we have already seen associated with the Spirit, and joy, one of his fruits, holiness, which bears his own name, and that restoration of relationship which is the heart of all that God is about and, in association with the Spirit, bears the name of 'fellowship'.

Conclusion: sacraments and the Incarnation

We can conclude where we began, with the observation that the reasons for the sacraments are the reasons for the Incarnation. In the fourth book of his *Summa Contra Gentiles*, Aquinas lists eight angles on the logic of the Incarnation.[1]

First, the Incarnation encourages us. It shows that seeking God face to face is possible. God demonstrates in the Incarnation 'with greatest clarity' that the human being can be united to God.

Second, the Incarnation puts us right about the 'worthiness' of human nature. On the one hand it shows us that we are more than animals, and should seek something better that the no-more-than-animal happiness of the pleasures of the flesh. The Incarnation has shown us the dignity of being human and teaches us to seek for human greatness. However, it also teaches us only to find that greatness in relation to God.

Third, nothing could be more important than knowing where our destiny and final happiness lies, but really only God can be certain about these things. In the Incarnation, the truth about God, and about human beings in relation to God, has been made known to us by the very one for whom all of this is perfectly clear, namely God himself. The One who was eternally 'in the bosom of the Father' (John 1.18 AV) 'came into the world, to testify to the truth' (John 18.37).[2]

Fourth, what applies to knowing also applies to loving. Our truest happiness consists in enjoying God (a point on which the very Reformed *Westminster Confession* perfectly agrees). We are made to love God, but we do not always realize it. We needed, Aquinas says, an 'inducement'. God, who is love itself, took love to its furthest conclusion in the Incarnation: 'for it is proper to love to unite the lover with the beloved so far as possible'.[3]

Next we encounter one of Aquinas's most daring and beautiful ideas: that God wants to be friends with us. Friendship consists in a sort of equality, which means that things greatly unequal do not seem able to be joined in friendship. For that reason, so that there could

148

be greater familiarity in friendship between human beings and God, it was helpful for us that God became one of us, since it is natural for human beings to be friends with one another.[4]

With each of us, God has a project on his hands and we have a journey to make. The sixth angle notes that we are inspired to grow in virtue by 'words and examples', and the better the person they come from, the more they inspire us. That only goes so far, however, since everyone has failings. In order to be really 'solidly grounded' in virtue, the example had to come from God made human, giving us both teaching and example. This is what Christ did: 'I have set you an example, that you also should do as I have done to you' (John 13.15).

That sixth point may seem in danger of neglecting quite how sinful each of us can be, and indeed quite how sinful we all are. With the seventh point, Aquinas tackles this directly. Sin blocks us from our final happiness, both as an obstacle and because it offends God. It destroys charity and means that we have no confidence to turn to God. In short, we need a remedy from sin, and that had to come from God, since he is the one we have offended. It was 'suitable' that God should become one of us, accomplishing the remission of our sins with certainty. Jesus clearly wanted both to forgive our sins and for us to be clear about it by virtue of tangible demonstration. Thomas quotes Matthew 9.6, where Jesus makes it clear that he wants us to *know* 'that the Son of Man has authority on earth to forgive sins'.

Finally, while that discussion of sin had the individual in mind, the last point is more global, dealing with 'the whole human race'. It follows from divine justice that God will not remit without satisfaction, but that is beyond the power of any of us. The incarnate Christ can save us because he is both a human being and yet also more than that. Christ is that one person who can take away the sin of the whole world (John 1.29), the one person who can bring justification for all (Rom. 5.16).

Reasons for the sacraments

Just two chapters after the discussion for the 'reasons' for the Incarnation – and the chapters in this work are quite short – Aquinas turns to explore why it is that God works in and through sacraments. His answer mirrors what he has said about the Incarnation: God works with us according to our condition. We are disposed in time and space, we are finite, we are creatures and we are cultural. Our salvation, therefore, is accomplished and communicated in time and space, by finite, creaturely and cultural means. Christ's death, Aquinas has just noted, is the 'universal cause of salvation'. This then needs to be appropriated by each person as each person is.[5] This requires 'remedies through which the benefit of Christ's death could somehow be conjoined to them'.[6] These are the sacraments.

Aquinas is particularly interested in why it is that God deals with us sacramentally through 'visible' means: why is it that the 'remedies' of our salvation are so very tangible, involving words, gestures, water, bread, wine, oil, and so on. Again he gives several interlocked answers.

First, this is about God providing for us according to our condition, 'just as He does for all other things'.[7] It is at the heart of our condition that we grasp everything, both the spiritual and intelligible, through the senses. For this reason, 'spiritual remedies' are given to human beings through the sensory means of 'sensible signs'.[8] Centuries later, John Calvin was to reiterate just this point.

Next, our salvation flows from the incarnate Word, and the means he uses line up with who he is. Just as the Word was incarnate, the salvation he offers us comes to us, and takes hold of us, 'under visible signs'.[9] There is a beautiful harmony to God's plan.

Third, the origin of our fall in the Genesis story was 'clinging unduly to visible things'. Against the backdrop of that story, it was fitting in God's wisdom that our remedy should also come to us through visible things. This demonstrates that there is nothing wrong with physical ('visible') things in themselves: far from it. Our problem is simply clinging to them in a 'disordered way'. The remedy comes through using them in 'an ordered way', through the sacraments.[10]

Aquinas points out that down Church history 'heretics' have occasionally tried to do away with sacraments. He adds that it is no accident that they are the same heretics who taught that visible, physical things are evil in themselves.[11] To rejoice in the sacraments is a sure defence against any such dualistic ('Gnostic') hatred of God's Creation. In God's hands, the material world can become an 'instrument' of the God who 'was made flesh and suffered'.[12]

The parallels with the dimensions of the Incarnation are clear. With the sacraments we are left in no doubt that the world is saveable, even (perhaps particularly) in its materiality, and that this salvation can reach us in a world of space and time. We are reminded of the dignity of humanity and of matter, and warned not to run from it, either in the direction of the beasts or the angels. We are also given certainty: God's love for us is as substantial as bread and wine; we know that we are forgiven because we know we got wet.[13] Aquinas deploys a striking turn of phrase here: although God is not bound by the sacraments, he does bind himself to them.[14]

God wishes to capture our love as well as our understanding, so he operates with things to which we are easily drawn: water, bread, wine, oil, the comfort of words and gestures. That the sacraments use both words and gestures is also important, since they carry on the work of Christ, who came to instruct us both by his words and by his deeds.

In the sacraments, as with the Incarnation, God comes to be with the lowly in a humble fashion, working with and through the most basic, material things of life. This aligns with the depths of God's love for us, such that he became equal to us so that we could become his friends. That equality, and that offer of friendship, is shown most of all in Christ condescending to be baptized, although sinless, and in that most basic act of companionability (*con-pan*-ionability): sharing bread. In these sacraments, and their penumbral five, we encounter him today.

> Behold: Fire and Spirit in the womb that bore you:
> Behold: Fire and Spirit in the river where you were baptized.
> Fire and Spirit in our baptism:
> In the Bread and the Cup, Fire and Holy Spirit.
> In your Bread is hidden a Spirit not to be eaten,
> In your Wine dwells a Fire not to be drunk.
> Spirit in your Bread, Fire in your Wine,
> A wonder set apart, yet received by our lips.
>   (Ephraim the Syrian)[15]

Notes

1 Why sacraments?

1 In the words of the *Catechism* from the Book of Common Prayer, a sacrament is 'An outward and visible sign of an inward and spiritual grace given unto us; ordained by Christ himself, as a means whereby we receive the same, and a pledge to assure us thereof'.

2 *Nicholas Cabasilas: The Life in Christ*, trans. Carmino J. De Cantazaro. (Crestwood, NY: St Vladimir's Seminary Press, 1974), p. 133, quoted in Stanley Burgess, *The Holy Spirit: Eastern Christian Traditions* (Peabody: Hendrickson), p. 75. Translation slightly amended.

3 Thomas Aquinas, *Summa Contra Gentiles* (hereafter *SCG*), trans. Anton C. Pegis and others, 5 vols (New York: Hanover House, 1955), IV.56.4.

4 Tom Wright, *Simply Jesus* (London: SPCK, 2011), p. 176.

5 The *Common Worship* translation of what is an ancient Western text.

6 Kenan Osborne, *Sacramental Theology: A General Introduction* (New York: Paulist Press, 1988), ch. 5.

7 His death, for Aquinas, is 'the universal cause of human salvation' (*SCG* IV.56.1).

8 Adrienne von Speyr, *The Cross: Word and Sacrament* (San Francisco: Ignatius Press, 1983).

9 If you find yourself in Madrid rather than Antwerp, there is a similar depiction, although by a lesser artist, in the Prado gallery.

10 'There are four parts to every sacrifice – the one we offer it to, the one it is offered by, what is offered and the one it is offered for': Christ is all four in his offering (Augustine, *De Trinitate* IV.14).

11 A point that Edwin Muir makes beautifully in his poem 'The Incarnate One' in *Collected Poems* (London: Faber, 1960), p. 228.

12 I have written on this in Andrew Davison and Alison Milbank (eds), *For the Parish* (London: SCM Press, 2010), ch. 1.

13 Friedrich Schleiermacher, *The Christian Faith* (London: Continuum, 1999), pp. 429–31, 650.

14 Thomas Aquinas, *Summa Theologiae* (hereafter *ST*) III.60.7 *resp.*, trans. Fathers of the English Dominican Province, 22 vols (London: Burns, Oates & Washbourne, 1912).

15 Friedrich Schelling, *Stuttgart Private Lectures*, I/7, quoted by Andrew Bowie, *Schelling and Modern European Philosophy: An Introduction* (London: Routledge, 1993), p. 92.

16 Slavoj Žižek, *The Indivisible Remainder: An Essay on Schelling and Related Matters* (London: Verso, 1996), p. 89, n. 81.
17 Henri de Lubac, *Paradoxes of Faith* (San Francisco: Ignatius Press, 1987), p. 66.
18 Schleiermacher distinguishes something very close to these two objections – a refusal of mediation and a rejection of a serious sense of sin – in a highly perceptive passage in *The Christian Faith*, §100.3.
19 Evelyn Underhill, *The Mystery of Sacrifice* (London: Longmans, Green and Co., 1938), p. xi.
20 *Thirty-Nine Articles of Religion*, Article 6.
21 I have written about this in Davison and Milbank (eds), *For the Parish*, ch. 2.

2 Baptism

1 The patristic confirmation of this interpretation of the scriptural message is inexhaustible. Consider, for instance, *Shepherd of Hermas*, mandate 4.3.1 and Tertullian, *On Baptism*, 12.
2 Martin Luther, *Large Catechism*, trans. John Nicholas Lenker, *Luther's Works* (Minneapolis: Luther Press, 1907), vol. 24, §4.6.
3 Although faith ranks before works, 'faith' in the Bible is never purely external. Abraham, the great hero of faith, showed that faith in his willingness to journey from his city to a foreign land and by his willingness to sacrifice his son. Heb. 11 presents us with one practical example of faith after another. The message of James, that living faith expresses itself in action, is not at all alien to the thought of Paul. For Paul, after all, even faith is outranked by love or charity (1 Cor. 13).
4 Since the middle years of the twentieth century, the Roman Catholic Church has been particularly clear about its belief that salvation is open to those outside the faith. See the Vatican II document *Lumen Gentium*, §16 and Paul VI's declaration *Nostra Aetate*.
5 This is argued, for instance, by Cyril of Jerusalem in *Catechetical Oration*, 3.10.
6 Karl Barth, *Wolfgang Amadeus Mozart* (Eugene: Wipf and Stock, 2003), pp. 54–5.
7 That said, not all early baptisms were by full immersion, since some baptisteries would be too shallow for that. We need not necessarily even infer that Jesus went right under the water at his baptism. The phrase 'coming up out of the water' (Mark 1.10; cf. Matt. 3.16) describes him walking out of the river rather than emerging from under the water. The earliest account of baptism from outside the New Testament, in the *Didache*, §7, seems to envisage immersion but is happy with pouring water three times in the name of the Trinity if insufficient water is to hand.

153

8 Dietrich Bonhoeffer, *The Cost of Discipleship* (London: SCM Press, 2001), p. 5.

9 The blessing of the water at every baptism is preserved in the Book of Common Prayer with a beautiful and unapologetic prayer beginning: 'Almighty, everliving God, whose most dearly beloved Son Jesus Christ, for the forgiveness of our sins, did shed out of his most precious side both water and blood . . .'

10 If we find it difficult to rejoice in the death of the Egyptians then we might be reassured to find a part of the Jewish tradition which interprets the story with a certain chasteness of heart. Rabbi Johanan bar Nappaha (died *c.*279) has God responding to the calls upon him to rejoice with the words 'The work of my hands is being drowned in the sea, and you want to sing songs?' Babylonian Talmud, trans. Isidore Epstein (London: Soncino Press, 1938), Megillah 10b.

11 A setting of this text is among the most beautiful of compositions by Josquin des Prés. It has been recorded by the Tallis Scholars, along with a Mass setting by Cipriano de Rore based on Josquin's piece.

12 Bede, *In Lucae Evangelium Expositio* I.3.

13 Irenaeus, *Against Heresies* II.22.4, trans. Henry Bettenson, *The Early Christian Fathers* (London: OUP, 1956). Slightly adapted.

14 Augustine, *Literal Commentary on Genesis* X.39.

15 Augustine, *The Guilt and Remission of Sins, and Infant Baptism.*

16 Lawrence Mick, *Understanding the Sacraments: Baptism* (Collegeville: Liturgical Press), p. 18.

17 Canon B22.4, 6.

18 The occasional practice of 'reaffirmation of baptismal vows by immersion' is highly problematic. Visually, it looks like baptism and is therefore in danger of bringing the person's real baptism into disrepute.

19 Augustine, *On Baptism, Against the Donatists*, 15.23.

20 Many Christians also have the opportunity to enter into the wonders of God's lifelong baptismal work through the honour of serving as a godparent.

3 Sacramental character

1 John Macquarrie, *A Guide to the Sacraments* (London: Continuum, 1998), p. 185.

2 Trans. Percy Dearmer.

3 There are other possibilities. In Catholic countries we find a particular enthusiasm for names made out of events, such as the Spanish Concepción, from the conception of the Blessed Virgin Mary, or even Pilar, because of devotion to Our Lady of the Pillar in Zaragosa. In Protestant countries, there was once enthusiasm for names made out of Christian virtues:

Prudence, Faith or Charity, or Verity, from the Latin word for truth, or Lettice, from the Latin word for joy.

4 This has always been the case in Spain, for instance, with the added charm that you can have as many surnames as you want, recapitulating your family tree, when you wish, with the four surnames of your grandparents or the 16 of your great grandparents.

5 John Paul II, *Familiaris Consortio*, §21, 49, 51, 60–1, 65 and the Second Vatican Council, *Lumen Gentium*, §11.

6 Thomas Aquinas, *SCG* V.58.6.

7 The remarkable thing is not that some apostatized but that so few did. The names of the martyrs who remained firm, and the laity too, adorn the calendar of the Church. A full list is too long ever to be compiled, although an impressive sense of it is found in the *Roman Martyrology*. It is also worth remembering that, by some accounts, the honour roll of martyrs grew longer in the twentieth century than in any other, even than in those early days.

8 Aquinas, *SCG* IV.77.6.

9 Talk about grace resorts to hydraulic imagery from time to time. This is rarely a helpful direction for it to take, but on this occasion I stand by the bucket-versus-hosepipe analogy for sacraments that impart character.

4 The Eucharist

1 Augustine, *Confessions* VII.10, trans. Henry Chadwick (Oxford: OUP, 2008), p. 124.

2 J. N. D. Kelly, *Early Christian Doctrines* (London: A. & C. Black, 1958), p. 440.

3 Ignatius of Antioch, *Letter to the Smyrnaeans*, 7, trans. W. A. Jurgens, in *The Faith of the Early Fathers* (Collegeville: Liturgical Press, 1970), vol. 1.

4 E.g. Irenaeus, *Against Heresies*, V.2.

5 Justin Martyr, *First Apology*, 66, trans. Jurgens, *Early Fathers*, vol. 1.

6 The Roman Catholic Church upheld transubstantiation as the best approach to eucharistic transformation at the Council of Trent (session 13, ch. 2).

7 *Catechism of St Philaret of Moscow*, §340, trans. Philip Schaff, *The Creeds of Christendom with a History and Critical Notes* (New York: Harper & Brothers, 1877), vol. 2, pp. 497–8.

8 As an authority Philaret cites St John of Damascus, for whom the consecration brings it about that 'the bread and wine themselves are changed into the Body and Blood of God' although the manner is unknown: 'let it suffice thee to be told that it is by the Holy Ghost . . . nor know I aught

more than this, that the Word of God is true, powerful, and almighty, but its manner of operation unsearchable' (*On the Orthodox Faith* IV.13.7).

9 Wolfhart Pannenberg argues that the reformers were recapitulating the discussion of the early Church over Christology, and its various tendencies, associated with Antioch and Alexandria, in their Eucharistic theology (*Jesus, God and Man* (London: SCM Press, 1982), pp. 298ff.).

10 T. W. Coleman, *The Free Church Sacrament and Catholic Ideals* (London: Dent, 1930), p. 78. Coleman cites Oliver Chase Quick, *The Christian Sacraments* (London: Nisbet, 1932), p. 206.

11 John Calvin, *Institutes* IV.17.1. Trans. of the *Institutes* are by Henry Beveridge (Edinburgh: Calvin Translation Society, 1845).

12 Calvin, *Institutes* IV.17.4. Within Calvin's chain, bread, body, spiritual nourishment, it is inevitable that the body should be marginalized, as being neither the thing received physically, nor the thing received spiritually. We can have 'communion' but 'communion is something different from the body itself' (*Institutes* IV.17.22).

13 This is underlined by canon B12.1.

14 Coleman, *Free Church Sacrament*, p. 79.

15 Coleman, *Free Church Sacrament*, p. 78.

16 P. T. Forsyth, *Lectures on the Church and the Sacraments* (London: Longmans, Green and Co., 1917), p. 165, quoted by Coleman, *Free Church Sacrament*, p. 79.

17 This is stressed in the *Thirty-Nine Articles*: 'The Cup of the Lord is not to be denied to the lay-people: for both the parts of the Lord's Sacrament, by Christ's ordinance and commandment, ought to be ministered to all Christian men alike' (Article 30).

18 Second Vatican Council, *General Instruction on the Roman Missal*, §281.

19 Council of Trent, session 13.

20 'the said most blessed Sacrament be hereafter ... commonly delivered and ministered unto the people within the Church of England ... under both kinds, that is to say, of bread and wine except necessity otherwise require' (English Sacrament Act, §8, modernized spelling). The legal opinion delivered to General Synod in response to the 2009 outbreak of 'swine flu' argued that this clause 'explicitly recognises that there may be circumstances when the requirement for delivery of both bread and wine need not be complied with'. See *Common Worship: Pastoral Services*: 'Communion should normally be received in both kinds separately, but where necessary may be received in one kind, whether of bread or, where the communicant cannot receive solid food, wine' (p. 73).

21 This was expressed both in a letter from the two archbishops and a document from the Legal Advisory Commission of the General Synod entitled 'Holy Communion: Administration of the Sacrament'.

22 Timothy Thibodeau, 'Western Christendom', in Geoffrey Wainwright and Karen B. Westerfield Tucker (eds), *The Oxford History of Christian Worship* (New York: OUP, 2005), p. 236.

23 Frederick Bauerschmidt, 'The Theological Sublime', in John Milbank, Catherine Pickstock and Graham Ward (eds), *Radical Orthodoxy* (London: Routledge, 1999), p. 215.

24 The phrase is used by writers such as Lawrence Cunningham in *The Catholic Experience: Space, Time, Silence, Prayer, Sacraments, Story, Persons, Catholicity, Community and Expectations* (New York: Crossroad, 1987), p. 20 and Willem Speelman, 'Liturgy and Theatre', in Jozef Lamberts, *'Ars Celebrandi': The Art to Celebrate the Liturgy* (Leuven: Peeters, 2003), pp. 121ff.

25 Fortunately, this is not now the situation.

26 Promotional copy for Peter Craig-Wild, *Tools for Transformation: Making Worship Work* (London: Darton, Longman & Todd, 2002).

27 Bauerschmidt, 'Sublime', p. 215.

28 Augustine, *De Trinitate* IV.14.

29 As the heavens and earth are full of God's glory so God is asked, 'fill also this Sacrifice [the Eucharist] with your power and your participation [or communion]'; trans. from John McKenna, *The Eucharistic Epiclesis* (Chicago: Hillenbrand, 2009), p. 18.

30 *Saepius Officio: Answer of the Archbishops of Canterbury and York to the Bull Apostolicae Curae of H. H. Leo XIII*, §11.

31 John Chrysostom, *Homilies on the Second Epistle to Timothy*, 2.4.

32 Gregory Dix, *The Shape of the Liturgy* (London: Continuum, 2005), p. 661.

33 William H. H. Jervois, 'Wherefore, O Father', *The English Hymnal* (London: OUP, 1906).

34 Set as an anthem, for instance, by Edward Bairstow (1874–1946).

35 Emphasis added.

36 Emphasis added.

37 Cyril of Jerusalem, *Mystagogic Catechesis*, 23.5–7. See also §10.

38 Liturgy of St James, trans. Evelyn Underhill, *The Mystery of Sacrifice* (London: Longmans, Green and Co., 1938), p. 37.

39 Underhill, *Sacrifice*, p. 63.

40 The phrase is Underhill's paraphrase of Irenaeus, *Against Heresies* IV.18.2, from *Sacrifice*, p. 15.

41 From *Divine Hymns or Spiritual Songs*, compiled by Joshua Smith (New Hampshire, 1784). Set as an anthem by Elizabeth Poston (1905–87).

42 The Church of England's *Common Worship* links the bread of life and the tree of life in a slightly strained post-Communion prayer: 'God our creator, by your gift the tree of life was set at the heart of the earthly paradise, and the bread of life at the heart of your Church: may we who

have been nourished at your table on earth be transformed by the glory of the Saviour's cross and enjoy the delights of eternity; through Jesus Christ our Lord.'

43 Augustine, *Confessions* X.20, trans. Albert C. Outler (Philadelphia: Westminster Press, 1955).

44 Liturgy of St James, trans. Underhill, *Sacrifice*, p. 73.

45 The response of the Samaritan woman to Christ's promise of water that never leaves us thirsty is directly comparable: 'Sir, give me this water, so that I may never be thirsty or have to keep coming here to draw water' (John 4.15). The author of John's Gospel seems to like misunderstandings which penetrate to the heart of the truth, as we also see with the prophecy of Caiaphas. When Caiaphas argues that 'it is better for you to have one man die for the people' (John 11.50), the evangelist points out that he is saying more than he understands: 'He did not say this on his own, but being high priest that year he prophesied that Jesus was about to die for the nation, and not for the nation only, but to gather into one the dispersed children of God' (vv. 51–52, picked up in John 18.14). I am grateful to Johanna Kershaw for pointing out this link.

46 Underhill, *Sacrifice*, p. 64.

47 Vincent Donovan, *Christianity Rediscovered: An Epistle from the Masai* (London: SCM Press, 2001), p. 98.

48 Donovan, *Christianity*, p. 99.

49 Text from *The Way*, 4(1), 1961, p. 313.

50 Augustine, *Confessions* X.20, trans. Albert C. Outler.

51 Julian of Norwich, *Revelations of Divine Love* I.5, trans. Elizabeth Spearing (London: Penguin, 1998).

52 Henri de Lubac, *Catholicism* (San Francisco: Ignatius Press, 1988), p. 35, a point that was later to be an important topic in Pauline scholarship.

53 Henri de Lubac, *Corpus Mysticum* (London: SCM Press, 2006), pp. 79–80. We might explore what it means for the Eucharist to *make* the Church in terms of Aristotle's fourfold dissection of causation. The Eucharist gives shape to the Church whose *form* is to be the body of Christ; the Eucharist displays the *purpose* of the Church, as a foretaste of the worship to which God calls all Creation; it is the founding rite, the beginning, by which Christ gathered his Church before his Passion (an 'efficient' cause); it is something like what Aristotle calls the 'material cause' inasmuch as the celebration of the Eucharist week by week is the scaffolding of the Church, around which its life is built, or out of which its life emerges.

54 *Pesahim* 10.5, trans. Herbert Danby (Peabody: Hendrickson, 2012), p. 151.

55 Augustine seems to refer to the communion of infants in *Sermon* 174.

56 Cited for instance by Justin Martyr in the *Dialogue with Trypho*, 41.8–10.

57 Reception of Communion and of other sacraments can be extended beyond the usual barriers in certain cases. John Paul II wrote that 'it is a source of joy to note that Catholic ministers are able, in certain particular cases, to administer the Sacraments of the Eucharist, Penance and Anointing of the Sick to Christians who are not in full communion with the Catholic Church but who greatly desire to receive these sacraments, freely request them and manifest the faith which the Catholic Church professes with regard to these sacraments' (John Paul II, *Ut Unum Sit*, §46). The 'particular cases' include danger of death and occasions when someone is 'unable to have recourse for the sacrament desired to a minister of his or her own Church or ecclesial Community' (*Directory for the Application of Principles and Norms on Ecumenism*, §131). See *Code of Canon Law*, 844.

58 Augustine, *Sermon* 272, trans. Edmund Hill, *Works of St Augustine, Sermons III/7* (New York: New City Press, 1993), p. 300.

59 Justin Martyr, *First Apology*, §66.

60 *Didache* 9.10.

61 Canons B13 and B14, unless a parish has an explicit dispensation from the bishop.

62 Friedrich Schleiermacher, *The Christian Faith*, §139.1.

63 Remembering that the 'holy mysteries' that God has 'instituted and ordained . . . as pledges of his love' come at the cost of the death of his Son, and that 'the danger is great, if we receive the same unworthily'. The exhortation is a meditation on 1 Cor. 11.27–34.

64 Arguing, for instance, that 'as the Son of God did vouchsafe to yield up his soul by death upon the Cross for your salvation; so it is your duty to receive the Communion in remembrance of the sacrifice of his death, as he himself hath commanded' and that to refuse to come to Communion is to 'separate from your brethren, who come to feed on the banquet of that most heavenly food'. This exhortation is a meditation on Luke 14.16–24.

65 Preface to the Service of Holy Communion.

66 In such extraordinary circumstances, the priest is to inform the bishop within a week.

67 Underhill, *Sacrifice*, pp. 65–6.

5 The anatomy of the sacraments I: signs, matter and form

1 As an example of this distinction, St Thomas will call certain rites from before the Incarnation 'sacraments' but only in the sense of pointing and promising. Those which come after the Incarnation *bring about* what they promise.

2 Lawrence Mick, *Baptism* (Collegeville: Liturgical Press, 2007), p. 4.

3 The contrast here is with a sense of *ex opere operantis*, which is to say 'by virtue of the agent': literally 'from the work of the worker', which is here the human 'worker'.

4 For a discussion of the philosophical background to the terms 'form' and 'matter' see my *The Love of Wisdom* (London: SCM Press, 2013).

5 Word and matter are similarly the focus of the opening of Genesis.

6 David Jones, epigram in the essay 'Art and Sacrament', in *Epoch and Artist* (London: Faber, 1959). In that volume he attributes the quotation to Maurice de la Taille.

7 See two important essays by Janet Martin Soskice, 'Calling God "Father"' and 'Trinity and the "Feminine Other"' in *The Kindness of God* (Oxford: OUP, 2007), pp. 66–83, 100–24.

8 Out of charity, some priests might wish to make this baptism conditional, using the form '*N*, if you have not already been baptized, I baptize you in the name of the Father, and of the Son, and of the Holy Spirit. Amen.'

9 Tertullian, *On the Resurrection of the Flesh*, 8, trans. Alexander Roberts and others, *Ante-Nicene Fathers* (New York: Charles Scribner's Sons, 1896), vol. 3, p. 551.

10 Another example of a physical dimension that is highly appropriate without being necessary is use of the sign of the cross in baptism. This was one of those elements of ceremonial over which the Church of England would not yield in face of Puritan opposition at the Hampton Court Conference (1604). Other Puritan objections at this time furnish additional examples, including rings at weddings and bowing at the name of Jesus. This principled resistance to Puritan demands set England on the path to the Civil War and eventually forced the Church of England to go underground.

11 'The material for the priesthood is the cup with the wine and the paten with the bread; for the deaconate, the books of the Gospel' (Council of Florence, *Decree for the Armenians*). Quotations from this decree, here and below, are taken from James Harvey Robinson (ed.), *Readings in European History* (Boston: Ginn, 1904), vol. 1.

12 '[T]he matter of the holy orders of diaconate, presbyterate and episcopate is the laying on of hands alone . . . if other provisions have been legitimately made in the past at any time, we now determine that, at least in future, the handing over of the instruments is not necessary for the validity of the holy Orders of the diaconate, the presbyterate and the episcopate' (Pius XII, *Sacramentum Ordinis*). Pius XII went so far as to justify his change of the matter of ordination with the phrase 'all know that the Church has the power to change and abrogate what she has determined'.

13 The first explicit application of the phrase 'living water' to baptism is in the *Didache*, which was probably written at the beginning of the second century. In the *Apostolic Tradition* of Hippolytus, he describes the proper water for baptism as 'pure and flowing, that is, the water of a spring or a flowing body of water' (§21).

14 Or, even more technically, what is the substance and what is the accident.

15 Roman Catholic *Code of Canon Law*, §925 and the instruction *Redemptionis Sacramentum*, §48: the bread must be 'purely of wheat ... bread made from another substance, even if it is grain, or if it is mixed with another substance different from wheat to such an extent that it would not commonly be considered wheat bread, does not constitute valid matter'. Church of England Canon B17: the bread 'shall be of the best and purest wheat flour that conveniently may be gotten'.

16 These are considered 'valid matter, provided that they contain the amount of gluten sufficient to obtain the confection of bread, that there is no addition of foreign materials and that the procedure for making such hosts is not such as to alter the nature of the substance of the bread', *Letter from the Congregation for the Doctrine of the Faith*, 19 June 1995.

17 Canon B17.2.

18 It has been suggested that 'wine' might be provided for those who cannot consume alcohol (for instance, for alcoholics) in the form of wine from which the alcohol has been removed. The Legal Advisory Commission of the General Synod of the Church of England has written, however, that 'wine from which all the alcohol has been removed would be contrary to the Canon and its use during Holy Communion contrary to ecclesiastical law'. The rationale is that 'the addition of the word "fermented" must also have been included for good reason ... By the removal of all ... alcohol the required results of that fermentation are nullified and the resultant beverage then not only ceases to be "wine" as commonly understood but also ceases to be "the fermented juice of the grape" ... If, however, some alcohol remains, such wine may legally be used.'

6 How many sacraments?

1 William Shakespeare, *Romeo and Juliet*, act II, scene 2.

2 Jacques Depuis, *The Christian Faith* (New York: Alba House, 1996), p. 518.

3 I think it is a lost cause to argue for eight, so I will stick to seven. However, among rites with a sacramental character that are not listed as sacraments, coronation has a very sacramental character indeed. The coronation

of Elizabeth II was televised and can be viewed on YouTube. Only her reception of Communion, and her anointing, was not filmed. Coronation was the only rite for which the Church of England retained the consecration of the oil of chrism, until its recent restoration to routine use in confirmation and ordination. Conversely, the monarch of the Commonwealth Realms is the only surviving anointed monarch in the world. Coronation seems to share in the anointing of Christ as king, just as religious profession seems to share in the anointing of Christ as prophet, and priestly ordination shares in his anointing as a priest. The noble example of the nonjuring bishops provides us with an example of coronation seen as imparting an indelible character, very much not dependent on the recipient's character.

4 Thomas Aquinas, *SCG* V.58.

5 'the sacrament of matrimony knitteth man and wife in perpetual love', First Book of Homilies, 7.

6 Marcus Donovan, *Sacramentals* (London: Society of SS. Peter & Paul, 1925). More recent books, from a Roman Catholic perspective, include Ann Ball, *A Handbook of Catholic Sacramentals* (Huntington: Our Sunday Visitor Publishing, 1991) and Richard Whinder, *Sacramentals: Explaining Actions, Signs and Objects That Catholics Use* (London: Catholic Truth Society, 2009).

7 However, the requirement that the Eucharist be celebrated by a priest or bishop – no minister in apostolic orders, no Eucharist – means that one of the sacraments 'necessary for salvation' would die out without ordination.

8 Reprinted with a commentary by A. W. Evans (London: Constable, 1933).

9 Candidates at baptism are sometimes anointed with the oil of chrism in the rites of the Church of England (*Common Worship: Christian Initiation*, p. 100). There is no accompanying delegation of authority from bishops to priests that would allow us to consider this equivalent to confirmation, nor are any words provided (the 'form') related to confirmation.

10 The Christian tradition will often talk of rites of the Old Testament as sacraments, or sacramental, *in a certain sense*. Both Hugh of St Victor (*On the Sacraments*, 1) and Aquinas (*ST* I-II.101.4) will refer to some rites in the Old Testament as 'sacraments' while not giving them the same degree of efficacy as those of the New Testament. Calvin described circumcision and sacrifice as 'Sacraments of the Old Testament' (*Institutes* IV.14.21). The *Catechism of the Catholic Church* lists 'circumcision, anointing and consecration of kings and priests, laying on of hands, sacrifices, and above all the Passover' as 'liturgical signs' that prefigure the sacraments of the New Covenant (§1150). In general the reformers saw less

of a distinction between the rites of the Old and New Testaments than had the mediaeval tradition.

11 George B. Timms (1910–97). These are the opening lines of the hymn.

12 'Sing, ye faithful, sing with gladness', by John Ellerton (1826–93). The first two lines of this verse pick up Heb. 2.9.

13 The Greek was interpreted differently by the translators of the NRSV: 'everyone whose name has not been written from the foundation of the world in the book of life of the Lamb that was slaughtered'.

14 From the hymn *Hostis, Herodes impie* by Caelius Sedulius (*c.*450), trans. Percy Dearmer (1867–1936).

7 Confirmation

1 Second Vatican Council, *Lumen Gentium*, 11.

2 Second Vatican Council, *Apostolicam Actuositatem* (Decree on the Apostolate of the Laity), 2.

3 Thomas Aquinas, *ST* I.1.8 *ad* 2.

4 I have written about this in Andrew Davison and Alison Milbank (eds), *For the Parish* (London: SCM Press, 2010), ch. 3, on the 'theology of mediation'.

5 There is some question over the proper interpretation of this passage. The Greek could mean either 'we are God's fellow workers' (RSV) or 'we are God's servants, working together' (NRSV). Christ makes it clear, however, from the passage just quoted from John, that we share in God's work. In Colossians we even read the extraordinary statement that 'in my flesh I am completing what is lacking in Christ's afflictions for the sake of his body, that is, the church' (Col. 1.24).

6 Aquinas, *ST* III.72.11. The 'catechism' associated with Aquinas, based on Neapolitan sermons, describes confirmation by priests in the 'Greek' Church as an 'error'.

7 Roman Catholic *Code of Canon Law*, §882.

8 The other oils used in the Church – the oil of catechumens and the oil of the sick – can be blessed by a priest, although they are usually also blessed by the bishop, with the oil of chrism, at the 'Chrism Mass' on Maundy Thursday.

9 The form and matter of confirmation have been particularly hotly contested. The Council of Florence taught that the proper matter was sealing with the sign of the cross on the forehead with the oil of chrism. The council gave good, if poetic, reasons for signing on the brow and the sign of the cross: the forehead is where we blush; we are sealed there so that we 'may never blush to confess the name of Christ and especially his cross' (*Decree for the Armenians*). The use of oil was replaced by the simple laying on of hands in the Church of England after the

Reformation. The use of chrism has, however, been widely and officially restored, which is to be welcomed. In more disputative times, differences in emphasis over anointing and laying on of hands divided East and West. Today the spirit is to see these differences as just this: differences in emphasis within a fundamentally similar rite.

10 The opening prayer of the 1662 Publick Baptism of Infants asks that the child 'be baptized with Water and the Holy Ghost'.

8 Ordination

1 John Calvin, *Institutes* IV.3.2, quoted in John Macquarrie, *A Guide to the Sacraments* (London: SCM Press, 1997), p. 169.

2 *Doctrine in the Church of England* (London: SPCK, 1928), p. 115.

3 This was the position of Bonaventure, for instance, and Duns Scotus.

4 Aquinas held that a priest should be understood as the instrument of Christ (*SCG* IV.74).

5 Peter Anson, *Bishops at Large* (London: Faber and Faber, 1964), republished by Apocryphile Press (Berkeley, 2006). There are earlier surveys by A. J. Macdonald and Henry R. T. Brandreth.

6 For instance Eph. 4.4–7, 11–12 and 1 Cor. 12.28, where we read of prophets, evangelists, pastors, teachers, apostles, miracle workers, healers, helpers, administrators, and speakers in tongues.

7 Macquarrie, *Sacraments*, p. 168.

8 Priests join in with the laying on of hands at an ordination, as a gesture of solidarity, but without a bishop there is no ordination.

9 Canon 4.

10 *1 Clement* 44.3; Leo, *Letter* 10.6.

11 Strictly speaking, the ordinal is not part of the Book of Common Prayer but rather published with it.

12 A few churches ordain straight to the priesthood, without first ordaining someone as a deacon. The Church of Sweden is an example. This is sometimes known as a *per saltam* ordination, from the Latin for 'by a leap': the candidate leaps over the diaconate. Most episcopal churches, however, proceed by steps: the diaconate first, then the priesthood (if someone is to be a priest), and then the episcopacy (in a few cases). It is salutary for a priest or bishop to remember that he or she is also a deacon, or servant. Until the reforms of the Second Vatican Council, with this in mind, it was common for bishops to wear a thin dalmatic, the diaconal vestment, under the chasuble, the priestly garment, when celebrating Mass. The practice is retained by some Anglican bishops.

13 R. C. Moberly, *Ministerial Priesthood* (London: John Murray, 1910), p. 261.

14 *Catechism of the Catholic Church*, §1535, referring to the Vatican II documents *Lumen Gentium* 11.2 and *Gaudium et Spes*, 48.2.

15 Augustine, *Letter against Parmenian* II.13. Translation from W. A. Jurgens, *The Faith of the Early Fathers* (Collegeville: Liturgical Press, 1970), vol. 3, p. 64. Punctuation modernized.

16 See *Catechism of the Catholic Church*, §1581–4.

17 Canon C1.2.

18 See *Catechism of the Catholic Church*, §1583.

9 The anatomy of the sacraments II: setting, intention, minister and recipient

1 'in the visible Church the evil be ever mingled with the good . . . yet forasmuch as they [wicked ministers] do not the same in their own name, but in Christ's, and do minister by his commission and authority, we may use their Ministry, both in hearing the Word of God, and in the receiving of the Sacraments. Neither is the effect of Christ's ordinance taken away by their wickedness, nor the grace of God's gifts diminished from such as by faith and rightly do receive the Sacraments ministered unto them; which be effectual, because of Christ's institution and promise, although they be ministered by evil men' (Article 26).

2 Calvin stresses that the simplicity or 'familiarity' of the elements allows God to speak 'to minds however dull' (*Institutes* IV.17.1).

3 Introductory paragraph to *The Ministration of Private Baptism of Children in Houses*.

4 Second Vatican Council, *Sacrosanctum Concilium*, §59.

5 It is not a bad idea for a new priest to express to God the wish to have this intention *habitually*, which is to say, as his or her fundamental wish and inclination, in spite of mood or alertness. That way, if the priest pitches up at an 8 a.m. service feeling rather unfocussed, any lack of mindful intention that particular morning would be situated within a larger, overarching disposition.

6 'The ministrant of this sacrament [baptism] is the priest, for baptism belongs to his office. But in case of necessity not only a priest or deacon may baptize, but a layman or a woman – nay, even a pagan or a heretic, provided he use the form of the Church and intend to do what the Church effects' (Council of Florence, *Decree for the Armenians*). See *The Catechism of the Catholic Church*, §1256. The paragraph concludes: 'The Church finds the reason for this possibility in the universal saving will of God and the necessity of Baptism for salvation.'

7 It has generally been thought that a marriage between two unbaptized people, or where one is baptized and the other is not, is still a marriage, but that it does not enter into the full extent of its Christian sacramentality unless both are baptized.

8 Canon B22.

9 Aquinas, *ST* III.68.10; Scotus, *In Sententias* IV.4.9.

10 As Gregory Nazianzus wrote, 'what he did not assume, he did not heal' (*Epistle* 101). If, therefore, his humanity is his in such a manner as to be exclusively male humanity, then women are not redeemed.

11 In the words of a paragraph added to the 1928 proposed prayer book: 'let them not doubt, but that the child thus privately baptized either by the Minister of the Parish, or by some other Minister, or by one of them that be present, is lawfully and sufficiently baptized, and ought not to be baptized again'. See *Common Worship: Christian Initiation*, p. 105.

12 For instance, see the canon of the Church of England B21 'Of Holy Baptism' and B22.5.

13 See 'Lay-Baptism Censured by the Bishops' (§14H), in Francis Procter and Walter Howard Frere, *A New History of the Book of Common Prayer* (London: Macmillan, 1901).

10 Marriage

1 First Book of Homilies, §7.

2 The theme is taken up in Rev. 19.6–8.

3 *The Catechism of the Catholic Church*, §1602.

4 In the *Homily against Swearing and Perjury*.

5 Expressed, for instance, in the *Catechism of the Catholic Church*, §1623. In the theology of the Eastern Church, however, the priest *is* seen as the minister of the marriage.

6 *Common Worship*, alternative preface. As a parallel, among the teaching collected by Aquinas's students after his death, we read that 'Matrimony is instituted both as an office of nature and as a sacrament of the Church' (Aquinas, *ST*, supplement, 49.2, response).

7 *Catechism of the Catholic Church*, §1626.

8 Reported in Aquinas, *ST*, supplement, 49.2, quoting *Sent.* IV.D.31.

9 This is from the 1662 text. It is hardly changed from 1549.

10 *Code of Canon Law*, 1013.1.

11 Plato, *Symposium*, 193d–193e.

12 Aquinas, *ST* I.93.3.

13 Luce Irigaray, 'Questions to Emmanuel Lévinas', in Margaret Whitford (ed.), *The Irigaray Reader* (Oxford: Blackwell, 1991), p. 180. Quoted by Sarah Coakley, 'Living into the Mystery of the Holy Trinity: Trinity, Prayer, and Sexuality', *Anglican Theological Review* 80(2), 1998, pp. 223–32, p. 231.

14 Coakley, 'Living', p. 231.

15 Aquinas, *Nicomachean Ethics*, VIII.12.

16 1 Cor. 7.9. The AV has 'it is better to marry than to burn'.

17 'Keeping to one woman is a small price for so much as seeing one woman', G. K. Chesterton, *Orthodoxy* (New York: Bantam, 1996), p. 55; 'it is just because he loves one wife that he can have a hundred honeymoons', *Manalive* in *Collected Works of G. K. Chesterton* (San Francisco: Ignatius Press, 2005), p. 415. Louis MacNeice makes a similar point in his poem *Ode* (London: Faber, 1966), pp. 54–8.

18 Eph. 6.3, quoting Exod. 20.12/Deut. 5.16.

19 Aquinas, *Lectures on Ephesians*, 6.1.

20 Coakley, 'Living', p. 230.

21 Coakley, 'Living', p. 230.

22 Pseudo-Dionysius, *Divine Names*, 4.13, quoted in Coakley, 'Living', p. 230.

23 God is not abusive, but spouses and communities can be. On that account, the *eros–agape* link cannot be a recipe for always simply doing what a husband or wife, or a mother superior, wishes.

24 Eph. 4.22–24.

25 Terry Eagleton, *After Theory* (London: Penguin, 2004), pp. 101–2.

26 Eagleton, *After Theory*, p. 2.

27 John Paul II, *Familiaris Consortio*, 85.

28 John Paul II, *Familiaris Consortio*, 85, quoting Matt. 11.28.

29 John Chrysostom, *On Virginity*, 10, quoted by the *Catechism of the Catholic Church*, §1620.

30 John Paul II, *Familiaris Consortio*, §11 (amending punctuation of the official translation to better translate *hanc ad amorem vocationem personae humanae omnibus ex eius partibus*).

31 Among the books that represent this position are short works by Rowan Williams and Jeffrey John: Jeffrey John, *Permanent, Faithful, Stable: Christian Same-Sex Marriage* (London: Darton, Longman & Todd, 2012) – first published in 2000, the new edition has a preface and postscript for the 2010s; Rowan Williams, *The Body's Grace* (London: Lesbian and Gay Christian Movement, 2002). The essay by Williams is also found in a useful anthology: Eugene Rogers, *Theology and Sexuality: Classic and Contemporary Readings* (Oxford: Blackwell, 2002). Two works by the Dominican Gareth Moore deserve consideration: *A Question of Truth: Christianity and Homosexuality* (London: Continuum, 2003) and *The Body in Context: Sex and Catholicism* (London: Continuum, 2001). Over the question of how we use Scripture in ethics more widely, William Spohn has written wisely in *Go and Do Likewise: Jesus and Ethics* (London: Continuum, 2000).

32 Even those who think that same-sex relationships are not good might hold, as Oliver O'Donovan for instance has written, that faithfulness is preferable to promiscuity.

33 John Milbank is an example. See, for instance, 'The Gospel of Affinity', in Miroslav Volf and William Katerberg (eds), *The Future of Hope: Christian Tradition amid Modernity and Postmodernity* (Grand Rapids: Eerdmans, 2004), pp. 149–69.

34 The significance of nuptuality as an overarching theme in twentieth-century Roman Catholic theology is outlined by Fergus Kerr in *Twentieth-Century Catholic Theology: From Neoscholasticism to Nuptual Mysticism* (Oxford: Blackwell, 2005).

35 *Catechism of the Catholic Church*, §1604.

11 Anointing

1 There was, however, an ongoing sense that we should pray for the sick and a strong tradition of ongoing care of the sick and dying: consider, for instance, the rite for the Communion of the Sick in the Prayer Book, which includes a very forceful rite of confession and absolution.

2 Thomas Aquinas, *SCG* IV.73.2. See §1. This line was taken by the Council of Florence (*Decree for the Armenians*) and the Council of Trent, session 14, on extreme unction, ch. 2.

3 Aquinas, *SCG* IV.73.3.

4 Council of Florence, *Decree for the Armenians*.

5 Paul VI, *Sacram Unctione Infirmorum*.

6 Council of Florence, *Decree for the Armenians*.

7 Aquinas, *SCG* IV.73.4.

8 Paul VI, *Sacram Unctione Infirmorum*.

9 Perhaps picking up Rom. 14.7.

10 See Shirley Du Boulay and Marianne Rankin, *Cicely Saunders: The Founder of the Modern Hospice Movement* (London: SPCK, 2007).

11 From the 'Office of Commendation', in *Celebrating Common Prayer* (London: Mowbray, 1992).

12 For example, Article 6 of the *Thirty-Nine Articles*.

13 Aquinas, *ST* II-II.97.1 *ad* 3.

14 Augustine, *Contra Faust* XXII.36.

15 For the Church of England, see Canon B 37.

16 Christian ministry to the dying is discussed from a theological, medical and pastoral perspective in Sioned Evans and Andrew Davison, *Care for the Dying* (London: Canterbury Press, 2013).

12 Confession

1 *Guidelines for the Professional Conduct of the Clergy* (2003), 7.1.

2 The Roman Catholic Code of Canon Law puts it like this: 'To receive the salvific [saving] remedy of the sacrament of penance, a member of the Christian faithful must be disposed in such a way that, rejecting sins

committed and having a purpose of amendment, the person is turned back to God' (§987).

3 For instance, 1 John 3.9 and Heb. 6.4–6.

4 'Provided always, that if any man confess his secret and hidden sins to the minister, for the unburdening of his conscience, and to receive spiritual consolation and ease of mind from him; we do not in any way bind the said minister by this our Constitution, but do straitly charge and admonish him, that he do not at any time reveal and make known to any person whatsoever any crime or offence so committed to his trust and secrecy (except they be such crimes as by the laws of this realm his own life may be called into question for concealing the same), under pain of irregularity' (Proviso to Canon 113 of the Code of 1603). Since the abolition of capital punishment, no priest would ever even be in the position of having his or her own life 'called into question' by preserving secrecy.

5 *Nova, Nova: Ave Fit Ex Eva:* punning *Eva* (Eve) with its reverse, *Ave* ('Hail!'), which reversed Eve's doom. The Jewish philosopher Hannah Arendt linked forgiveness with both newness and the birth of Jesus in *The Human Condition* (Chicago: University of Chicago Press, 1998), p. 247.

6 'There is all the difference in the world between being lazy or a nuisance to your comrades and betraying the whole project; that is the difference between venial and moral sin. As St. Thomas says: one is about how you do the job; the other is about not doing it at all, but something else. The job, of course, is loving God', Herbert McCabe, *God Still Matters* (London: Continuum, 2005), p. 224.

7 Canon B29.

8 As spelt out in the Prayer Book service for the Visitation of the Sick.

9 The code of canon law of the Roman Catholic Church binds all of the faithful under the obligation to make use of this sacrament at least once per year if they are conscious of grave, or mortal, sin (§989), although who would wait, conscious of mortal sin? They are recommended to confess venial sins also (§988.2).

10 Note that he later writes that 'all must carry their own loads' (Gal. 6.5). The first Greek word, translated 'burden', is for a weight too heavy to bear; the second Greek word, translated 'load', is more like a soldier's pack, which each person has to be prepared to shoulder as part of his or her Christian discipleship. The burden of a sin committed is often crushing. Here the Church provides, through this sacrament, a means by which it can be lightened.

11 For priests of the Church of England, 'There can be no disclosure of what is confessed to a priest. This principle holds even after the death

of the penitent. The priest may not refer to what has been learnt in confession, even to the penitent, unless explicitly permitted' (*Conduct of the Clergy*, 7.4).

12 The seal is spelt out for Anglicans in *Conduct of the Clergy*, 7.4.

13 *Conduct of the Clergy*, 7.2.

14 *Conduct of the Clergy*, 7.3.

15 The contemporary Roman Catholic form is also beautiful and worth reproducing: 'God, the Father of mercies, through the death and resurrection of his Son has reconciled the world to himself and sent the Holy Spirit among us for the forgiveness of sins. Through the ministry of the Church may God give you pardon and peace. And I absolve you from your sins in the name of the Father, and of the Son, and of the Holy Spirit.'

16 When Aquinas tackled this question, he drew a parallel with medicine. Medicine always involves some sort of physical act, he writes. Sometimes that is a matter of applying a substance (such as an ointment), but sometimes we have to identify the act with the treatment as a whole, such as taking exercise. In a similar way, some sacraments are physical in that they involve some external matter (such as bread or wine) but others are material acts in the sense of what the human agent does as a whole, such as turning up to be married or to make one's confession. See *ST* III.84.1. The Council of Florence put the physical emphasis on 'the acts of penitence', which were 'contrition of heart', 'confession with the mouth' and the penance, such as 'prayer, fasting, and almsgiving' (*Decree for the Armenians*).

13 The sacraments and the Holy Spirit

1 On Mary and contemporary Christian experience of the Spirit, see Tom Smail, *The Giving Gift: The Holy Spirit in Person* (London: Darton, Longman & Todd, 1994).

2 Augustine, *Sermon* 267.4. 'However far we go back in the sequence of confessions of faith or creeds, we find the article on the Church linked to that on the Holy Spirit', Yves Congar, *I Believe in the Holy Spirit* (New York: Crossroad, 1997), vol. 2, p. 5.

3 Francis Hall, *Dogmatic Theology* (New York: Longmans, Green and Co., 1921), p. 27.

4 Hall, *Dogmatic Theology*, p. 25.

5 Hall, *Dogmatic Theology*, pp. 25–6.

6 Basil of Caesarea, *On the Holy Spirit*, §35, quoted by John Gordon Davies, *The Spirit, the Church and the Sacraments* (London: Faith Press, 1954), p. 94.

7 Clement of Alexandria, *Paschal Homily*, 10.

8 Clement of Alexandria, *In Nah.* II.2ff.
9 John of Damascus, *The Orthodox Faith* I.13. These translations are from Davies, *Spirit, Church and Sacraments*, p. 136.
10 John Calvin, *Institutes* III.1.1.
11 Congar, *I Believe*, III.262. Emphasis added.
12 Congar, *I Believe*, III.263.
13 Congar, *I Believe*, III.231.
14 Congar, *I Believe*, III.230.
15 Congar, *I Believe*, III.219.
16 Congar, *I Believe*, III.269.
17 For priests, the form in the Book of Common Prayer begins, 'Receive the Holy Ghost for the office and work of a Priest in the Church of God, now committed unto thee by the imposition of our hands.' The words of John 20 follow immediately. The making of bishops is similar. The words of ordination of the deacon do not mention the Holy Spirit, but the preceding prayer has: 'Fill them, we beseech thee, with the Holy Ghost, that, enabled by the sevenfold gift of his grace, they may be faithful to their promises, modest, humble, and constant in their ministration . . .'

Conclusion: sacraments and the Incarnation

1 Thomas Aquinas, *SCG* IV.54.
2 Aquinas, *SCG* IV.54.4.
3 Aquinas, *SCG* IV.54.5.
4 Aquinas, *SCG* IV.54.6.
5 Aquinas, *SCG* IV.55.29.
6 Aquinas, *SCG* IV.56.1.
7 Aquinas, *SCG* IV.53.3.
8 Aquinas, *SCG* IV.56.3.
9 Aquinas, *SCG* IV.56.4.
10 Aquinas, *SCG* IV.56.5. Similarly, it was fitting that God should have lived among us as a poor person without worldly honour. This makes it all the more clear that success lies with God, not with human power. Further, our problem is to be drawn away from God by 'devotion to earthly things'. Part of the remedy is to learn devotion to Christ as one who lived a 'needy and private life' (*SCG* IV.55.15). Both aspects are mirrored in the sacraments. The means involved, such as bread, wine and water, are humble; this puts the emphasis on the power of God. Similarly, our disordered desire for riches and power can be reoriented by a focus for the spiritual life with these humble means near its centre.
11 Aquinas, *SCG* IV.56.6.

12 Aquinas, *SCG* IV.56.7.
13 Perhaps this is a reason for not warming the baptismal water too much, not at least for those who are old enough to remember at first hand what happened: having cold water poured on us is an archetypally bracing experience.
14 Thomas Aquinas, *ST* III.66.6.
15 Canticle 80 in *Common Worship: Daily Prayer*.

Bibliography

Ambrose of Milan, *On the Sacraments* and *On the Mysteries*, trans. Thomas Thompson (London: SPCK, 1950).

Baillie, D. M., *The Theology of the Sacraments and Other Papers* (London: Faber and Faber, 1957).

Behrens, James, *Confirmation, Sacrament of Grace: The Theology, Practice and Law of the Roman Catholic Church and the Church of England* (Leominster: Gracewing, 1995).

Boersma, Hans, *Heavenly Participation: The Weaving of a Sacramental Tapestry* (Grand Rapids: Eerdmans, 2011).

Bouyer, Louis, *Christian Initiation*, trans. J. R. Foster (London: Burns and Oates, 1960).

Bradshaw, Paul, *Ordination Rites of the Ancient Churches of East and West* (New York: Pueblo, 1990).

Brown, David and Ann Loades (eds), *The Sense of the Sacramental: Movement and Measure in Art and Music, Place and Time* (London: SPCK, 1995).

Brown, David and Ann Loades (eds), *Christ: The Sacramental Word* (London: SPCK, 1996).

Chauvet, Louis-Marie, *Symbol and Sacrament: A Sacramental Reinterpretation of Christian Existence* (Collegeville: Liturgical Press, 1995).

Chauvet, Louis-Marie, *The Sacraments: The Word of God at the Mercy of the Body* (Collegeville: Liturgical Press, 2001).

Clark, Francis, *The Eucharistic Sacrifice and the Reformation* (Oxford: Blackwell, 1967).

Cocksworth, Christopher, *Evangelical Eucharistic Thought in the Church of England* (Cambridge: Cambridge University Press, 2002).

Cyril of Jerusalem, *Lectures on the Christian Sacraments*, trans. F. L. Cross (Crestwood: St Vladimir's Seminary Press, 1986).

Davies, John Gordon, *The Spirit, the Church and the Sacraments* (London: Faith Press, 1954).

Donnelly, Doris K. (ed.), *Sacraments and Justice* (Collegeville: Liturgical Press, 2013).

Dudley, Martin and Geoffrey Rowell (eds), *The Oil of Gladness: Anointing in the Christian Tradition* (Collegeville: Liturgical Press, 1993).

Macquarrie, John, *A Guide to the Sacraments* (London: SCM Press, 1997).

Meyendorff, Paul, *The Anointing of the Sick* (Crestwood: St Vladimir's Seminary Press, 2009) [From an Eastern Orthodox perspective].

Bibliography

Mick, Lawrence E., *Understanding the Sacraments Today* (Collegeville: Liturgical Press, 2006). [This book, written in the spirit of the years following the Second Vatican Council, has also been published as seven, cheap booklets, one on each sacrament.]

Moberly, R. C., *Ministerial Priesthood* (London: John Murray, 1897).

Osborne, Kenan B., *Christian Sacraments in a Postmodern World: A Theology for the Third Millennium* (New York: Paulist Press, 1999).

Ramsey, Michael, *The Christian Concept of Sacrifice* (Oxford: SLG Publications, 1974).

Schmemann, Alexander, *For the Life of the World: Sacraments and Orthodoxy* (Crestwood: St Vladimir's Seminary Press, 1973).

Stevenson, Kenneth, *Accept This Offering: The Eucharist as Sacrifice Today* (London: SPCK, 1989).

Sykes, Stephen, *Sacrifice and Redemption* (Cambridge: Cambridge University Press, 2007).

Underhill, Evelyn, *The Mystery of Sacrifice: A Meditation on the Liturgy* (London: Longmans, Green and Co., 1938).

Waddell, Peter, *Joy: The Meaning of the Sacraments* (London: Canterbury Press, 2012).

Weinandy, Thomas G., *The Sacrament of Mercy: A Spiritual and Practical Guide to Confession* (Boston: Pauline Press, 1997).

Williams, Rowan, *Eucharistic Sacrifice: The Roots of a Metaphor* (Cambridge: Grove Publications, 1982), a response to R. P. C. Hanson, *Eucharistic Offering in the Early Church* (Cambridge: Grove Publications, 1979).

Index of biblical references

Genesis
1.2 142
1.26 106
2.18 115
3 150

Leviticus
7 39
23 39

1 Kings
8 36

Psalms
34.8 45
80.7 78

Song of Solomon
8.6 6
2.3 44

Isaiah
1.6 125
43.19 134
55.5 6
61.1 73
61.1–2 143

Jeremiah
17.5 29

Ezekiel
47.12 125

Hosea
1—3 102

Malachi
1.11 49

Ecclesiasticus
38.1–2 125–6
38.4–8 125

Matthew
3.2 129
3.11 143
3.16 153
4.17 129
5.48 136
6.14–15 134
7.13 135
9.6 149
9.8 2, 131
9.14–15 71
9.25 2
10.7 70
11.4–5 120
11.5 3
11.28 167
13.11 55
19.12 116
20.28 95, 102
22.1–4 71
22.1–14 102
25.1–13 71, 102
25.31–45 136
26.10–12 72
28 70
28.19 59
28.20 31

Mark
1.10 153
1.5 129
2.5 24
2.7 131
2.9 4
2.9–11 2

2.18–20 71
4.39 4
5.41 3, 4
7.34 5
10.30 43, 110
10.38–39 121
10.45 102
14.6–8 72
16.16 13

Luke
1.26–38 73
1.35 142
1.41–45 73
2.22–39 73
2.40 77
2.42–51 77
2.52 77
3.3 129
3.7 14
4.18 73
4.18–19 143
4.35 4
7.22 120
10.34 125
11.4 133
12.50 14
14.16–24 159
22.19 34, 59
22.20 5
22.27 95
23.34 133

John
1 30, 36
1.16 137
1.18 146
1.29 73, 149
2.11 71

3.4 18, 134
3.5 13, 63, 70
3.29 102
4.13–14 61
4.15 158
4.23 26
5.17 78
6 34, 43
6.33 45
6.34 45
6.37 132
6.53 68
6.55 33, 72
7.37–39 61
8.1–11 3
8.11 24
10.10 14, 142
11.43 4
11.50 158
12.7 72
12.24 64
13.15 149
14.12 78
16.7 142
18.14 158
18.37 148
20 171
20.19–23 146
20.22–23 131
20.23 70

Acts
2.38 13, 60, 129
2.46 51
6 91
8.16 60
10.48 60
16.15 20
16.33 20

18.8 20
19.5 60
22.16 5

Romans
4.17 135
5.16 149
6.3, 5 57
6.4 13
8 110
8.29 23, 30,
   144
11.29 28
12.15 122
14.7 168
16.1 101
16.7 101

1 Corinthians
1.16 20
1.30 1
3.9 78
7 116, 117
7.9 109
7.17 115
7.29, 31 116
7.32–35 116
7.38 116
10.16 34, 57
10.17 48
11 46

11.27–34 159
11.29 47
12 147
12.26 123
12.27 47
12.28 164
13 136, 153
13.13 136

2 Corinthians
1.19–20 15
3.17 146
4.7 58
5.21 7, 74
12.14 108
13.13 146

Galatians
2.20 39, 112
3.27 13
4.4–6 142
4.19 23
5.22–23 146
6.2 137
6.5 170

Ephesians
2.8 136
2.8–9 78
2.12 16
4.4–7 164

4.12 23
4.22–24 113
4.32 133–4
5.28–30
   102–3
5.32 103
6.3 111

Philippians
2.12 78, 117
3 39
3.7–14 6
3.7–15 121

1 Timothy
2.4 98
2.5 7
4.14 82
5.23 125

2 Timothy
2.2 83
3.14 83

Hebrews
1.1–3 23
2.9 8, 163
3.1 26
4.1 95
6.1–2 57
6.2 82

6.4–6 169
7.25 39
9—10 43
9.27 16
11 153

James
1.27 136
2.15–16 136
5.14–15 68
5.15 121
5.16 70, 137

1 John
1.1 45, 70
1.8 130
2.10–11 136
3.9 169
3.17 136
4.8 136
5.17 135

Jude
1.20 77

Revelation
13.8 73, 163
19.6–8 71
21.3 30–1
21.5 134
22.2 125

Index of names and subjects

Abelard, Peter 67
absolution 18, 28, 67, 70, 89, 129, 131–4, 136–8, 140; withholding 138
abstinence 53, 116
abundance 14, 18, 29, 58, 63, 142
abuse: of children and the vulnerable 126–7, 138; by religious leaders and spouses 167; of the sacraments 40, 68, 84, 138
accident, Aristotelian category 32–3, 161
accommodation (divine) 11, 32, 45
accountability 83–4, 132–3
acolyte 92
Adam 106
adolescence 77, 111, 126
alcoholism 37, 64, 161–2
altar 41
altarpiece 6
Amaury de Bène 9
anabaptists 19
anatomy of sacrament see sacraments, anatomy of
angel 4, 6, 8–9, 17, 107, 123, 151
anger 53, 139
Anglicanism 19, 26, 34, 37, 49–50, 62–3, 79–80, 87–9, 92, 99–100, 104, 113, 118, 143, 145, 156, 160, 162, 165, 170
anointing 1, 4, 6–7, 61–2, 66–70, 72–3, 75, 79, 99, 120–8, 131–2, 143, 146–7
Anson, Peter 86
Anthony of Egypt 123
apostasy 28
Apostles 68–70, 79, 83, 86, 89–91, 101, 127, 131–2, 138
appetites 109

Aquinas, Thomas 1, 8–9, 11, 27–8, 67–8, 74, 80, 100, 105, 107–8, 111, 119–22, 125, 148–51, 152, 166, 169, 170
archangel 73, 123
archbishop 90, 92, 157
archdeacon 92
archimandrite 92
archpriest 92
Arendt, Hannah 169
Aristotle 32–3, 106, 108, 158
Arius 60
Articles, Thirty-Nine see Thirty-Nine Articles
Ascension 27, 41, 129
Ash Wednesday 27, 52, 67
atonement 38, 74
Augustine of Hippo 5, 7, 20–1, 28, 30, 39, 44, 46, 50, 94, 105, 125, 143
authority 2, 28, 50, 66, 70, 76, 79–80, 84–7, 91, 131–2, 140, 149

Bairstow, Edward 157
Baltic churches 67, 87
baptism 1, 5–6, 13–26, 29–30, 39, 47, 50–1, 57–63, 66–71, 73–7, 79–81, 87–8, 94, 96–101, 103, 121, 129–31, 143–5, 147, 162; adult 17, 20, 99; anniversary of 22; conditional 21, 160; continuity and discontinuity 16–18; emergency 21, 63, 96; formula and inclusivization 58–9; infant 19–20, 63, 100; 'no' and 'yes' 14–16; quantity of water 15, 62–3, 153–4, 161; rebaptism 19–21, 28, 166
Barth, Karl 15, 106
Basil 143
Basle, Council of 37
Bauerschmidt, Frederick 38

Bayeux Tapestry 5
beauty 15, 18–19, 24, 44, 106, 144, 148, 150
Bede, the Venerable 19
beer 63–4
bishop 18, 24, 26–8, 31, 54, 62–3, 70, 73, 78–80, 82–7, 89–95, 100–1, 103, 111, 127, 131–2, 146, 160, 162
blessing 17, 35, 41, 54, 57, 61, 63, 68, 71, 78, 89, 92, 100, 103–5, 118, 123, 144–5, 164
blood 4–6, 8, 14, 31–7, 39–41, 44, 57, 61, 63, 65, 68, 96, 145
body 4, 6, 8, 13, 17–19, 25, 30–5, 37–8, 42–4, 47–51, 53, 57, 61, 63, 65–7, 72, 76, 83, 94, 96–7, 105–6, 112–14, 120–2, 124, 126–7, 141, 145; *see also* flesh
Bonaventure 164
Bonhoeffer, Dietrich 16
Book of Common Prayer 35, 54, 68, 90, 97, 99, 103, 105, 109, 113, 130, 140, 145–6, 152, 154, 164, 166, 168, 170–1; the 'ordinal' 90
Book of Homilies 67, 102–3
bosom 6, 148
bread 7–10, 12, 31–7, 39, 43–5, 48, 51, 56–7, 61, 63–4, 68, 96, 140, 145, 147, 150–1, 155–6, 161
Brevint, Daniel 41
bride 71, 74, 102
bridegroom 71, 74, 102
buckwheat 64
burial 51, 72–3

Caiaphas 158
Calvary 54
Calvin, Jean 11, 19, 27, 33–5, 45, 83, 144, 150, 165
Cambuslang, revival of 53
Cana 71
candidature 92
canon, office of 66, 92
canon law 20, 60, 94, 106, 133, 137, 159, 161–2
cardinal 92

catechesis 20, 98
Catechism (of 1662) 55, 68, 152
Catechism of the Catholic Church 93, 102, 104, 119
Catechism of St Philaret of Moscow 33
Cathars 32
cathedra 84, 89
cathedral 84, 88–90, 97
causality 1, 54, 62, 64, 85–6, 97–8, 105–6, 116, 150, 158; instrumental 85–6
celibacy 117
ceremony 25, 68
chalice 36–7, 63, 156, 160–1
chaplain 92
character, sacramental *see* sacraments, character
charismatic 75, 120, 127, 146
charity 53, 97, 123, 136, 149
Chesterton, G. K. 110
children: admission to the Eucharist 48–9; baptism of 19–20, 25, 77, 97–8; and Christ 3; marriage and 27, 104–5, 107–9, 118–19
chrism 62, 75, 80, 162, 164
chrismation 62, 71, 80, 101
Christ *see* Jesus Christ
Christendom 52
christening 121; *see also* baptism
Christianity, pagan threat to 8
Christmas 6, 18, 26, 52, 134
Christology 2
Chrysostom, John 40, 46, 116
church 5–9, 11, 13–21, 26–8, 31–7, 39–43, 46–55, 58, 60–2, 64, 66–71, 74–6, 78–80, 82–94, 96–105, 108–9, 113–20, 122–3, 127–34, 136–8, 140, 143, 145–7, 150, 158, 171; organization 89
circumcision 8, 72
city 90, 123, 127, 139
cleansing 3, 18, 56, 61–2
Clement of Alexandria 144
clergy 27–8, 84, 88, 91, 101
clericalists 101
clothing 17

Coakley, Sarah 107, 112
coeliac disease 37
coffin 17
Coleman, T. W. 34–5
command 4, 13, 59, 69, 111
commission 25, 28, 73, 76, 82, 131, 127
Common Prayer, Book of *see* Book of
    Common Prayer
Common Worship 17, 42, 133, 140,
    158, 166
Commonwealth 52, 160
communicant 33–4, 36–7, 50–4, 57–8,
    124, 145, 150
communication 11, 32, 56–8
communion: Anglican 89; between
    churches 49–51, 62, 89, 159;
    frequency of 51–3; reception in both
    kinds 36–8; *see also* Eucharist; Holy
    Communion
community 26, 38, 43, 48, 69–70, 78,
    82–3, 90–2, 97, 99, 106, 109, 116,
    119, 130, 134
concomitance, doctrine of 37, 65,
    156–7
concupiscence 106
confession 18, 24, 26, 29, 52–3, 66–7,
    70, 97–9, 124, 129–41, 147–8
confessional 135, 138
confirmation 1, 23–4, 26, 29, 49, 52,
    62, 66–7, 70–1, 73, 75–81, 88, 98–9,
    111, 124, 126, 145–6, 12–13
conjugality 119
conscience 52, 123, 135, 137, 147
consecration 31–2, 35–6, 61, 80,
    86, 89–90, 92–3, 116, 144–6
consensus 14, 34
consent 90, 103
consubstantiation 33
consumption (of elements) 35, 45
contrition 70, 130, 138, 170
coronation 45, 146, 162, 163
courage 110
covenant 5, 8, 39, 72
Cranmer, Thomas 19, 40, 42, 105
creation 9, 102, 104, 111–12, 142, 150
creator 1, 7, 40, 58–9, 146

creature 11, 35, 40, 44, 145, 150
creed 13, 109, 142
cross 4–10, 17, 38–43, 54, 61, 63,
    95, 133, 152, 159, 160, 164
crucifixion 8
cult (worship) 27, 88
cults 83, 88
Cunningham, Conor 9
cup 57, 121, 144, 147
curate 86, 97
curse 29, 92

damnation 27, 139
Dante Alighieri 27
Davison, Andrew 153, 160, 163, 169
deacon 24, 27–9, 83, 89–92, 94–5,
    100–1, 103, 111, 146
dean, rural 92
death 3–6, 9–10, 13–17, 19–20, 35,
    39, 41, 43, 48, 57, 61, 64, 66, 69,
    72–3, 92, 98–9, 108, 113, 115,
    120–3, 126–7, 129, 133, 135,
    143, 150
dedication 66, 88
defrocking 28
demon 4
denomination 50
desire *see* erotic desire
devil 4, 17
diaconate *see* deacon
Didache 51, 154
diocese 89–90, 93, 116
Diocletian 94
Dionysius, Pseudo- *see* Pseudo-Dionysius
disciples 3–4, 28, 40, 48–9, 59, 70–2,
    78, 144
discipleship 16, 27, 71, 77, 80
discipline 46, 53, 132–3
dismissal 25, 119
doctor 28, 125; *see also* medicine
Dominicans 120
Donatists 28, 94
Donatus 28
Donovan, Marcus 68
Donovan, Vincent 46
doorkeepers 92

drink 17, 31, 33–4, 44–6, 51, 61, 68, 72, 83, 110, 121
drowning 15
drunkenness 139, 147
Duns Scotus, John 100, 164
duty 24, 26, 54, 93, 98, 101

Eagleton, Terry 113
Easter 6, 17, 21–2, 51–2, 145
Eastern churches 1, 19, 33, 36–7, 40, 48, 53, 55, 58, 62, 66, 74, 79–80, 86–7, 89, 92, 99–100, 115, 137, 144
eating 4, 30–1, 34, 43–4, 46, 51, 53, 68, 110, 147
economics 43
ecstasy 112
Elizabeth, mother of John the Baptist 73
Elizabeth II 45, 162
emergency baptism see baptism, emergency
Ephraim the Syrian 151
epiclesis 145
Epiphany 26
episcopal succession of order see order, episcopal succession of
episcope 91
epitaphs 20
eros 104, 111–13
erotic desire 112–13
eschatology 117
Eucharist 1, 6–7, 10–11, 19, 24–5, 27–8, 30–54, 56–7, 59, 61, 63–4, 66–9, 72, 76, 80, 85–7, 89–91, 95–6, 99, 103, 113–14, 126, 130, 132, 144–5; as food 43–7; incorporation 47–9; presence of Christ 30–6, 37–9, 47, 54, 113, 158; reservation of sacrament 36; sacrifice 38–42; see also communion; Holy Communion; incorporation; sacrifice
evangelical churches/people 35, 83, 143
evangelism 104, 109; see also mission
Evans, Sioned 169
evil 4, 9, 17, 53, 109, 113, 116, 121–2, 150

ex opere operantis 160
ex opere operato 56–7
excommunication 28, 49–51, 159
exodus 17
exorcists 92
Egyptians 17, 154

family 6, 15, 20, 27, 88, 104, 108–9, 113–14, 116
fasting 46, 53, 63, 87
feast 17, 26, 43, 46, 51–2, 71, 102, 132
feeding 1, 25, 30, 43–4, 47, 56, 61, 93, 132
fellowship 35, 83, 89, 124, 146–7
feminism 60, 107
Feuerbach, Ludwig 38
finance 89
First Letter of Clement 90
firstborn 30
fittingness 11, 97, 150
flesh 3–4, 6, 8, 12, 30–3, 58, 61, 63, 68, 110, 148, 150
font 17, 21
food 30–1, 33, 42–3, 45–6, 51, 53, 63–4, 72, 110; see also meal; nourishment
forgiveness 2–3, 13, 18, 24, 53, 70, 130–4, 136, 138, 140, 146, 149, 151
formulation 58–60, 63, 87, 98, 105, 134
fornication 106
Forsyth, P. T. 35
Fourth Lateran Council 32, 51
Francis 134
Frequency of Communion see communion, frequency of
Freud, Sigmund 112
friendship 70, 148–9, 151
funeral 3, 17, 20

Galilee 71
garden 132, 139, 141
Gehenna 3
gender 60
Geneva 23
Georgia 94

gesture 3–4, 18, 56–7, 61, 70, 72, 140, 150–1
gift(s) 9, 13, 16, 38, 45, 49, 54, 56, 75, 79, 81–2, 84–5, 97, 104, 106, 109–10, 125, 138, 140, 142–3, 146–7; irrevocable 28, 85; *see also* grace
gluttony 139
Gnosticism 8, 31–2, 58, 61, 83–4, 150
God 1–2, 5–16, 18–19, 21, 23–4, 26–8, 30–4, 36, 38–47, 49–50, 52–4, 56–61, 67–79, 82, 84–8, 93–4, 96–8, 102–8, 110–12, 115–16, 119–21, 123–6, 128–37, 139–40, 142, 144, 147–51, 163; likeness of 102, 119
gods 31, 59
Golgotha 39
Good Friday 6
gospel 8, 13, 15, 46, 87, 116
grace 2, 5–6, 11, 13, 15–16, 18, 20, 28–9, 34–5, 49, 54–5, 58, 66, 69, 72, 77–8, 87, 93–4, 96–8, 104, 107, 110, 122, 130, 132, 134–7, 140; cheap 16, 97; hydraulic imagery for 155
grave 4, 15, 53–4, 135, 139–40, 143
greed 139
Gregory IX 63
Gregory the Great 94
Gregory of Nazianzus 39, 166
guarantee 13, 87
guilt 50

habit 19, 24, 165
Hall, Francis 143
hallow 67, 74, 121; *see also* blessing
happiness 44, 46, 141, 243, 148–9
Harold (King) 5
healing 2–4, 6, 14, 99, 120–2, 124–7, 131–2, 145–7
health 84, 108, 120, 125, 128
hell 4
Henry VIII 114
Herbert, George 84
heresy 8, 21, 31–2, 37, 42, 94, 150
hermits 66
hierarchy 68

Hippo, Augustine of *see* Augustine of Hippo
Hippolytus 89, 145, 161
Hitler, Adolf 16
holiness 103, 135, 147
Holy Communion 5, 30, 34, 36–9, 41–2, 45–6, 48–54, 65, 68–9, 89, 99, 113, 123–4, 137, 144, 156, 157; receiving as soon as convenient 99, 113; withholding 54, 159–60; *see also* communion; Eucharist
Holy Spirit 13, 25, 31, 33–4, 58–61, 63, 70–1, 73, 75, 77–81, 85, 108–9, 122–3, 130–1, 142–7, 156, 171
Homilies, Book of *see* Book of Homilies
homily *see* sermon
hope 16, 24, 28, 43, 48, 127, 136
hosepipe 29; *see also* grace, hydraulic imagery for
hospice 123
hospitality 46, 50
household 20, 27, 76
Hugh of St Victor 66
hunger 4, 46, 54, 132
Hus, Jan 37

idolatry 38
Ignatius of Antioch 31–2, 34
ignorance 139
illness 99, 127–8, 139
Incarnation 1–4, 7–8, 10, 12, 14–16, 18, 23, 26, 30–2, 41, 44, 47, 58, 63, 66, 72, 82, 94, 102, 110, 120, 125–6, 129, 134–5, 142, 148–51, 173; overlap with sacraments 7, 33, 38, 72, 105; *see also* Jesus Christ
Incas 43
Inclusivization *see* baptism, formula and inclusivization
incorporation 13, 19, 30, 47, 50, 80
incumbent 97
indelibility *see* sacraments, indelibility
indissolubility *see* marriage, indissolubility
infants 19–21, 49, 68, 73, 77, 100–1

Index of names and subjects

Institutes of Christian Religion, The
34, 83
intention *see* sacraments, intention
intercession 27, 39, 41–2, 91, 97, 132
investments 99
Irenaeus of Lyons 19, 31–2, 34, 43
Irigaray, Luce 107–8

James, Liturgy of St *see* Liturgy of
St James
Jerusalem 3, 36
Jervois, William H. H. 41
Jesuits 47
Jesus Christ 1–8, 10, 12–21, 23–6,
29–51, 53–66, 68–80, 82–3, 85–7,
90, 93–7, 101–3, 105–6, 111–13,
115–17, 120–5, 128–9, 131–4,
136–7, 140, 142–6, 149–51, 172;
as child 7, 77; likeness of 131;
overlap of two natures of 33;
sacramentality in life of 2–4,
69–74; *see also* Incarnation
Jewish 10, 48, 77, 100
Johannine literature 30, 45
John the Apostle 6, 70
John the Baptist 3, 69, 73, 120, 143
John of Beverley 126
John of Damascus 144, 153
John Paul II 115, 117, 159
Jones, David 58
Jordan, River 14, 72, 74
Joseph, husband of Mary 19
Judaism 77
Julian of Norwich 47
Junia 101
jurisdiction 118
justice 82, 143, 149
justification 69, 149
Justin Martyr 31, 51

Kelly, J. N. D. 31
kingdom 3, 13, 55, 69–70, 75, 78,
83, 90, 116–18, 129

laity 37, 75–6, 86–8, 92, 94, 101,
133, 166

Lamb, Mystic *see* Mystic Lamb
language 11, 23, 58, 92, 108, 112;
see also communication
law 2, 8, 11, 60, 67, 69, 84, 94, 106,
131, 133, 137, 142
laying on of hands 57, 62–3, 70, 73,
75, 79, 82, 86, 89, 108, 126–7, 146,
156, 161, 164
Lazarus 4
leadership 82–3, 126
lectors 92
Lécuyer, Jacques 145
Lent 53
Leo the Great 90
lepers 3, 125–6
Lewis, C. S. 4
liturgy 24–5, 38–9, 42, 44–5, 52,
89, 91, 97, 105, 107, 144–6;
therapeutic 38; *see also* worship
Liturgy of Malabar 24
Liturgy of St James 42, 45, 144
Liturgy of Serapion 39
love 6, 9, 11, 24, 43, 46, 49, 53, 55, 59,
67, 102, 104–8, 111–13, 117, 119,
122, 126, 134, 136, 146, 148, 151;
erotic 107
Lubac, Henri de 10, 47–8
lust 106, 109, 117, 139
Luther, Martin 13, 19, 27, 33, 40
Lutheran churches 87, 100
lying 18

McCabe, Herbert 169
Macquarrie, John 23, 89
magic 58, 96–7, 124
Malabar, Liturgy of *see* Liturgy of
Malabar
marriage 6–7, 9, 23–4, 26–7, 29, 47,
52, 66–7, 71, 74, 76, 81, 93, 96,
98–119, 121, 124, 126, 134, 140,
146–7, 160, 166; consummation
of 104; and Holy Communion 113;
indissolubility 29, 105, 114–15;
remarriage 29, 115; three goods
of 105–11; same-sex 115–19
martyrdom 14, 16, 28, 31, 120, 155

Index of names and subjects

Mary, the Blessed Virgin 19, 142, 171
Marys, the three 6
Mass 18, 25, 40, 42, 52
materiality 7–9, 31, 34, 57–65, 142, 151; *see also* sacraments, matter of
Maundy Thursday 39, 52
meal 3, 34, 56, 69, 72, 113, 132; *see also* bread; food; meat; wine
meat 83
mediation 7, 11
medicine 50, 122, 125, 170; *see also* doctor
Melchizedek 39
memorial 34–5
metanoia 129
metaphor 18, 44, 109
Methodism 52–3, 133; *see also* Wesley, Charles and John
Mick, Lawrence 55
midwives 101; *see also* laity
Milbank, Alison 153, 163
Milton, John 114
minister 20–1, 28, 41, 79, 83, 84–7, 91, 94, 96, 98, 101, 103, 132, 146
ministry 8, 71–3, 82–4, 87–93, 99, 101, 126–7, 129, 131–3, 136–8
minor orders 91–2; *see also entries for individual minor orders*
miracle 2, 57, 71, 102, 120, 125–7
Mishnah 48, 77
mission 46, 69, 76, 78, 82, 86, 99, 102, 109, 134, 143; *see also* evangelism
Moberly, R. C. 92
modalism 59
Molokai, Damien 126
money 4, 125
moneychangers 3
monks 66, 92, 113
Mormonism 20
Mozart, Wolfgang Amadeus 15
Muir, Edwin 152
murder 135, 138–9
music 15, 96
mysteries 74, 98
mysterion 103
mysterium 5

mystery 6, 11, 25, 41, 43, 50, 55, 59, 67, 74, 77, 103, 106–7, 111
Mystic Lamb 73–4, 102
myth 106

names *see* sacraments, names
New Atheists 9
Newman, John Henry 68–9
Nicaea 13, 89, 142
Nicodemus 18, 134
Nonjurors 145
nourishment 34, 54, 63, 67, 97; *see also* food
nuptuality 119

oath 5
oblation 40–2
occasionalism 85
occult 88
offering 3–4, 5–7, 19, 21, 26–7, 38–43, 45, 49, 53–4, 56, 61, 63, 93, 96, 104–5, 109, 111, 114, 126–7, 132–3, 137, 144, 150–1; *see also* sacrifice
oil 1, 7, 62, 75, 80, 122, 125, 140, 150–1
ointment 122
Oneness Pentecostals 60
order: necessity of 82–3; episcopal succession of 50, 79, 86–7, 89–90, 100, 131, 162, 164
orders 82–6; *see also* ordination
ordination 23–4, 26–9, 52, 62–3, 66–70, 73, 76, 81–95, 98–101, 111, 124, 126–7, 131–2, 146; of women 100–1, 166
Orthodox Church *see* Eastern churches
overlap 7, 33, 38, 72, 105

pan-sacramentality 9–10
Pannenberg, Wolfgang 156
parables 3, 55, 102, 136
parent as name for God 60
parish 5, 37, 40, 52, 79, 84, 86, 88, 91, 97, 99–100, 116, 127
parliament 133
particularity, scandal of 63–4, 82, 111
Passover 48, 69, 72

pastors 86
paten 63, 160–1
Pelagianism 16
penance 122, 130, 137–8, 140, 147;
  vicarious 74
penitence 27, 53, 74, 115, 169
Pentecost 52, 145
Pentecostalism 19, 60, 81; oneness 60
Pentecostals *see* Oneness Pentecostals
per saltam ordinations 164–5
Philaret of Moscow 33
Phoebe 101
piety 21, 48, 52
pilgrimages 3
Pius X 48, 52,
Pius XII 63
Plato 106
polygamy 115
Poston, Elizabeth 158
prayer 4, 21, 25, 27, 31–2, 34–6, 40–2,
  46, 53–4, 67, 72–3, 75–6, 78–9, 81,
  84, 90–1, 97, 99, 103, 105, 109, 113,
  120, 122–7, 132–3, 140, 144–7;
  postures 67; *see also* liturgy, worship
preaching 13, 57, 70, 84, 91, 96, 129,
  132, 146
presbyter 79, 90–1
presence of God 6, 15, 30–1, 97;
  see also Eucharist, presence of Christ
prester 91
pride 117, 136, 139
priest and priesthood 6–8, 20–1, 24–9,
  33, 35–6, 39–40, 54, 56, 61, 63, 67,
  73, 76, 79–80, 84–96, 98, 100–1,
  103, 111, 123, 126–7, 129, 131–3,
  136–8, 140–1, 144–7, 160–1, 164
promise 5, 7, 15, 27, 45, 55–6, 63,
  110–11, 120, 133–4, 138
prophecy 49
prophet 76, 88, 102
prophetess 73
Protestantism 8, 15, 19, 27, 34, 37,
  40, 42, 67, 100–1, 106
providence 128, 147
Pseudo-Dionysius 112
Puritanism 52, 112, 160

reaffirmation 20, 22
rebaptism *see* baptism, rebaptism
rebirth 18, 64, 96
receptionism 35
recipient *see* sacraments, recipient of
reconciliation 49–50, 82, 129–30,
  132–3, 135, 140; *see also* confession
rector 92, 100
rededication 128
redemption 1, 4, 7–10, 13, 17, 25, 31,
  35, 58–9, 73, 111, 123; *see also*
  salvation
Reformation 19, 27, 33, 36–7, 52,
  62, 67, 114, 120, 135
reformers 13, 19, 33–4, 40, 67, 103,
  136
religion 38, 88, 113
religious (members of religious
  orders) 92, 113, 117, 120
remarriage *see* marriage, remarriage
repentance 13, 21, 50, 54, 69–70, 74,
  129–30, 133, 137–8, 140, 143
representation 87–8
reserved sacrament *see* Eucharist,
  reservation of sacrament
Restoration of Crown and
  Episcopacy 52
resurrection 3–5, 7, 10, 13–15, 17, 19,
  22, 26, 39, 43, 51–2, 57, 61, 64, 69,
  110, 124, 129, 134
resurrection of Christ 1, 17
romance 102, 111–12
rubric 113
rule 11, 34, 51, 59, 97, 108, 126

sacerdos 92
sacramental (rite not a
  sacrament) 67–8
sacramentality 2, 9–10, 118–19, 126
Sacramentis 66
sacraments: anatomy of 55–65,
  96–101; certainty of 56–8, 151;
  character 23–9, 39, 80, 85–6, 91–4,
  110, 127, 144, 146; definition of 5,
  32, 68; dominical 47, 68–9; efficacy
  28, 57, 62, 69, 143–4; form of 55,

57–65, 80, 114, 121–2, 140, 146; indelibility 27–9, 93–4, 98; intention 98–9, 165; licit and illicit 28, 85–6, 93–4, 115; matter of 57–8, 60–5, 80, 114, 121–2, 140–1, 160–1, 170; names 25–6, 154–5; number of 66–74; preparation for 14, 20, 22, 51–3, 56, 84, 98–100, 114–15; recipients of 5, 72, 96, 99–100, 121–2, 128, 134; setting of 96–9; surety 1, 35, 56–7, 87, 96, 132, 136; valid and invalid 60, 62, 85–6, 101; *see also* communication; gesture; materiality
sacramentum 5, 55
sacrifice 3–4, 7–8, 11, 30–1, 38–43, 54, 70, 72, 111, 113; *see also* offering
salt 62, 64
salvation 1, 3, 7, 11–16, 18, 21, 31, 41, 47, 55, 57, 61, 63, 68, 73, 78, 98, 117, 120–1, 124, 128, 131, 136–7, 142, 150, 166; *see also* redemption
Samaritan woman 26, 158
same-sex marriage *see* marriage, same-sex
sanctification 1, 19–20, 35, 40, 58–9, 61, 97, 115, 143–5
Sarum rite 40
Saunders, Dame Cicely 123
scandal 42, 50, 54, 63–4, 72, 82, 110–11, 131
scandalon 54
Scandinavian churches 67, 87
Schelling, Friederich 9
schism 50, 94
Schleiermacher, Friederich 8, 52, 153
Scripture 10–12, 57, 68, 90, 102–3, 117; *see also* Index of biblical references
sea 4, 14, 17, 61–2, 70
seal 39, 133, 138
Serapion, Liturgy of *see* Liturgy of Serapion
sermon 34, 44, 134
sexual relationships 99, 107, 109–10, 112, 118, 126
Shakespeare, William 104

sickness 9, 42, 67, 122, 126, 128, 147
signs 2, 8, 34, 55–7, 58, 71, 97, 150
Sigurd of Norway 63–4
Simeon 73
Simon the Pharisee 4
sin 2–3, 7, 10, 13, 16, 18, 24, 28, 31, 40, 43, 45–6, 50, 51–4, 63, 69–70, 73–4, 98–9, 106, 109–11, 117–18, 122, 124, 129–33, 135–40, 143–4, 146–7, 149; capital (or deadly) 138–9; mortal and venial 135–6, 139–40, 169, 170; *see also* anger; concupiscence; fornication; gluttony; greed; heresy; idolatry; lust; lying; pride; scandal; slander; sloth; suicide; theft; vice
singleness 115–16
sins, litany of 140
slander 53
sloth 139
smell 45, 66
soldier 42, 5, 56
solemnization 103–4
solidarity 74
Soskice, Janet Martin 160
soul 8, 24, 37, 42, 44, 61, 95, 101, 117, 123, 127, 143, 144–7
Speyr, Adrienne von 6
spillage 36
Spirit, Holy *see* Holy Spirit
subdeacons 92
suffering 6–7, 9, 31, 39, 41, 113, 121–4, 134, 150
suicide 139
supernatural: God as 11, 45, 120; natural and 124–6
surety of sacraments *see* sacraments, surety
symbol 3, 17, 35, 37, 62, 71, 89, 144, 146

tabernacle 36
Talmud 154
teetotalism 64
temperance 53, 110
temple 3, 8, 19, 26, 36, 51, 77, 81
Tertullian 61–2

thanksgiving 27, 40, 52–3, 75, 97, 103
theft 135, 139
Thirty-Nine Articles 21, 68, 96, 165
threefold office 76
threefold order 90–2, 100
tomb *see* grave
tongue 53
torture 21, 28, 42
tradition 9, 13, 17, 20, 22, 26–30, 33, 37, 48, 53, 57, 60, 62–3, 66, 73, 79, 87, 92–3, 96, 100, 103–4, 105, 112, 118, 120, 124–5, 127, 135–7, 144–5
transcendence 107–8
transfiguration 10
transfinalization 36
transignification 36
transubstantiation 32–3, 35
Trinitarian faith 59–60
Trinitarian form 60
Trinitarian formula 63, 87, 98
Trinity 21, 32, 34, 43, 58–60, 90, 106–8; subsistent relations 59
tritheism 59

Underhill, Evelyn 11, 43, 45, 54
unworthiness 28, 96, 165

vestments 66, 96
vice 47, 59
virginity 116–17
virtualism 34, 156

virtue 21, 85, 96, 110, 149; *see also* charity; courage; hospitality; justice; love; piety; temperance
virtus 34
visitation of the sick (Prayer Book) 67, 79, 140
vocation 29, 75–6, 87–8, 94–5, 115–17, 119, 129, 133
vows 21–2, 92

wafers 64
washing 1, 3–4, 17–18, 51, 56, 61–2, 74, 121
water 3, 7, 12–15, 17, 21, 29, 56, 61–4, 66, 70–1, 74, 87, 96, 98, 125, 140, 143–4, 150–1, 161
wax 23
wedding *see* marriage
Wesley, Charles and John 41, 52
Weyden, Rogier van der 6
Williams, Ralph Vaughan 45
wine 3, 7–9, 12, 31–7, 39, 43, 45, 56, 61, 63–5, 71, 96, 125, 140, 144, 147, 150–1, 155–6, 161–2
worship 17, 26–7, 38, 42, 52, 76, 82, 88, 91, 93, 97, 105, 133; *see also* liturgy
worthiness 94, 148
Wright, N. T. 3

Zacchaeus 4
Žižek, Slavoj 9
Zwingli, Huldrych 8, 19, 34–5